ASHES

WRITTEN BY **MARIO CANDELARIA**

ART BY **KARL SLOMINSKI**

LETTERS BY **ZAKK SAAM**

EDITOR **JOEY ESPOSITO**

COVER BY **KARL SLOMINSKI & IVAN PLASCENCIA**

DESIGN BY **TAYLOR ESPOSITO & TYLER BOSS**

Z2 COMICS

"To my rock, Erin. Without you none of this would have been possible"
-Mario

"For you. Even in the slightest way, you've picked me up when I had fallen down. I LOVE you."
-Karl

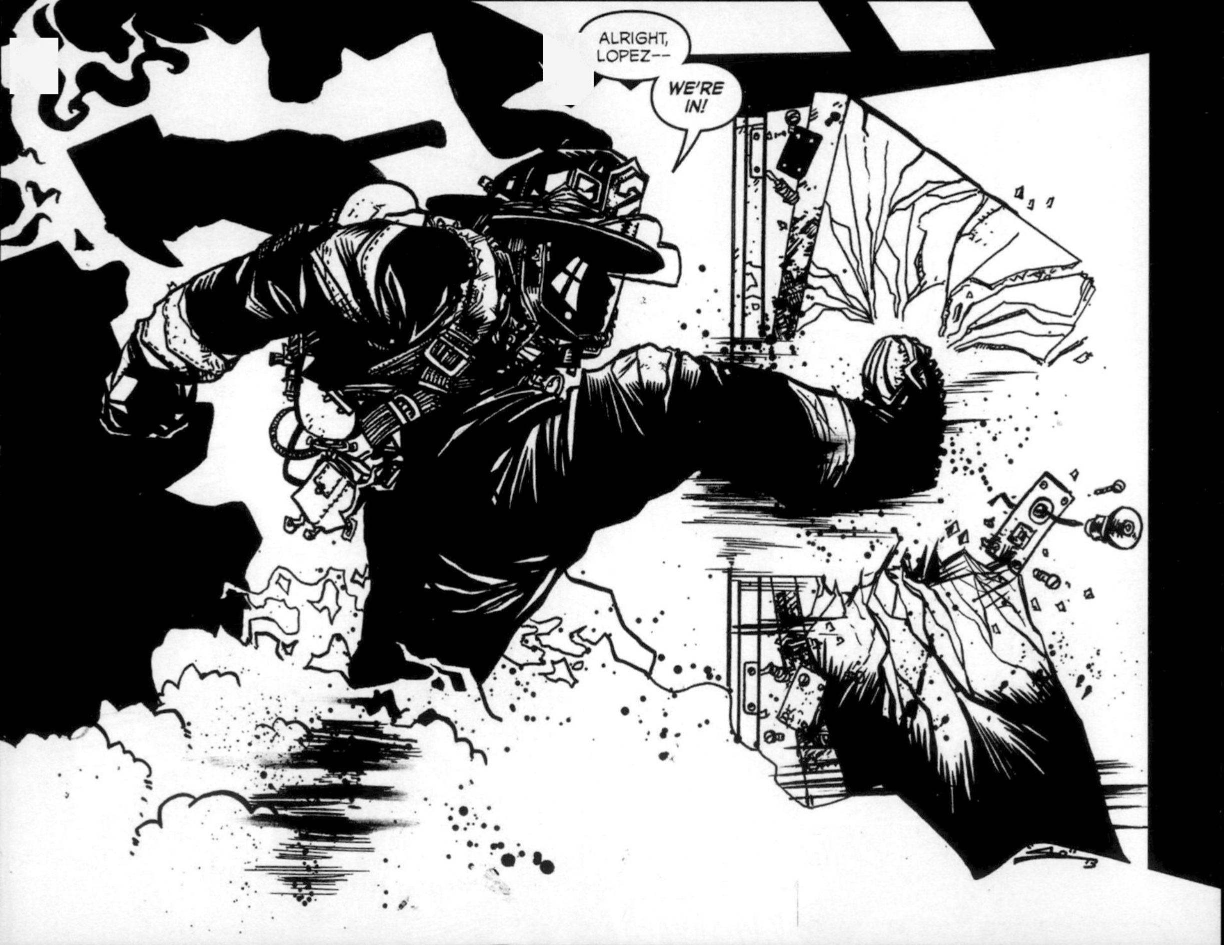
ALRIGHT, LOPEZ--
WE'RE IN!

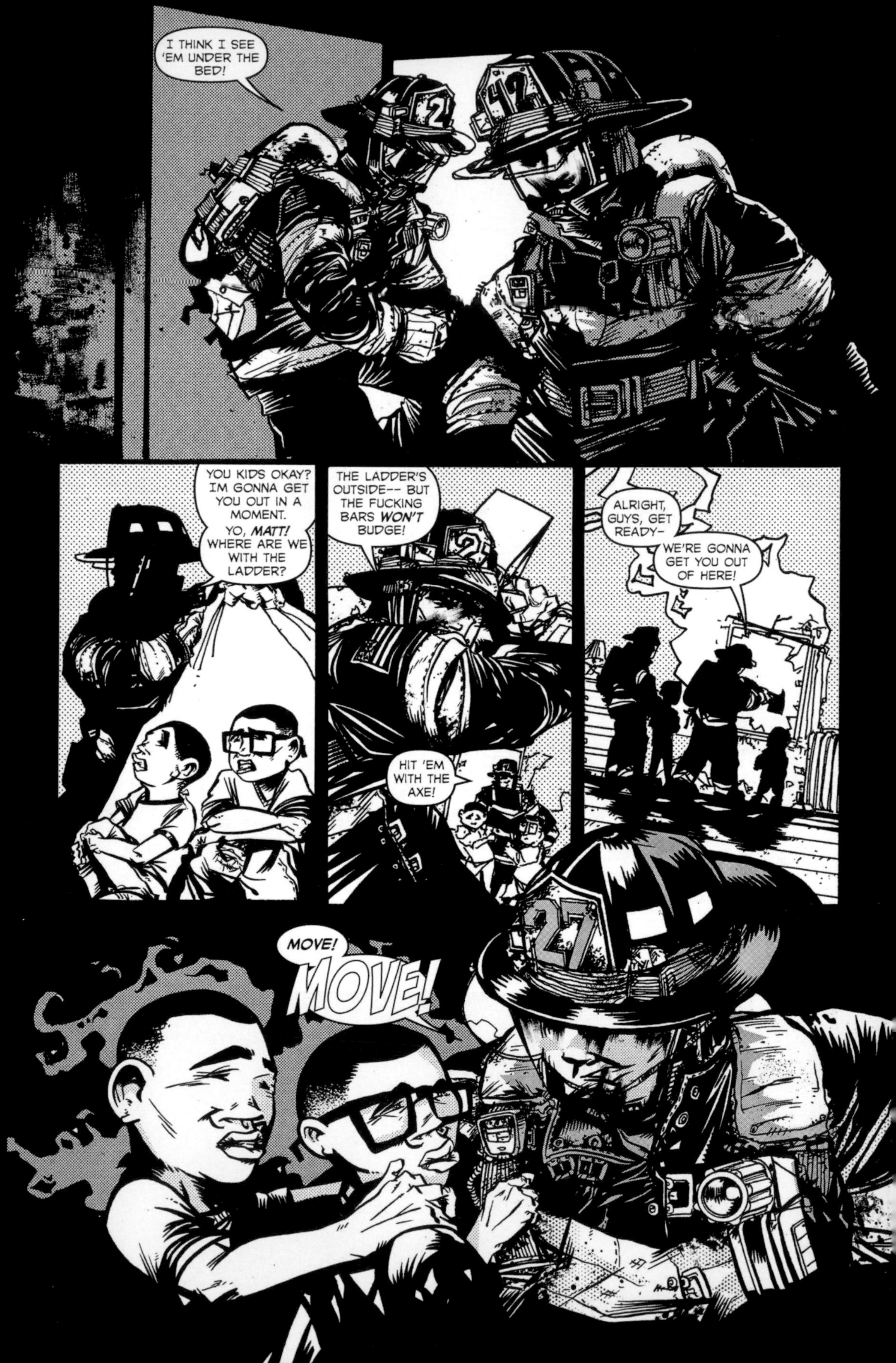
I THINK I SEE 'EM UNDER THE BED!
YOU KIDS OKAY? IM GONNA GET YOU OUT IN A MOMENT.
YO, MATT! WHERE ARE WE WITH THE LADDER?
THE LADDER'S OUTSIDE-- BUT THE FUCKING BARS WON'T BUDGE!
HIT 'EM WITH THE AXE!
ALRIGHT, GUYS, GET READY-
WE'RE GONNA GET YOU OUT OF HERE!
MOVE!
MOVE!

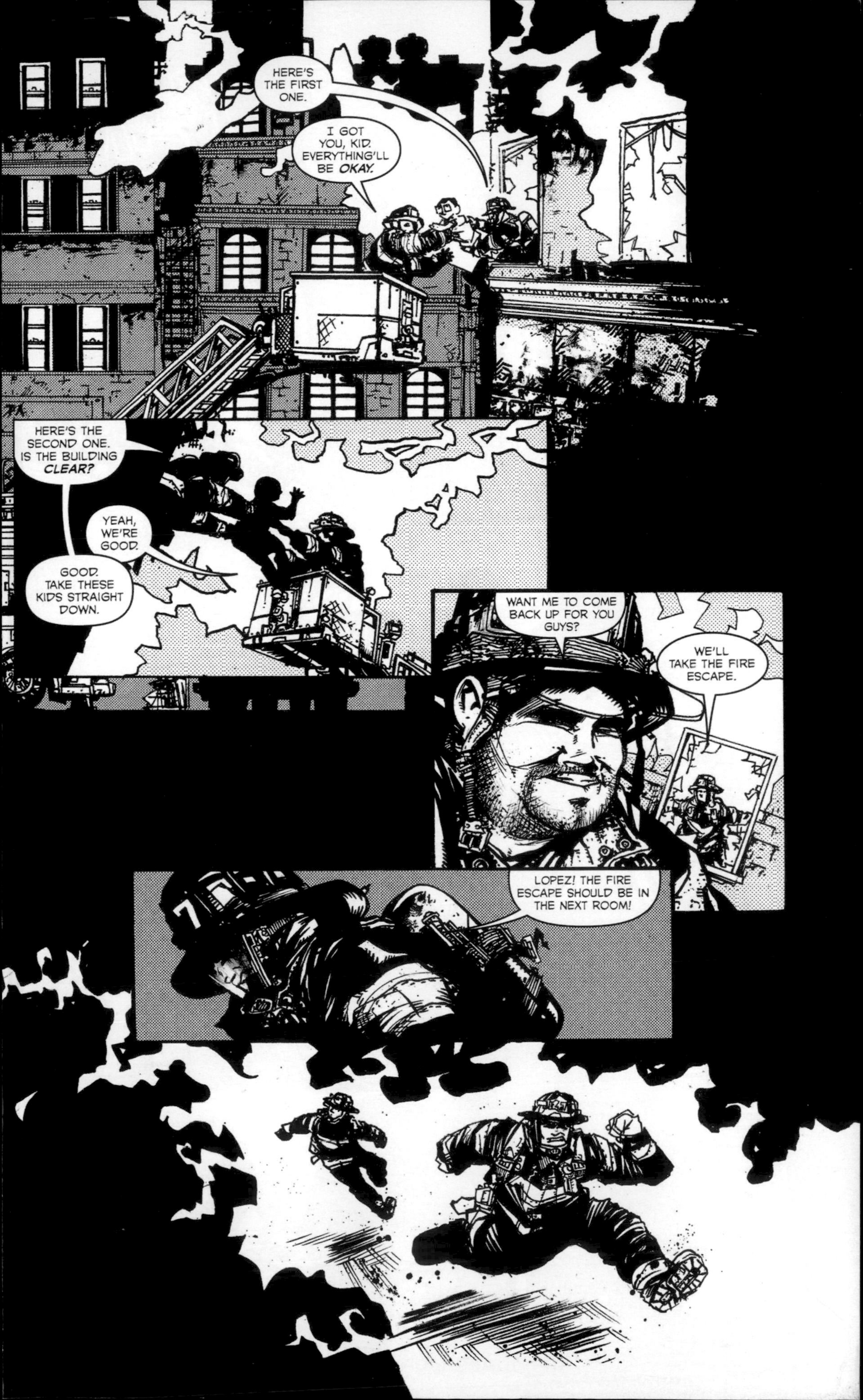
HERE'S THE FIRST ONE.
I GOT YOU, KID. EVERYTHING'LL BE OKAY.
HERE'S THE SECOND ONE. IS THE BUILDING CLEAR?
YEAH, WE'RE GOOD.
GOOD. TAKE THESE KIDS STRAIGHT DOWN.
WANT ME TO COME BACK UP FOR YOU GUYS?
WE'LL TAKE THE FIRE ESCAPE.
LOPEZ! THE FIRE ESCAPE SHOULD BE IN THE NEXT ROOM!

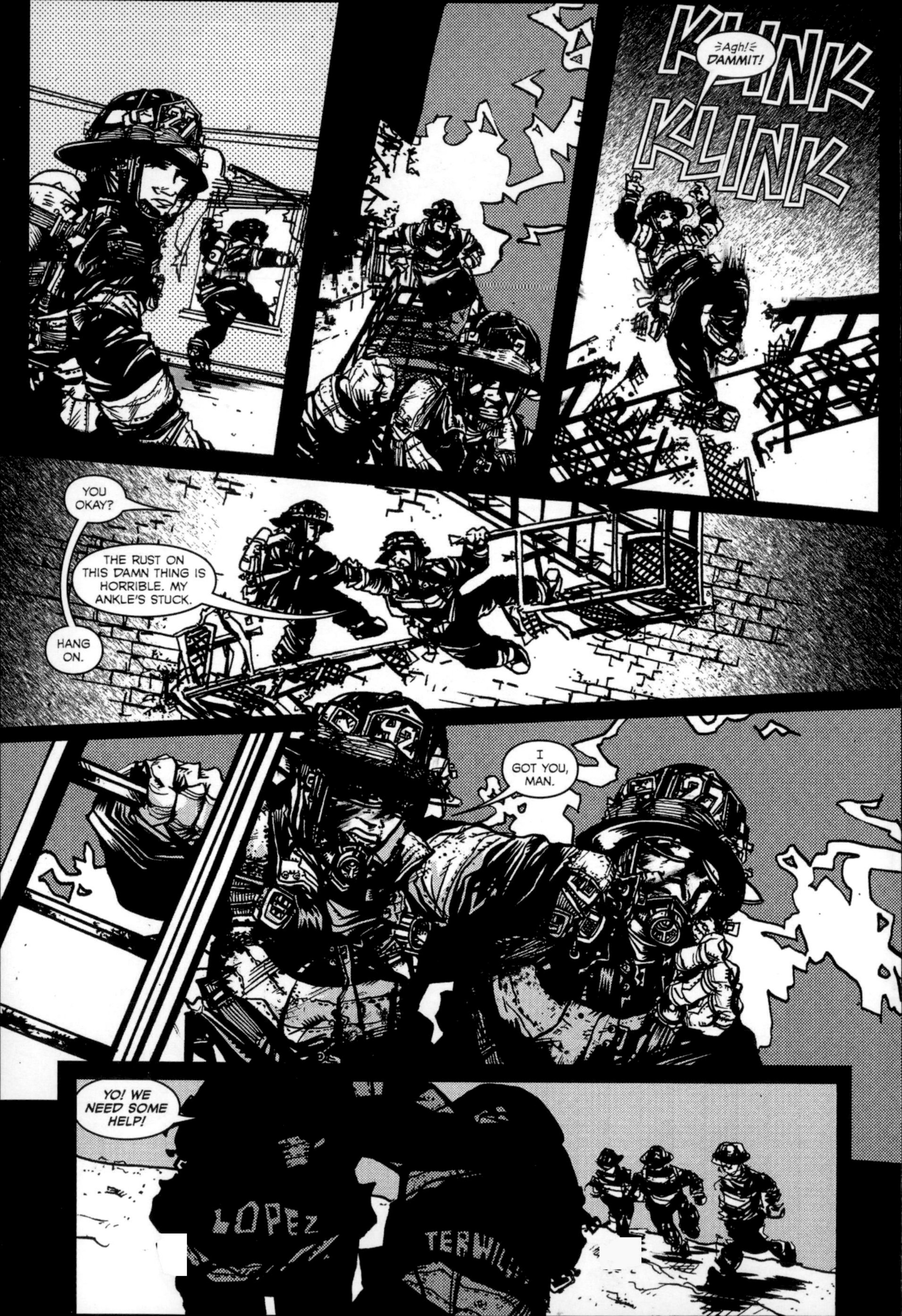

KLINK
Agh! DAMMIT!
KLINK
YOU OKAY?
THE RUST ON THIS DAMN THING IS HORRIBLE. MY ANKLE'S STUCK.
HANG ON.
I GOT YOU, MAN.
YO! WE NEED SOME HELP!
LOPEZ

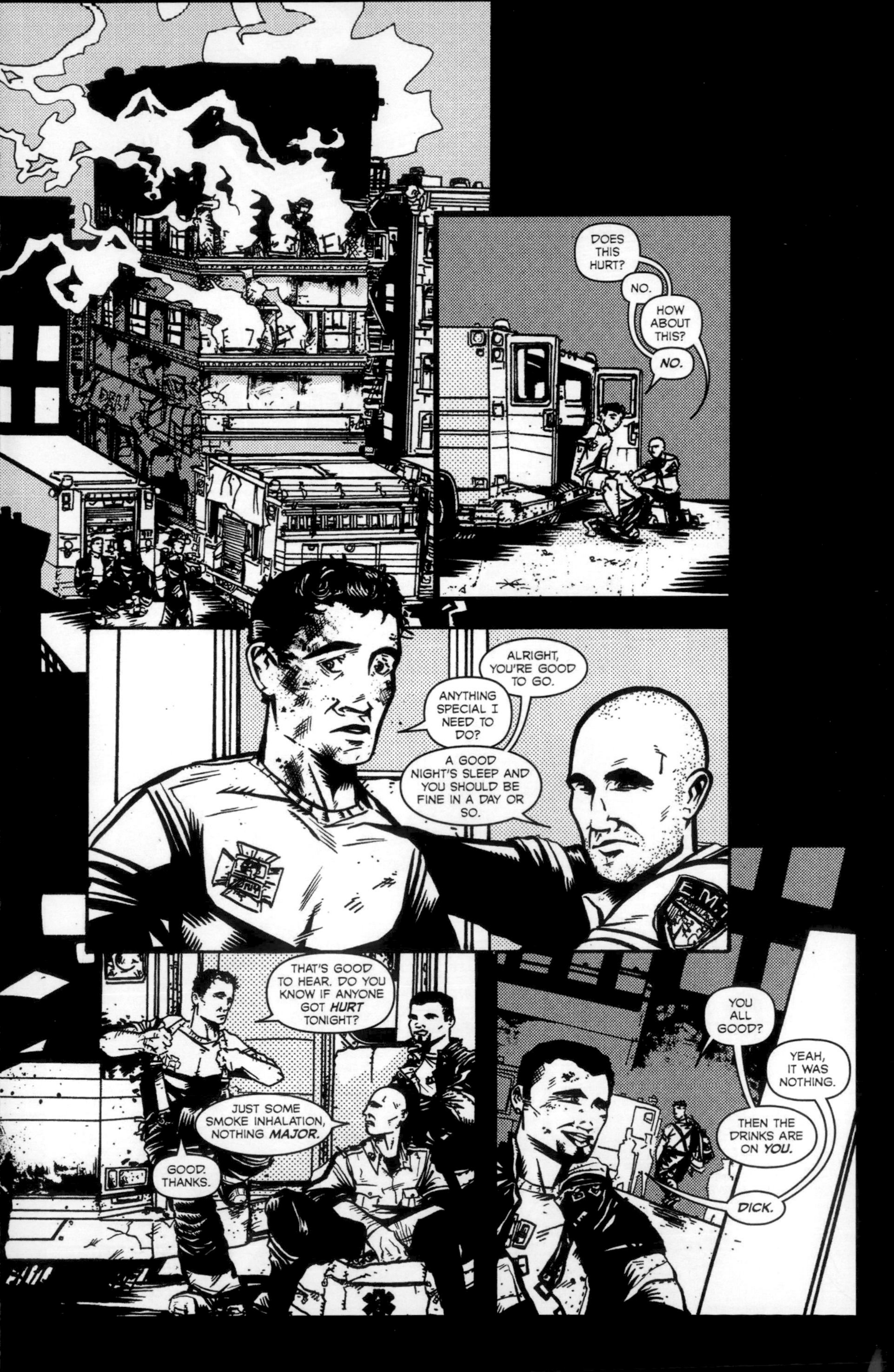
DOES THIS HURT?
NO.
HOW ABOUT THIS?
NO.
ALRIGHT, YOU'RE GOOD TO GO.
ANYTHING SPECIAL I NEED TO DO?
A GOOD NIGHT'S SLEEP AND YOU SHOULD BE FINE IN A DAY OR SO.
THAT'S GOOD TO HEAR. DO YOU KNOW IF ANYONE GOT HURT TONIGHT?
JUST SOME SMOKE INHALATION, NOTHING MAJOR.
GOOD. THANKS.
YOU ALL GOOD?
YEAH, IT WAS NOTHING.
THEN THE DRINKS ARE ON YOU.
DICK.

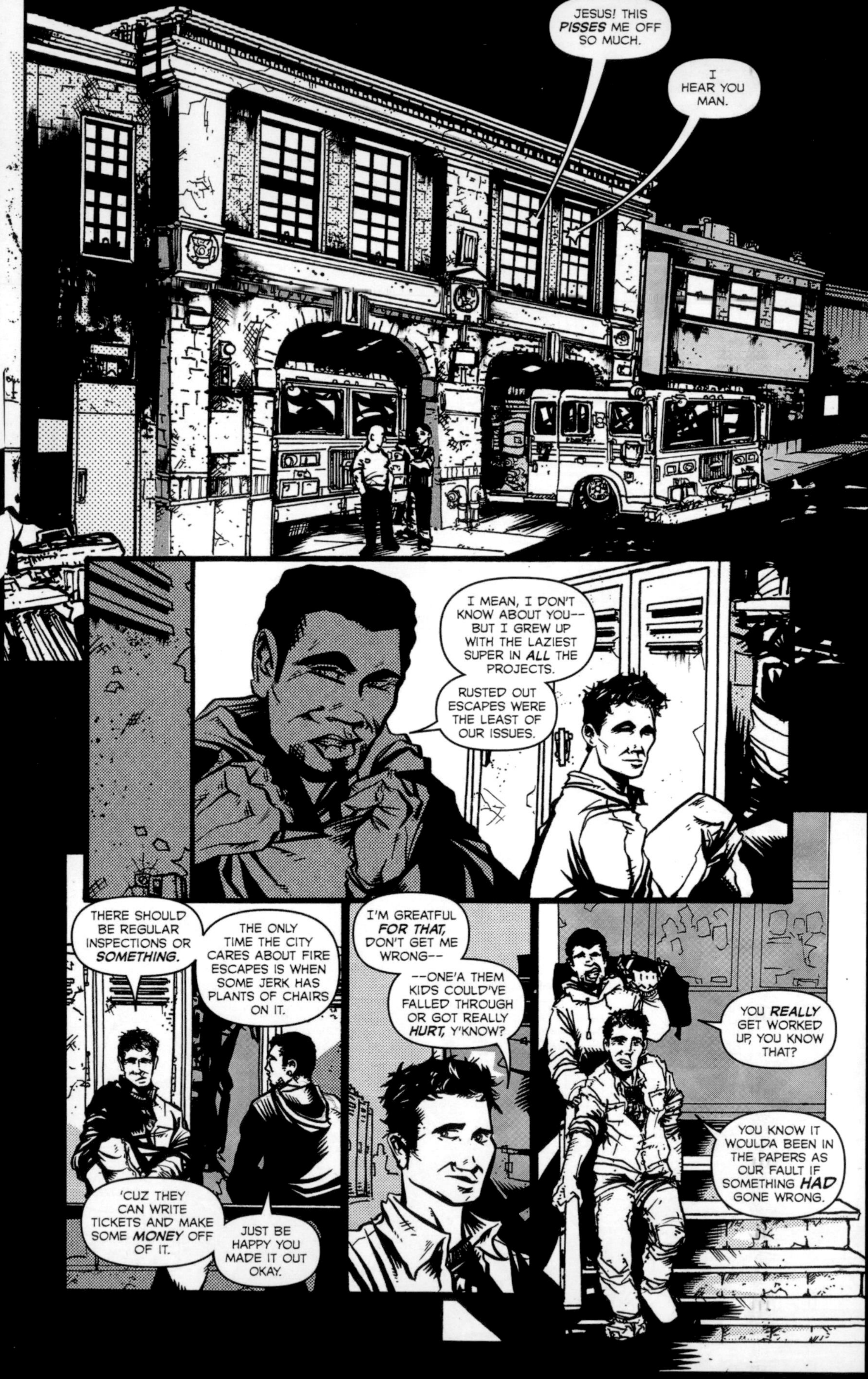
JESUS! THIS PISSES ME OFF SO MUCH.
I HEAR YOU MAN.
I MEAN, I DON'T KNOW ABOUT YOU-- BUT I GREW UP WITH THE LAZIEST SUPER IN ALL THE PROJECTS.
RUSTED OUT ESCAPES WERE THE LEAST OF OUR ISSUES.
THERE SHOULD BE REGULAR INSPECTIONS OR SOMETHING.
THE ONLY TIME THE CITY CARES ABOUT FIRE ESCAPES IS WHEN SOME JERK HAS PLANTS OF CHAIRS ON IT.
'CUZ THEY CAN WRITE TICKETS AND MAKE SOME MONEY OFF OF IT.
JUST BE HAPPY YOU MADE IT OUT OKAY.
I'M GREATFUL FOR THAT, DON'T GET ME WRONG--
--ONE'A THEM KIDS COULD'VE FALLED THROUGH OR GOT REALLY HURT, Y'KNOW?
YOU REALLY GET WORKED UP, YOU KNOW THAT?
YOU KNOW IT WOULDA BEEN IN THE PAPERS AS OUR FAULT IF SOMETHING HAD GONE WRONG.

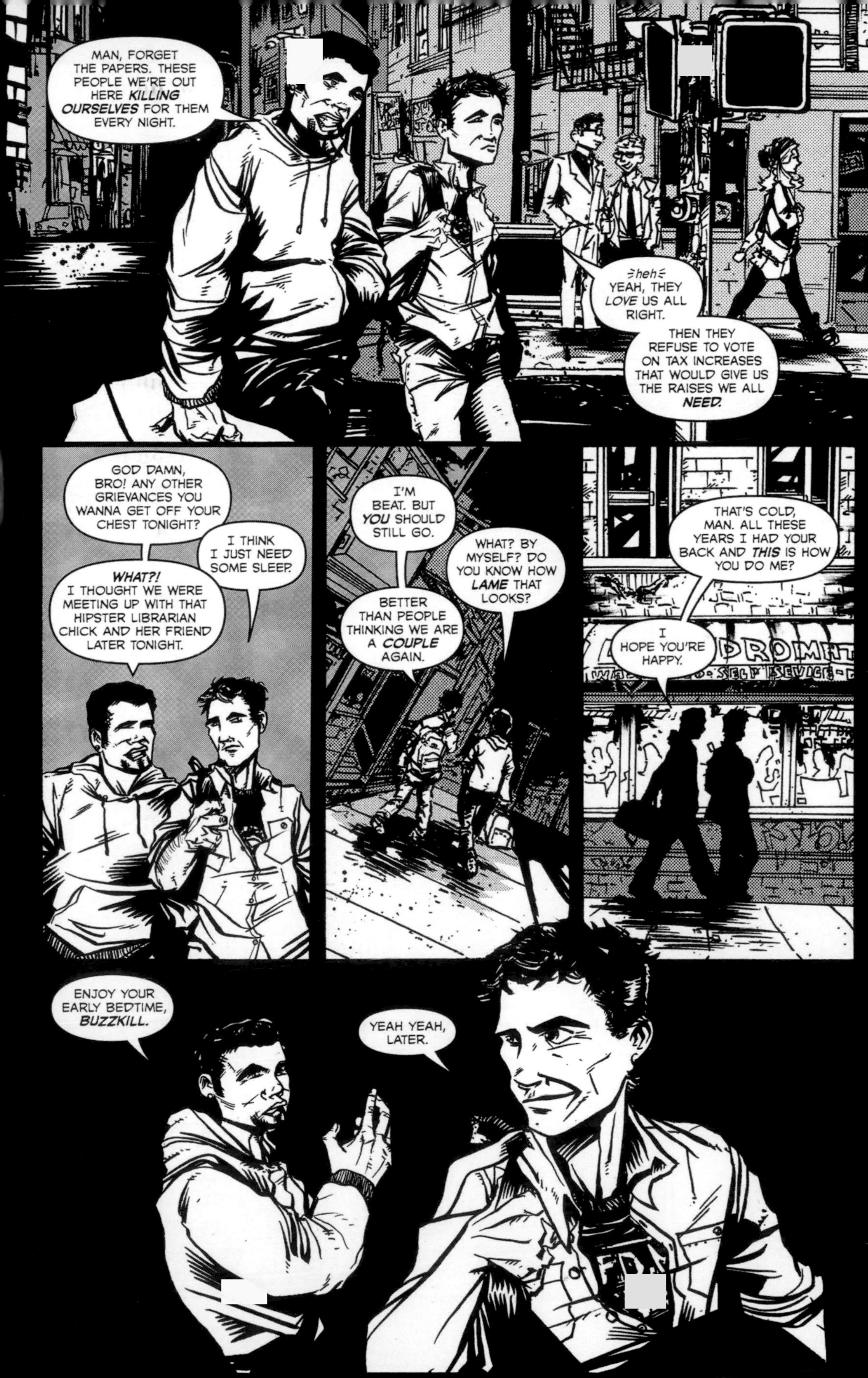
MAN, FORGET THE PAPERS. THESE PEOPLE WE'RE OUT HERE KILLING OURSELVES FOR THEM EVERY NIGHT.
heh
YEAH, THEY LOVE US ALL RIGHT.
THEN THEY REFUSE TO VOTE ON TAX INCREASES THAT WOULD GIVE US THE RAISES WE ALL NEED.
GOD DAMN, BRO! ANY OTHER GRIEVANCES YOU WANNA GET OFF YOUR CHEST TONIGHT?
I THINK I JUST NEED SOME SLEEP.
WHAT?! I THOUGHT WE WERE MEETING UP WITH THAT HIPSTER LIBRARIAN CHICK AND HER FRIEND LATER TONIGHT.
I'M BEAT. BUT YOU SHOULD STILL GO.
WHAT? BY MYSELF? DO YOU KNOW HOW LAME THAT LOOKS?
BETTER THAN PEOPLE THINKING WE ARE A COUPLE AGAIN.
THAT'S COLD, MAN. ALL THESE YEARS I HAD YOUR BACK AND THIS IS HOW YOU DO ME?
I HOPE YOU'RE HAPPY.
ENJOY YOUR EARLY BEDTIME, BUZZKILL.
YEAH YEAH, LATER.

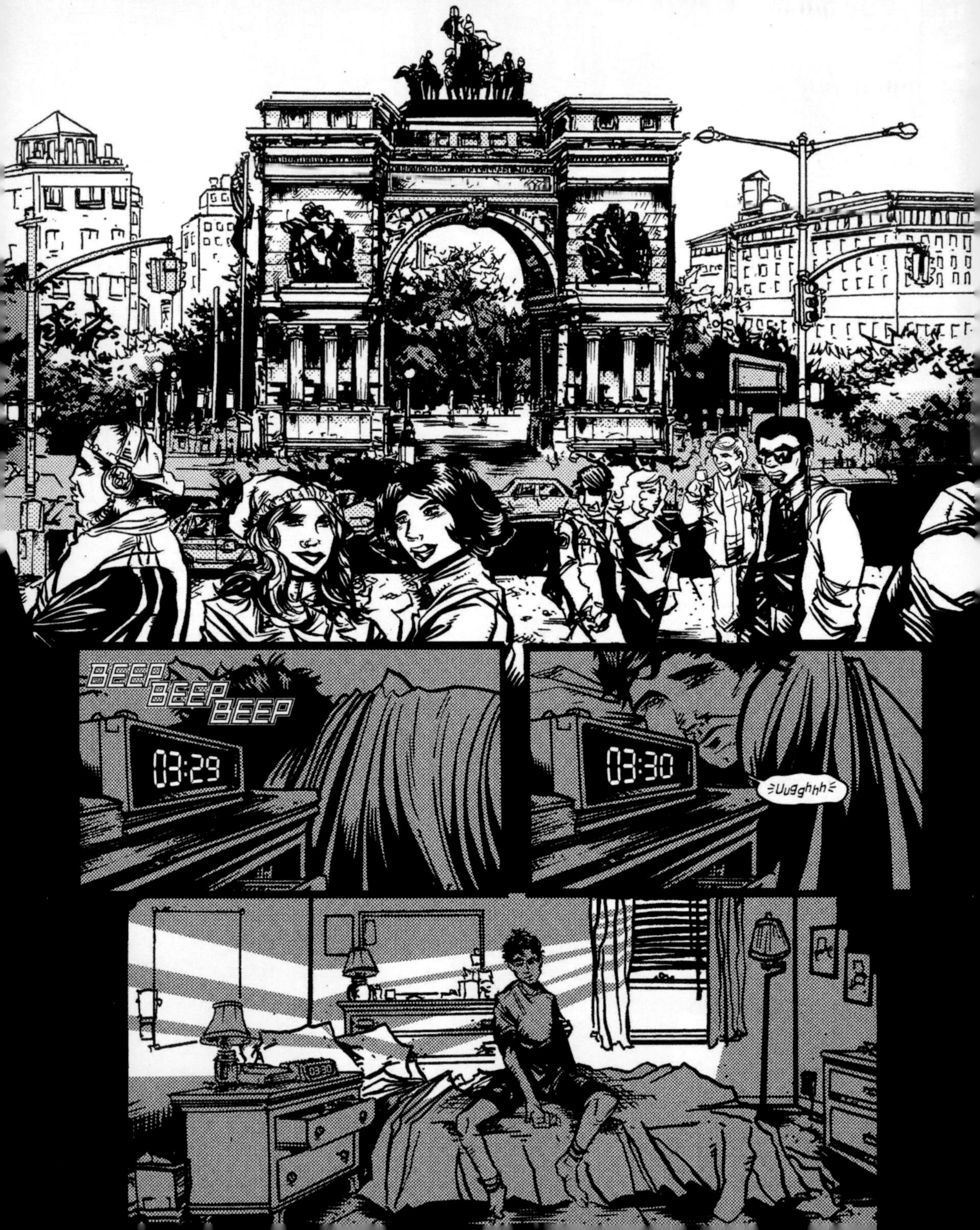
BEEP BEEP BEEP
03:29
03:30
Uugghhh
03:30

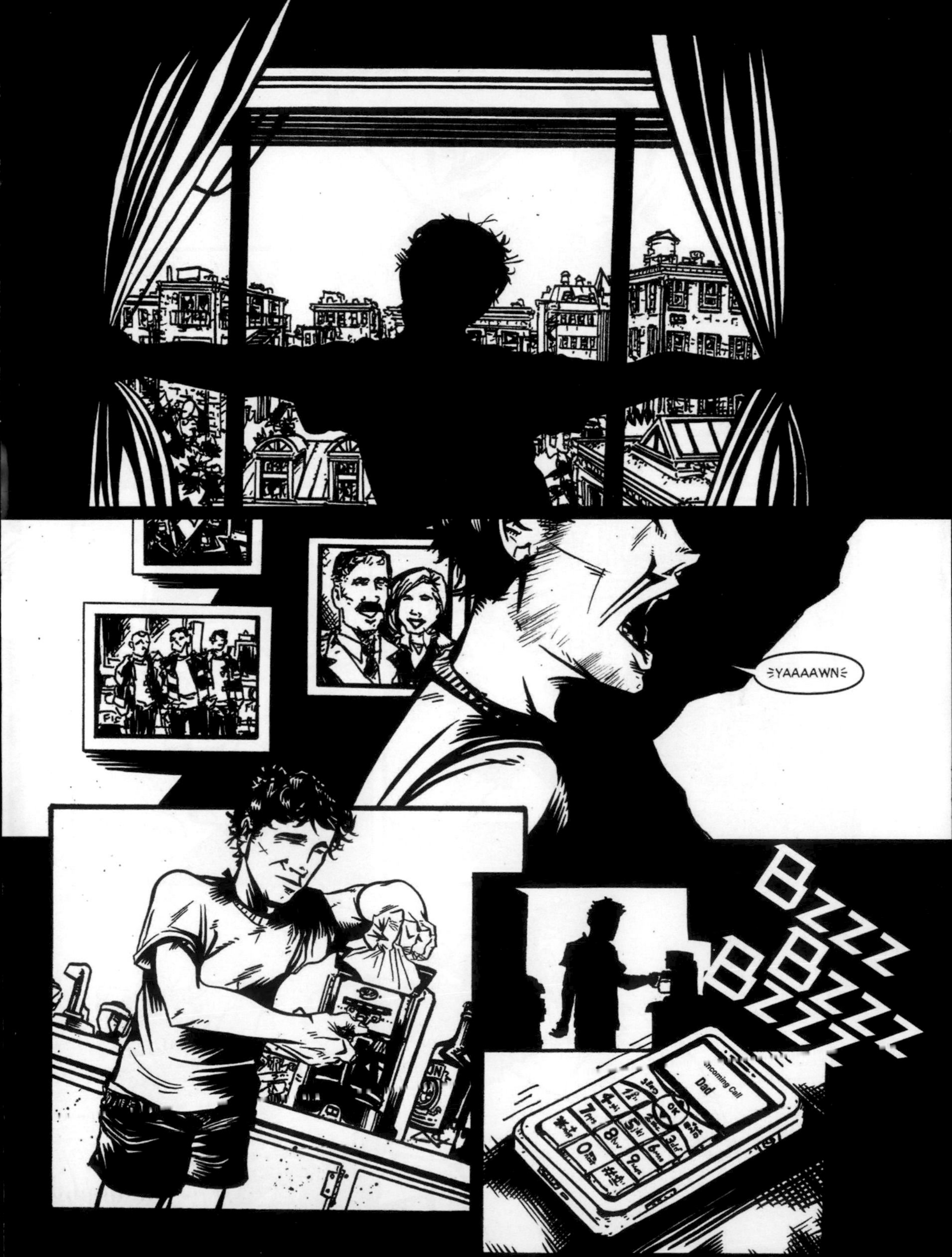
YAAAAWN
BZZZZ
BZZZZ
BZZZZ
Incoming Call
Dad

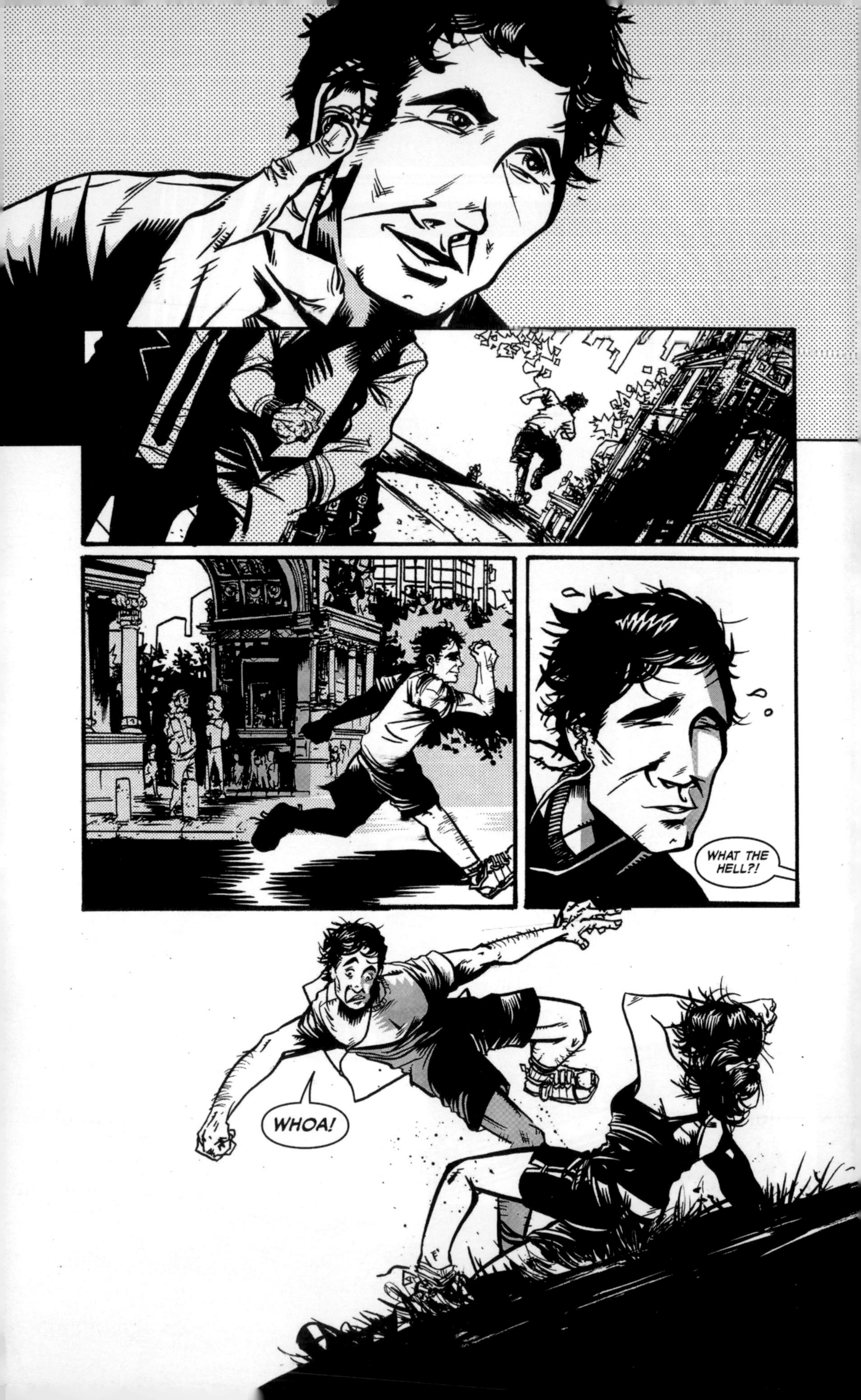
WHAT THE HELL?!
WHOA!

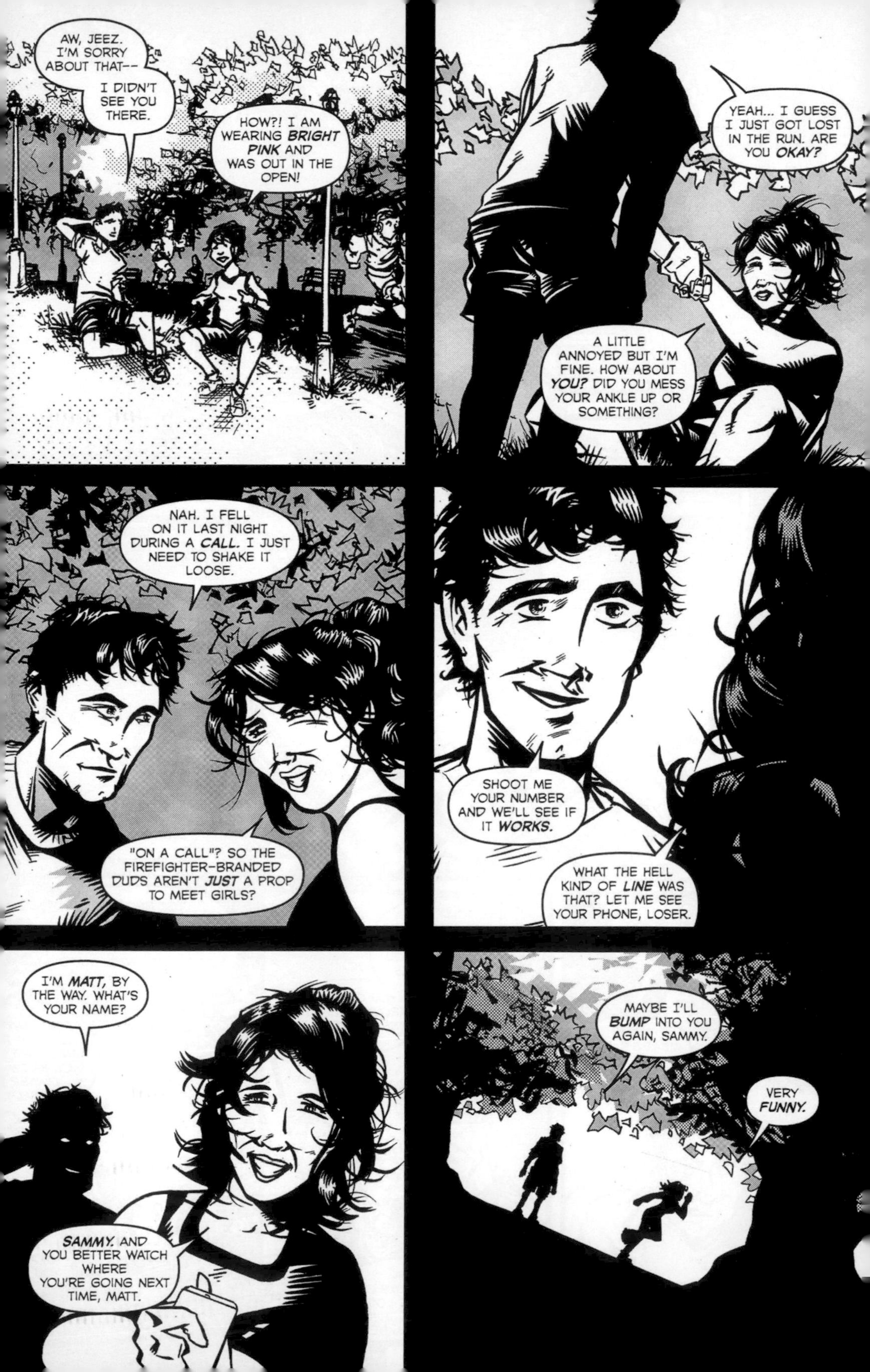
AW, JEEZ. I'M SORRY ABOUT THAT--
I DIDN'T SEE YOU THERE.
HOW?! I AM WEARING BRIGHT PINK AND WAS OUT IN THE OPEN!
YEAH... I GUESS I JUST GOT LOST IN THE RUN. ARE YOU OKAY?
A LITTLE ANNOYED BUT I'M FINE. HOW ABOUT YOU? DID YOU MESS YOUR ANKLE UP OR SOMETHING?
NAH. I FELL ON IT LAST NIGHT DURING A CALL. I JUST NEED TO SHAKE IT LOOSE.
"ON A CALL"? SO THE FIREFIGHTER-BRANDED DUDS AREN'T JUST A PROP TO MEET GIRLS?
SHOOT ME YOUR NUMBER AND WE'LL SEE IF IT WORKS.
WHAT THE HELL KIND OF LINE WAS THAT? LET ME SEE YOUR PHONE, LOSER.
I'M MATT, BY THE WAY. WHAT'S YOUR NAME?
SAMMY. AND YOU BETTER WATCH WHERE YOU'RE GOING NEXT TIME, MATT.
MAYBE I'LL BUMP INTO YOU AGAIN, SAMMY.
VERY FUNNY.

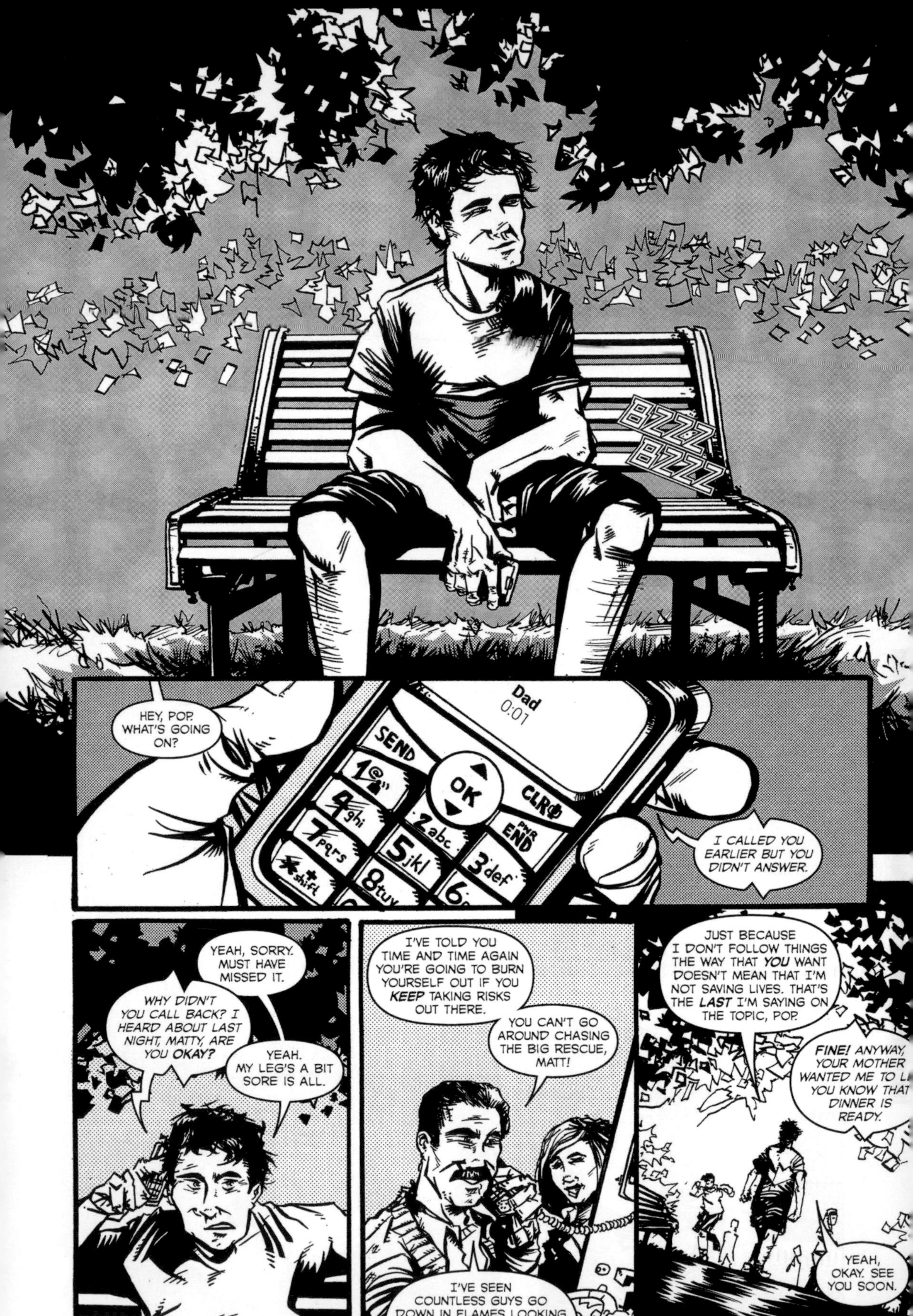
BZZZ BZZZ
Dad
0:01
SEND
OK
CLR
PWR END
HEY, POP. WHAT'S GOING ON?
I CALLED YOU EARLIER BUT YOU DIDN'T ANSWER.
YEAH, SORRY. MUST HAVE MISSED IT.
WHY DIDN'T YOU CALL BACK? I HEARD ABOUT LAST NIGHT, MATTY, ARE YOU OKAY?
YEAH. MY LEG'S A BIT SORE IS ALL.
I'VE TOLD YOU TIME AND TIME AGAIN YOU'RE GOING TO BURN YOURSELF OUT IF YOU KEEP TAKING RISKS OUT THERE.
YOU CAN'T GO AROUND CHASING THE BIG RESCUE, MATT!
I'VE SEEN COUNTLESS GUYS GO DOWN IN FLAMES LOOKING FOR THAT GLORY. THINK OF YOUR OWN WELL BEING.
JUST BECAUSE I DON'T FOLLOW THINGS THE WAY THAT YOU WANT DOESN'T MEAN THAT I'M NOT SAVING LIVES. THAT'S THE LAST I'M SAYING ON THE TOPIC, POP.
FINE! ANYWAY, YOUR MOTHER WANTED ME TO L YOU KNOW THAT DINNER IS READY.
YEAH, OKAY. SEE YOU SOON.

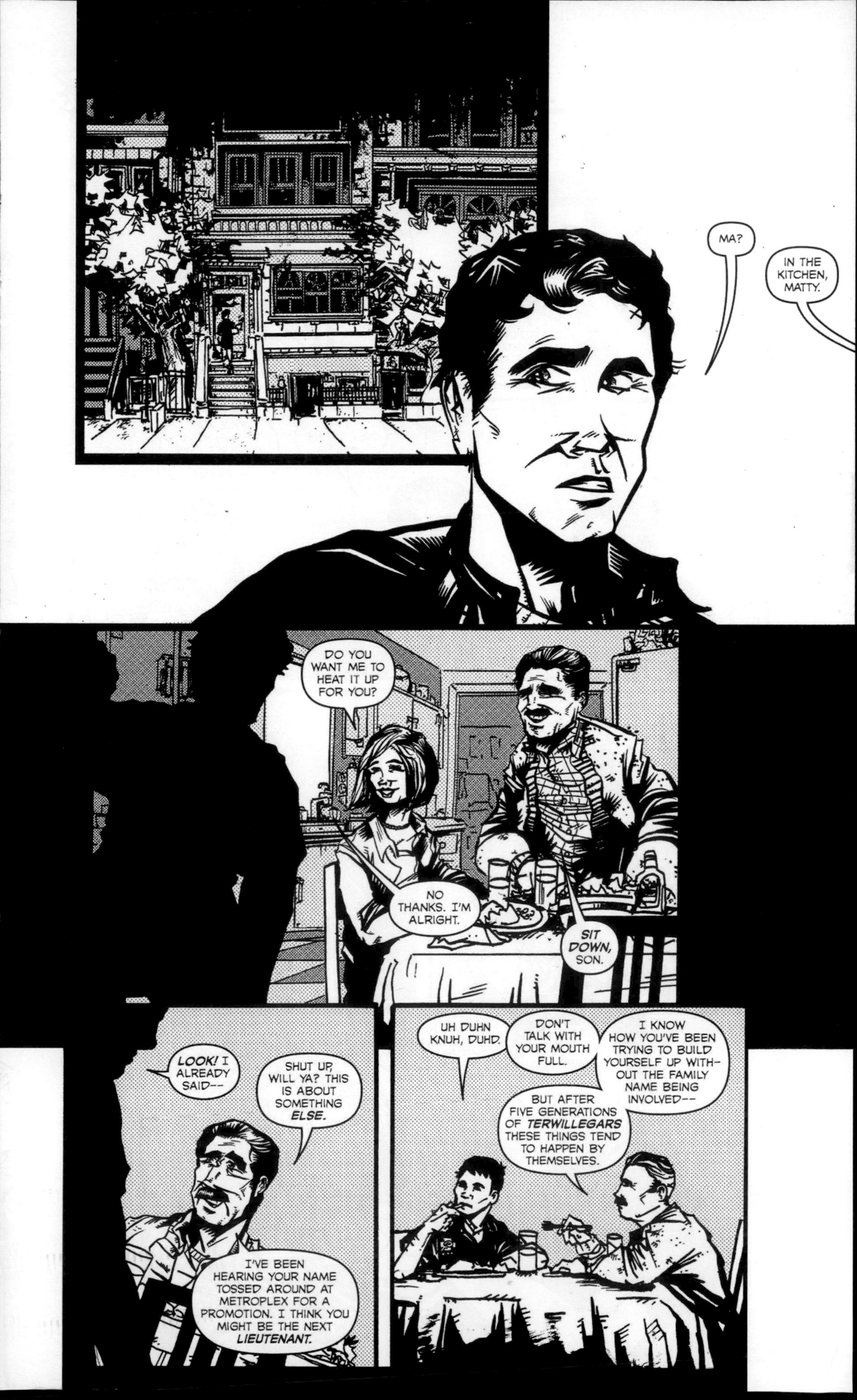
MA?
IN THE KITCHEN, MATTY.
DO YOU WANT ME TO HEAT IT UP FOR YOU?
NO THANKS. I'M ALRIGHT.
SIT DOWN, SON.
LOOK! I ALREADY SAID--
SHUT UP, WILL YA? THIS IS ABOUT SOMETHING ELSE.
I'VE BEEN HEARING YOUR NAME TOSSED AROUND AT METROPLEX FOR A PROMOTION. I THINK YOU MIGHT BE THE NEXT LIEUTENANT.
UH DUHN KNUH, DUHD.
DON'T TALK WITH YOUR MOUTH FULL.
I KNOW HOW YOU'VE BEEN TRYING TO BUILD YOURSELF UP WITH-OUT THE FAMILY NAME BEING INVOLVED--
BUT AFTER FIVE GENERATIONS OF TERWILLEGARS THESE THINGS TEND TO HAPPEN BY THEMSELVES.

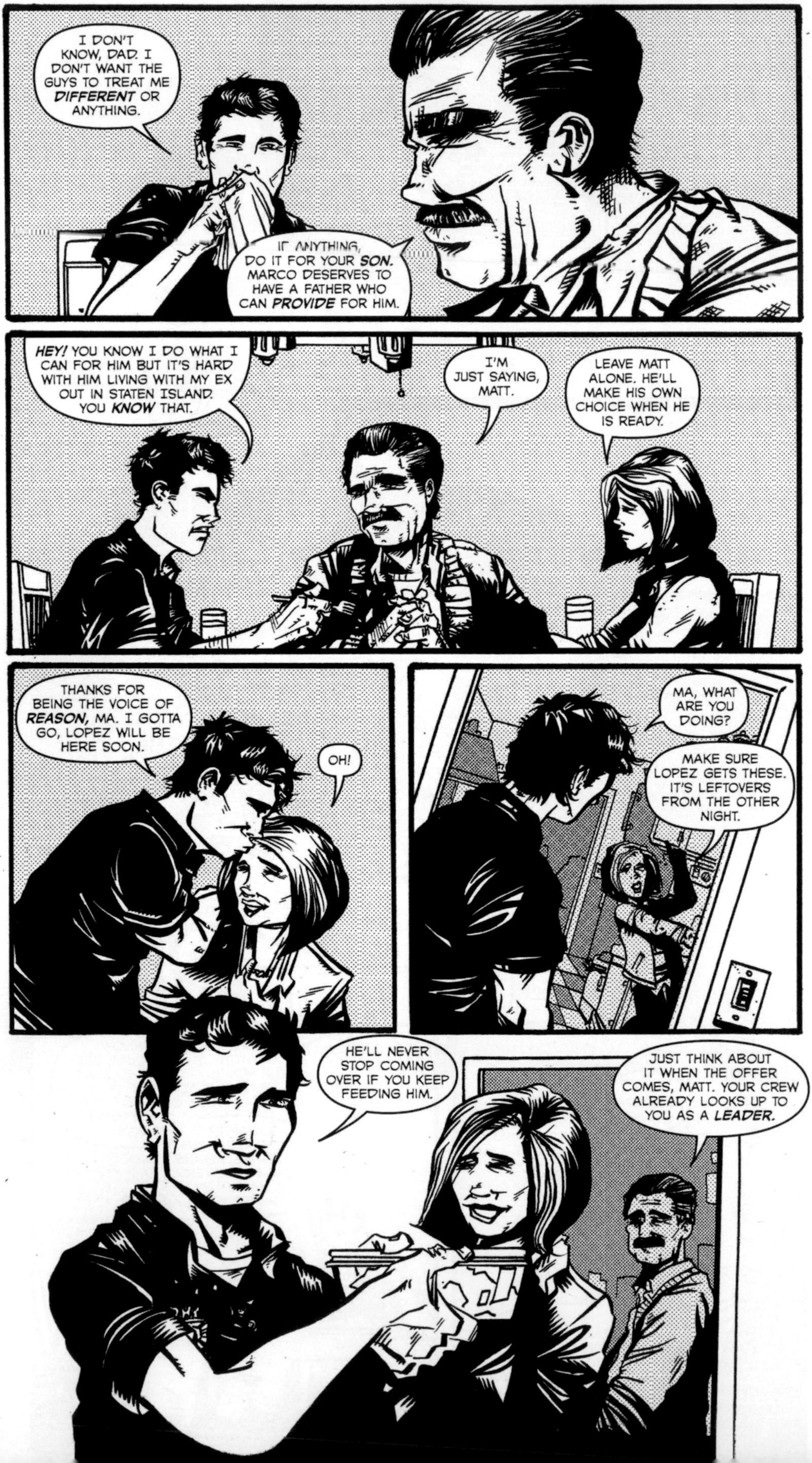
I DON'T KNOW, DAD. I DON'T WANT THE GUYS TO TREAT ME *DIFFERENT* OR ANYTHING.
IF ANYTHING, DO IT FOR YOUR *SON.* MARCO DESERVES TO HAVE A FATHER WHO CAN *PROVIDE* FOR HIM.
HEY! YOU KNOW I DO WHAT I CAN FOR HIM BUT IT'S HARD WITH HIM LIVING WITH MY EX OUT IN STATEN ISLAND. YOU *KNOW* THAT.
I'M JUST SAYING, MATT.
LEAVE MATT ALONE. HE'LL MAKE HIS OWN CHOICE WHEN HE IS READY.
THANKS FOR BEING THE VOICE OF *REASON,* MA. I GOTTA GO, LOPEZ WILL BE HERE SOON.
OH!
MA, WHAT ARE YOU DOING?
MAKE SURE LOPEZ GETS THESE. IT'S LEFTOVERS FROM THE OTHER NIGHT.
HE'LL NEVER STOP COMING OVER IF YOU KEEP FEEDING HIM.
JUST THINK ABOUT IT WHEN THE OFFER COMES, MATT. YOUR CREW ALREADY LOOKS UP TO YOU AS A *LEADER.*

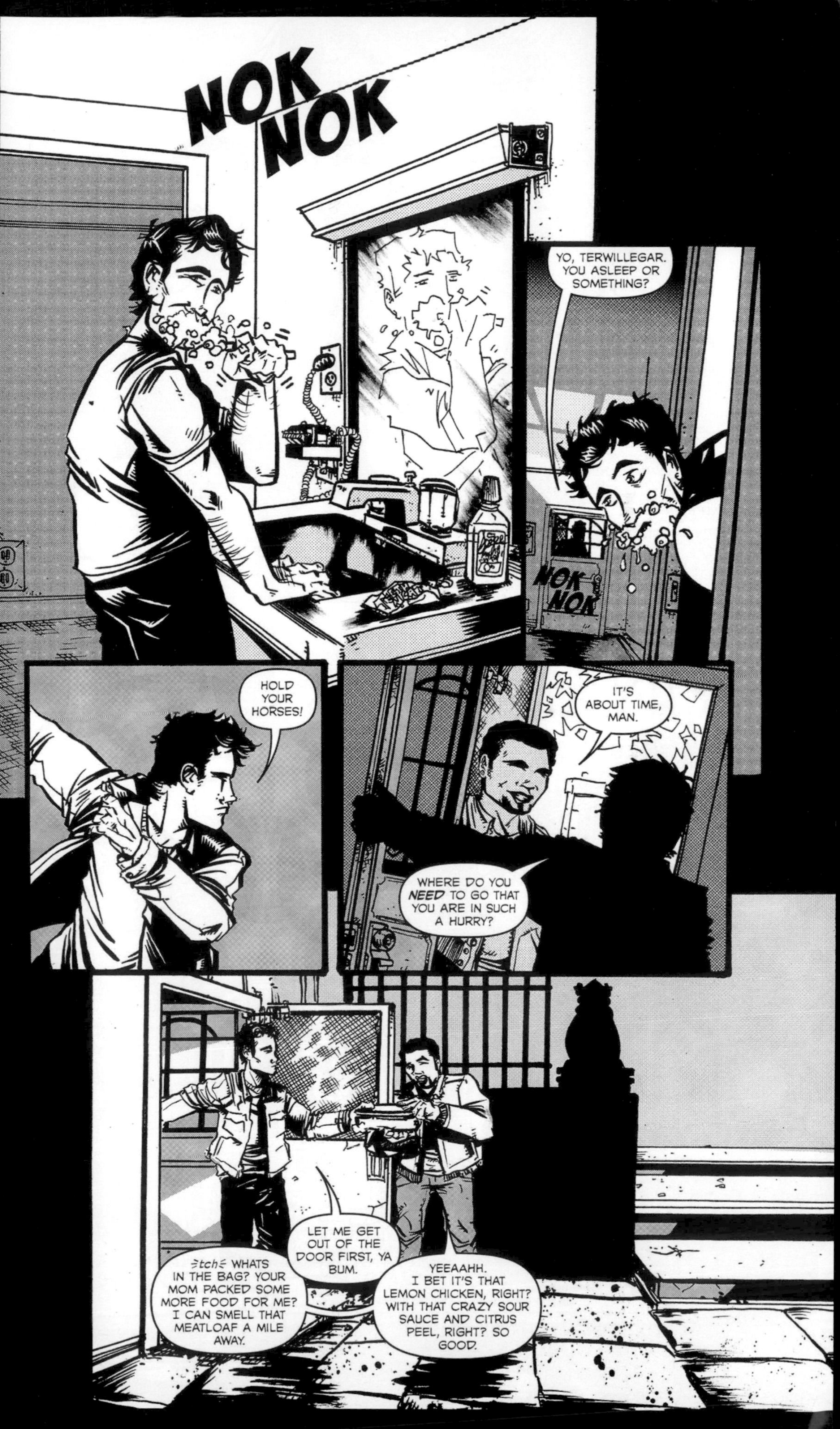
NOK NOK
YO, TERWILLEGAR. YOU ASLEEP OR SOMETHING?
NOK NOK
HOLD YOUR HORSES!
IT'S ABOUT TIME, MAN.
WHERE DO YOU *NEED* TO GO THAT YOU ARE IN SUCH A HURRY?
LET ME GET OUT OF THE DOOR FIRST, YA BUM.
=tch= WHATS IN THE BAG? YOUR MOM PACKED SOME MORE FOOD FOR ME? I CAN SMELL THAT MEATLOAF A MILE AWAY.
YEEAAHH. I BET IT'S THAT LEMON CHICKEN, RIGHT? WITH THAT CRAZY SOUR SAUCE AND CITRUS PEEL, RIGHT? SO GOOD.

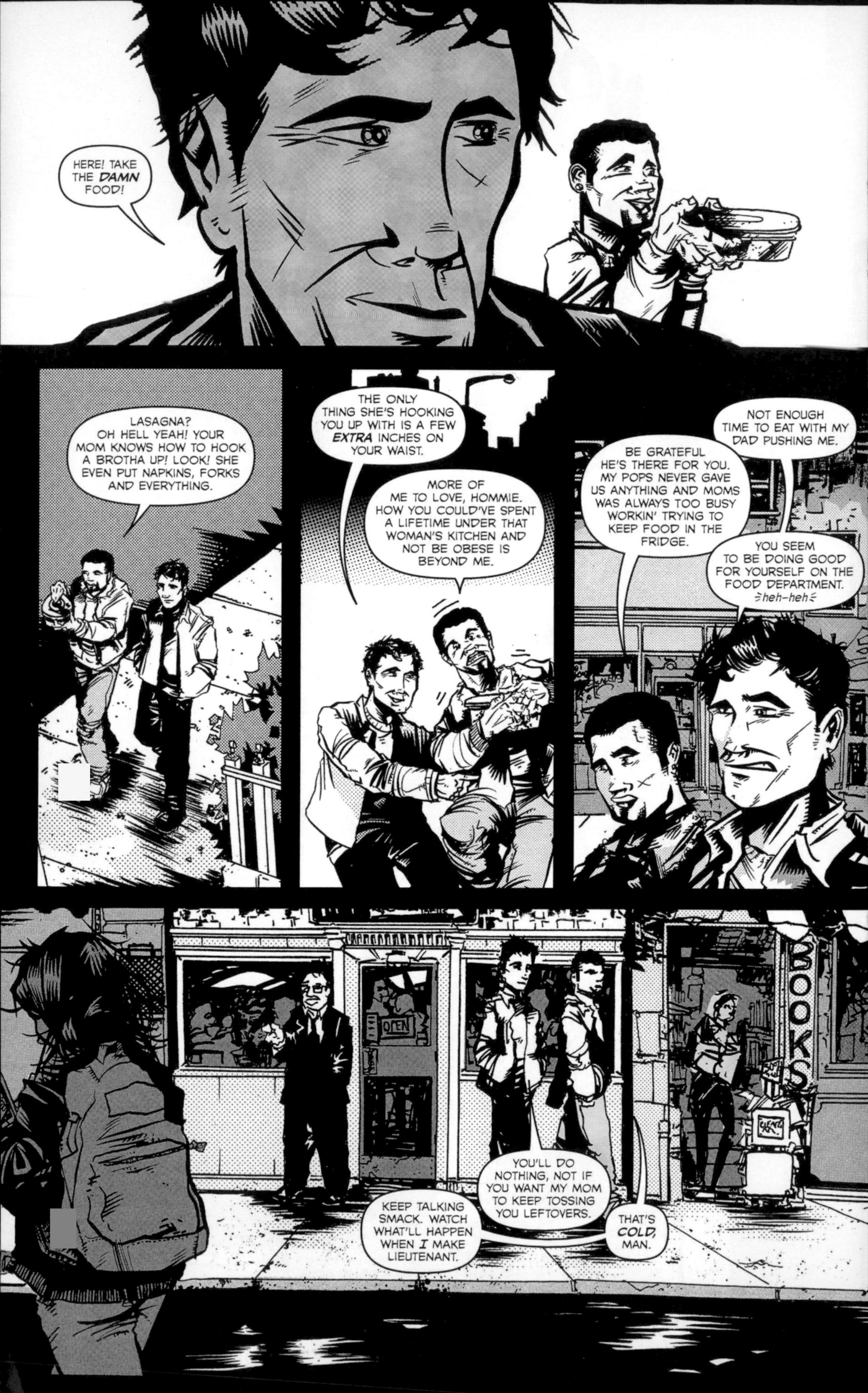
HERE! TAKE THE *DAMN* FOOD!
LASAGNA? OH HELL YEAH! YOUR MOM KNOWS HOW TO HOOK A BROTHA UP! LOOK! SHE EVEN PUT NAPKINS, FORKS AND EVERYTHING.
THE ONLY THING SHE'S HOOKING YOU UP WITH IS A FEW *EXTRA* INCHES ON YOUR WAIST.
MORE OF ME TO LOVE, HOMMIE. HOW YOU COULD'VE SPENT A LIFETIME UNDER THAT WOMAN'S KITCHEN AND NOT BE OBESE IS BEYOND ME.
NOT ENOUGH TIME TO EAT WITH MY DAD PUSHING ME.
BE GRATEFUL HE'S THERE FOR YOU. MY POPS NEVER GAVE US ANYTHING AND MOMS WAS ALWAYS TOO BUSY WORKIN' TRYING TO KEEP FOOD IN THE FRIDGE.
YOU SEEM TO BE DOING GOOD FOR YOURSELF ON THE FOOD DEPARTMENT. *heh-heh*
OPEN
BOOKS
KEEP TALKING SMACK. WATCH WHAT'LL HAPPEN WHEN *I* MAKE LIEUTENANT.
YOU'LL DO NOTHING, NOT IF YOU WANT MY MOM TO KEEP TOSSING YOU LEFTOVERS.
THAT'S *COLD*, MAN.

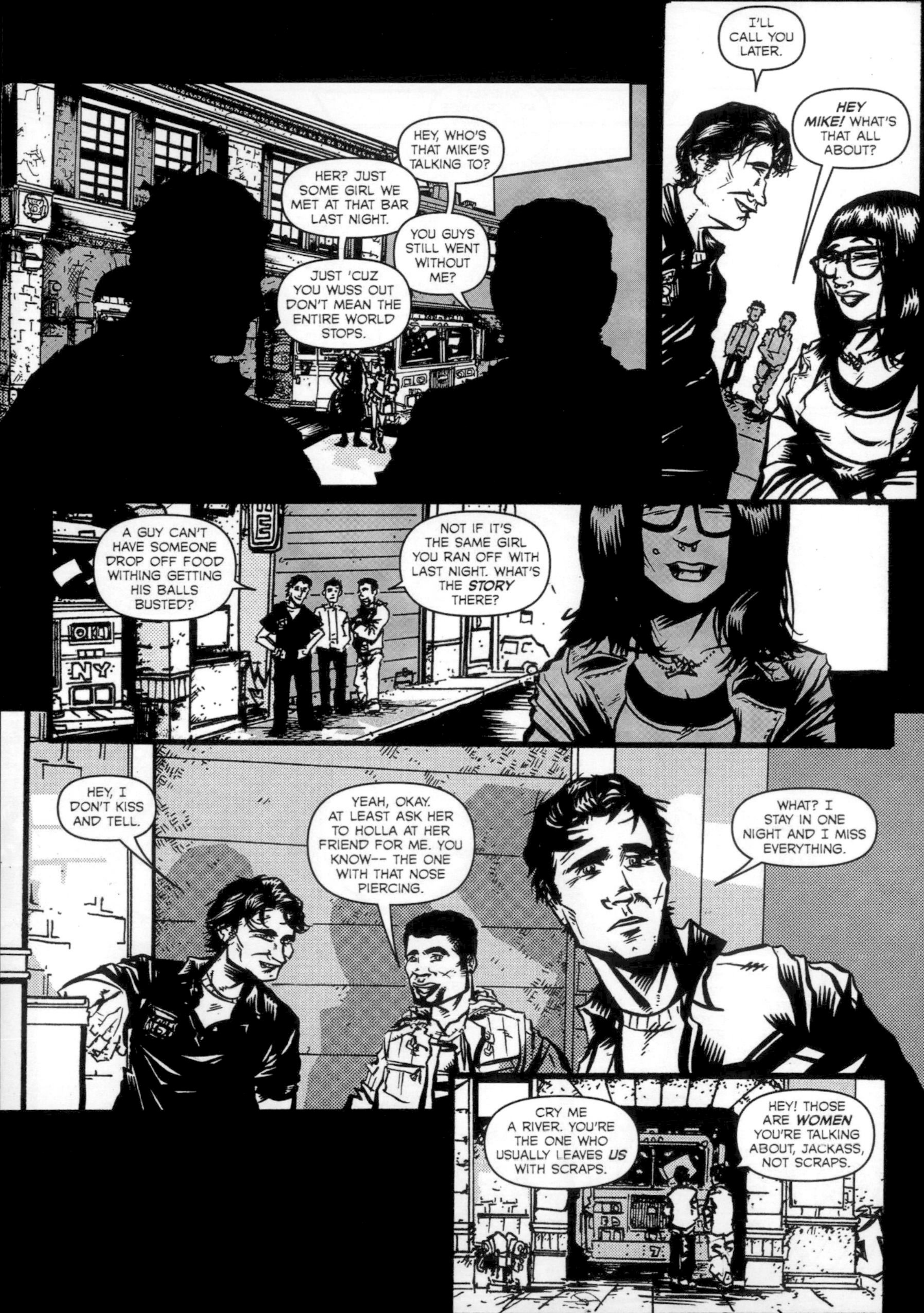
HEY, WHO'S THAT MIKE'S TALKING TO?
HER? JUST SOME GIRL WE MET AT THAT BAR LAST NIGHT.
YOU GUYS STILL WENT WITHOUT ME?
JUST 'CUZ YOU WUSS OUT DON'T MEAN THE ENTIRE WORLD STOPS.
I'LL CALL YOU LATER.
HEY MIKE! WHAT'S THAT ALL ABOUT?
A GUY CAN'T HAVE SOMEONE DROP OFF FOOD WITHING GETTING HIS BALLS BUSTED?
NOT IF IT'S THE SAME GIRL YOU RAN OFF WITH LAST NIGHT. WHAT'S THE STORY THERE?
OKI
NY
HEY, I DON'T KISS AND TELL.
YEAH, OKAY. AT LEAST ASK HER TO HOLLA AT HER FRIEND FOR ME. YOU KNOW-- THE ONE WITH THAT NOSE PIERCING.
WHAT? I STAY IN ONE NIGHT AND I MISS EVERYTHING.
CRY ME A RIVER. YOU'RE THE ONE WHO USUALLY LEAVES US WITH SCRAPS.
HEY! THOSE ARE WOMEN YOU'RE TALKING ABOUT, JACKASS, NOT SCRAPS.

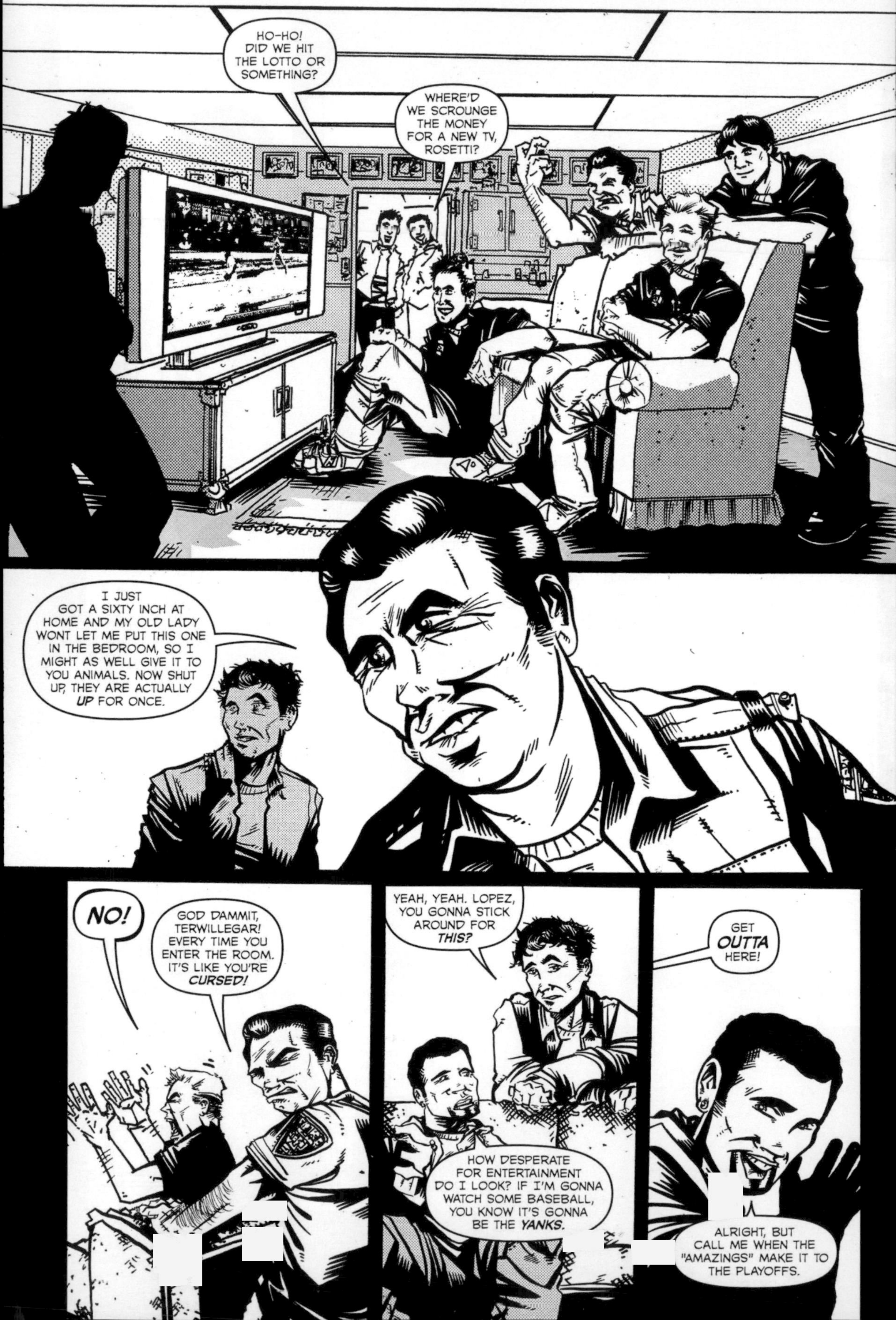
HO-HO! DID WE HIT THE LOTTO OR SOMETHING?
WHERE'D WE SCROUNGE THE MONEY FOR A NEW TV, ROSETTI?
I JUST GOT A SIXTY INCH AT HOME AND MY OLD LADY WONT LET ME PUT THIS ONE IN THE BEDROOM, SO I MIGHT AS WELL GIVE IT TO YOU ANIMALS. NOW SHUT UP, THEY ARE ACTUALLY *UP* FOR ONCE.
NO!
GOD DAMMIT, TERWILLEGAR! EVERY TIME YOU ENTER THE ROOM. IT'S LIKE YOU'RE *CURSED!*
YEAH, YEAH. LOPEZ, YOU GONNA STICK AROUND FOR *THIS?*
HOW DESPERATE FOR ENTERTAINMENT DO I LOOK? IF I'M GONNA WATCH SOME BASEBALL, YOU KNOW IT'S GONNA BE THE *YANKS.*
GET *OUTTA* HERE!
ALRIGHT, BUT CALL ME WHEN THE "AMAZINGS" MAKE IT TO THE PLAYOFFS.

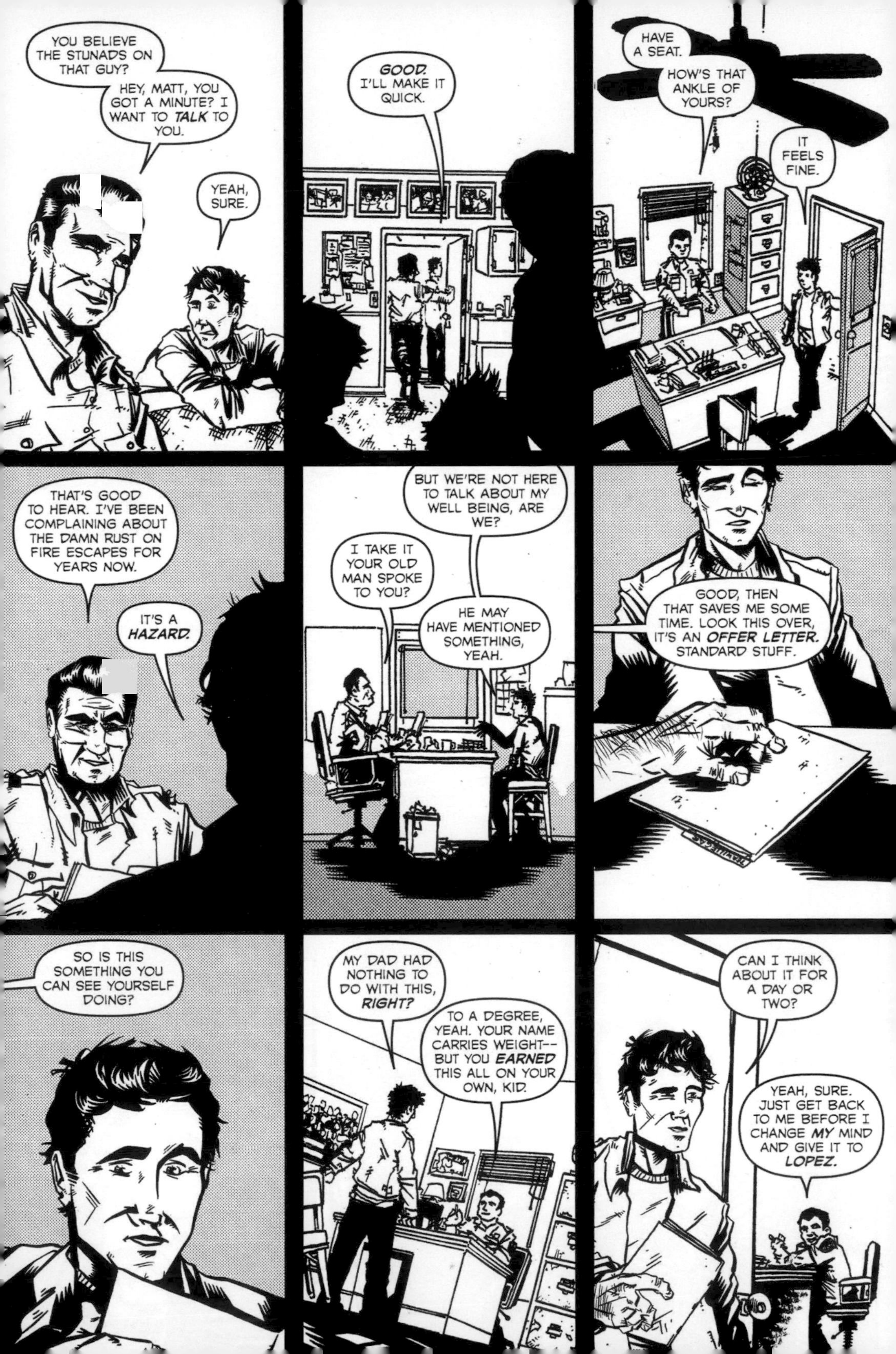
YOU BELIEVE THE STUNADS ON THAT GUY?
HEY, MATT, YOU GOT A MINUTE? I WANT TO *TALK* TO YOU.
YEAH, SURE.
GOOD. I'LL MAKE IT QUICK.
HAVE A SEAT.
HOW'S THAT ANKLE OF YOURS?
IT FEELS FINE.
THAT'S GOOD TO HEAR. I'VE BEEN COMPLAINING ABOUT THE DAMN RUST ON FIRE ESCAPES FOR YEARS NOW.
IT'S A *HAZARD.*
BUT WE'RE NOT HERE TO TALK ABOUT MY WELL BEING, ARE WE?
I TAKE IT YOUR OLD MAN SPOKE TO YOU?
HE MAY HAVE MENTIONED SOMETHING, YEAH.
GOOD, THEN THAT SAVES ME SOME TIME. LOOK THIS OVER, IT'S AN *OFFER LETTER.* STANDARD STUFF.
SO IS THIS SOMETHING YOU CAN SEE YOURSELF DOING?
MY DAD HAD NOTHING TO DO WITH THIS, *RIGHT?*
TO A DEGREE, YEAH. YOUR NAME CARRIES WEIGHT-- BUT YOU *EARNED* THIS ALL ON YOUR OWN, KID.
CAN I THINK ABOUT IT FOR A DAY OR TWO?
YEAH, SURE. JUST GET BACK TO ME BEFORE I CHANGE *MY* MIND AND GIVE IT TO *LOPEZ.*

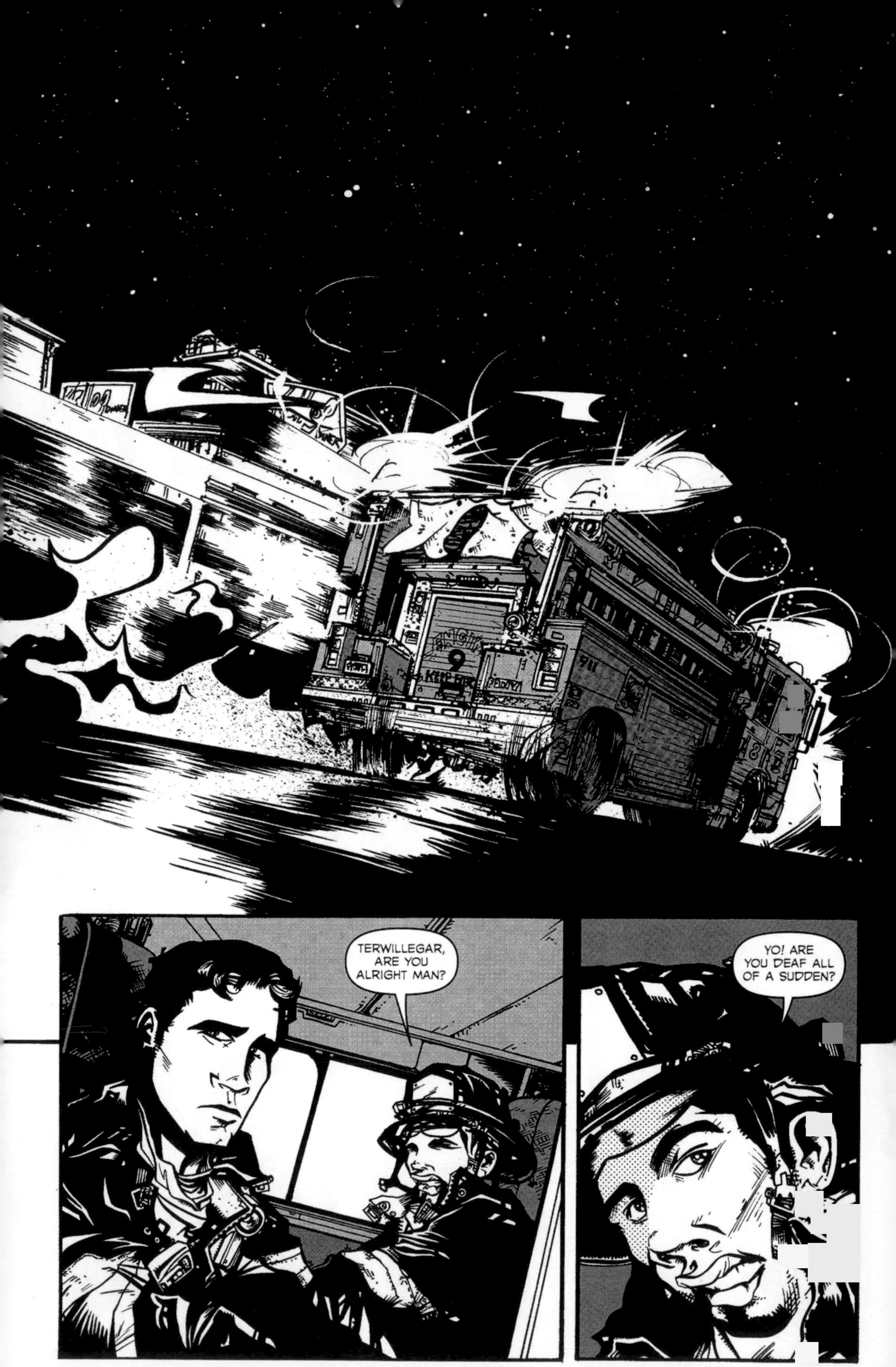
TERWILLEGAR, ARE YOU ALRIGHT MAN?
YO! ARE YOU DEAF ALL OF A SUDDEN?

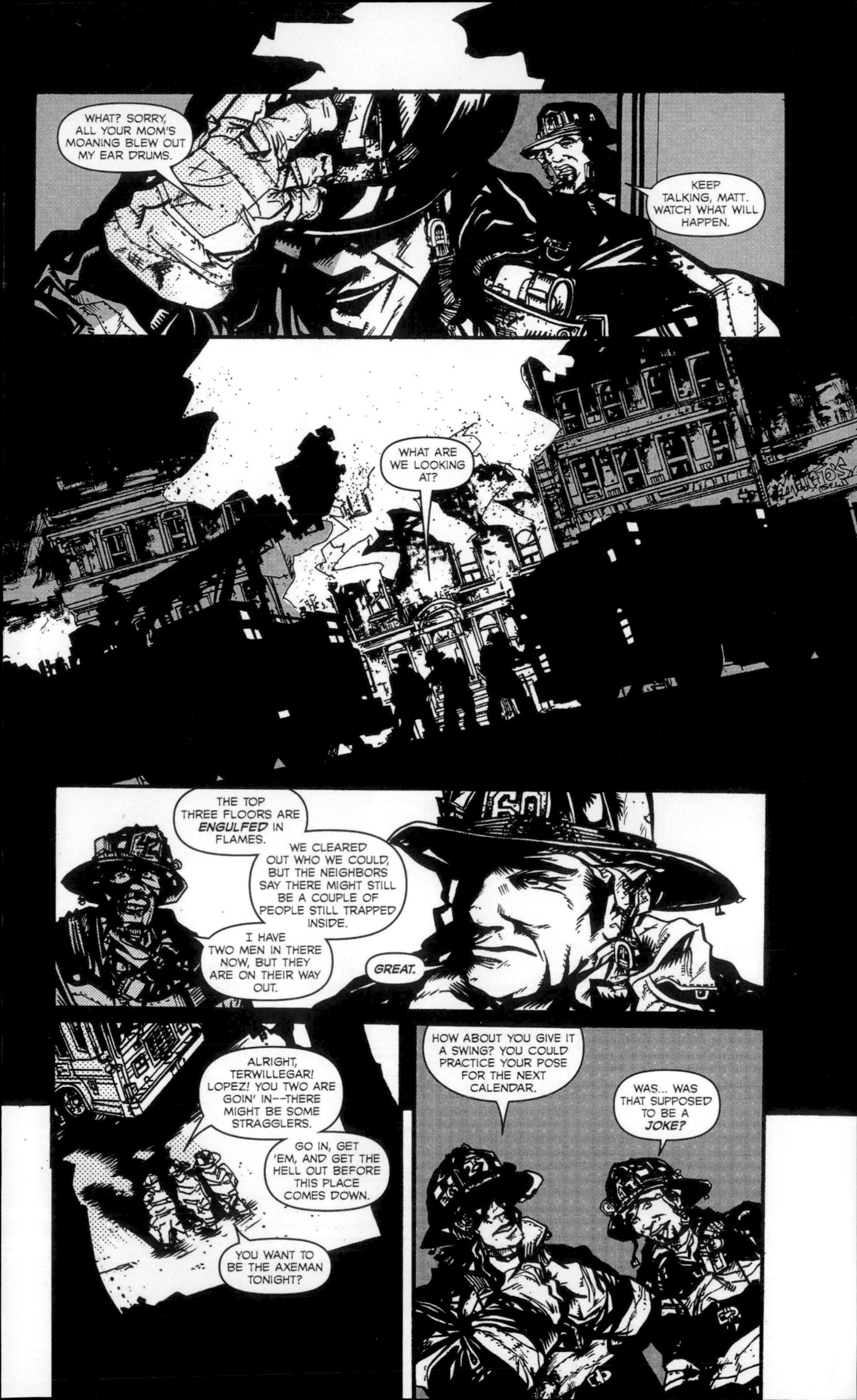
WHAT? SORRY, ALL YOUR MOM'S MOANING BLEW OUT MY EAR DRUMS.
KEEP TALKING, MATT. WATCH WHAT WILL HAPPEN.
WHAT ARE WE LOOKING AT?
THE TOP THREE FLOORS ARE *ENGULFED* IN FLAMES.
WE CLEARED OUT WHO WE COULD, BUT THE NEIGHBORS SAY THERE MIGHT STILL BE A COUPLE OF PEOPLE STILL TRAPPED INSIDE.
I HAVE TWO MEN IN THERE NOW, BUT THEY ARE ON THEIR WAY OUT.
GREAT.
ALRIGHT, TERWILLEGAR! LOPEZ! YOU TWO ARE GOIN' IN--THERE MIGHT BE SOME STRAGGLERS.
GO IN, GET 'EM, AND GET THE HELL OUT BEFORE THIS PLACE COMES DOWN.
YOU WANT TO BE THE AXEMAN TONIGHT?
HOW ABOUT YOU GIVE IT A SWING? YOU COULD PRACTICE YOUR POSE FOR THE NEXT CALENDAR.
WAS... WAS THAT SUPPOSED TO BE A *JOKE?*

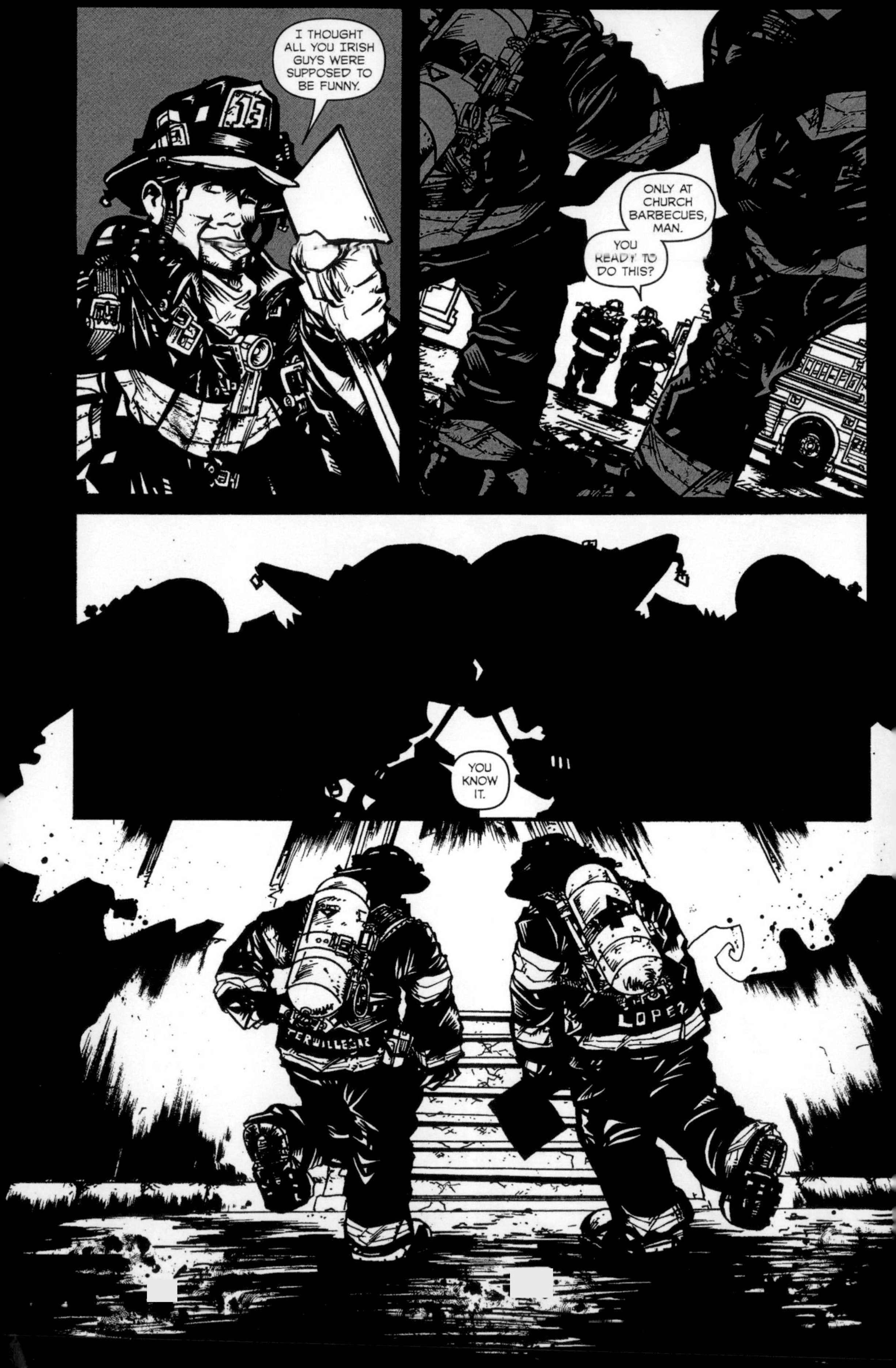
I THOUGHT ALL YOU IRISH GUYS WERE SUPPOSED TO BE FUNNY.
ONLY AT CHURCH BARBECUES, MAN.
YOU READY TO DO THIS?
YOU KNOW IT.
LOPEZ

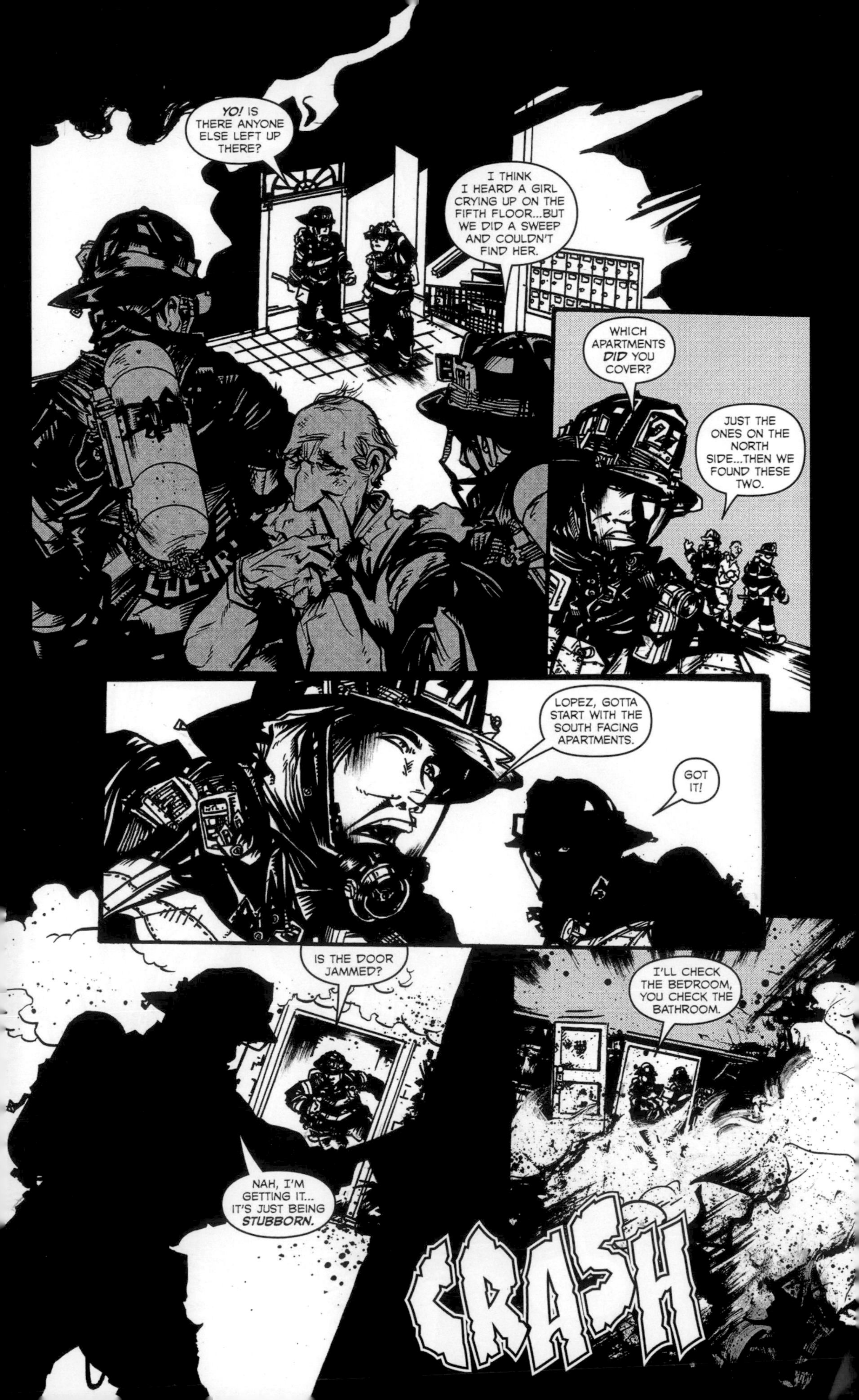
YO! IS THERE ANYONE ELSE LEFT UP THERE?
I THINK I HEARD A GIRL CRYING UP ON THE FIFTH FLOOR...BUT WE DID A SWEEP AND COULDN'T FIND HER.
WHICH APARTMENTS DID YOU COVER?
JUST THE ONES ON THE NORTH SIDE...THEN WE FOUND THESE TWO.
LOPEZ, GOTTA START WITH THE SOUTH FACING APARTMENTS.
GOT IT!
IS THE DOOR JAMMED?
NAH, I'M GETTING IT... IT'S JUST BEING STUBBORN.
I'LL CHECK THE BEDROOM, YOU CHECK THE BATHROOM.
CRASH

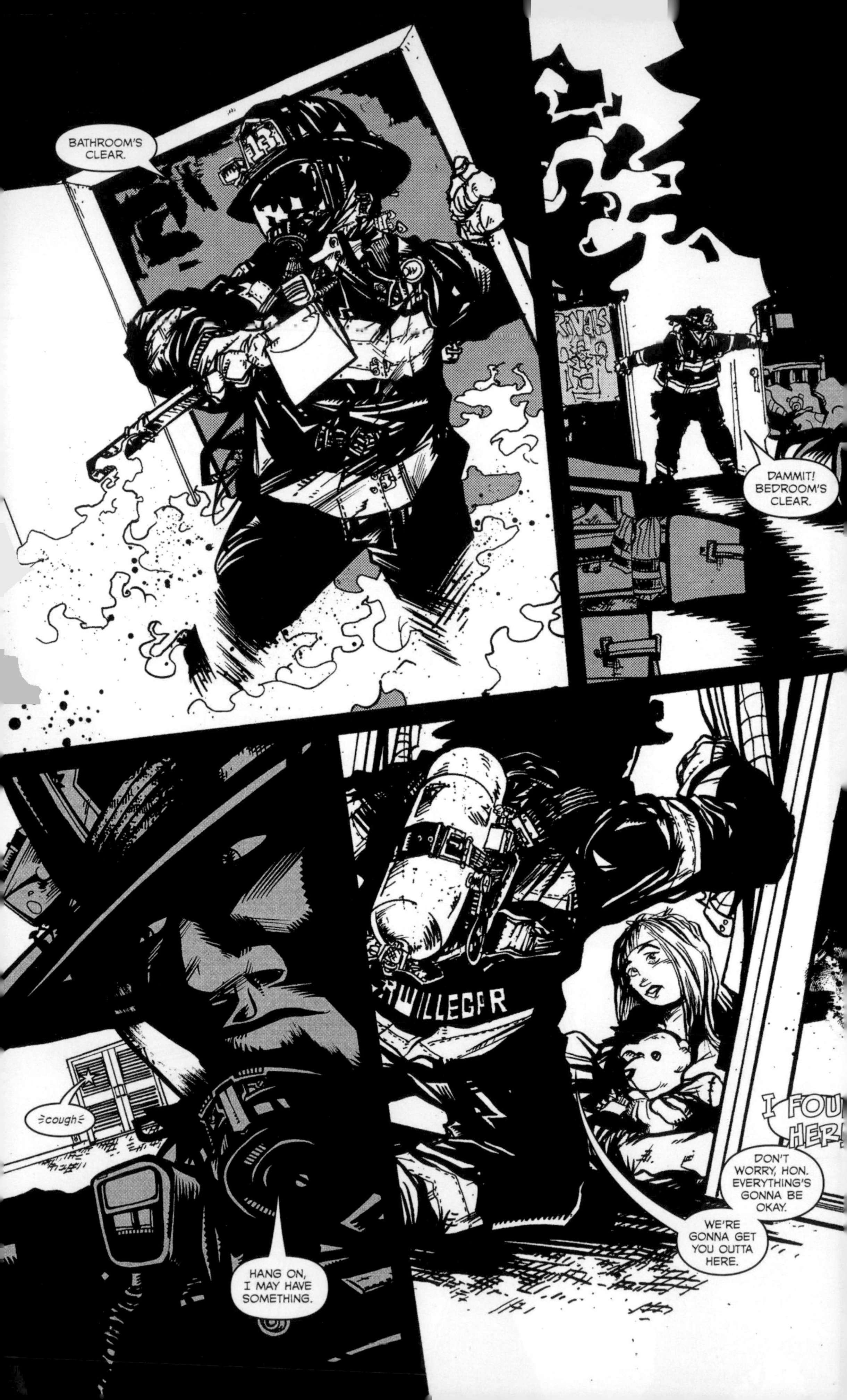

BATHROOM'S CLEAR.
DAMMIT! BEDROOM'S CLEAR.
cough
HANG ON, I MAY HAVE SOMETHING.
I FOU
HER
DON'T WORRY, HON. EVERYTHING'S GONNA BE OKAY.
WE'RE GONNA GET YOU OUTTA HERE.

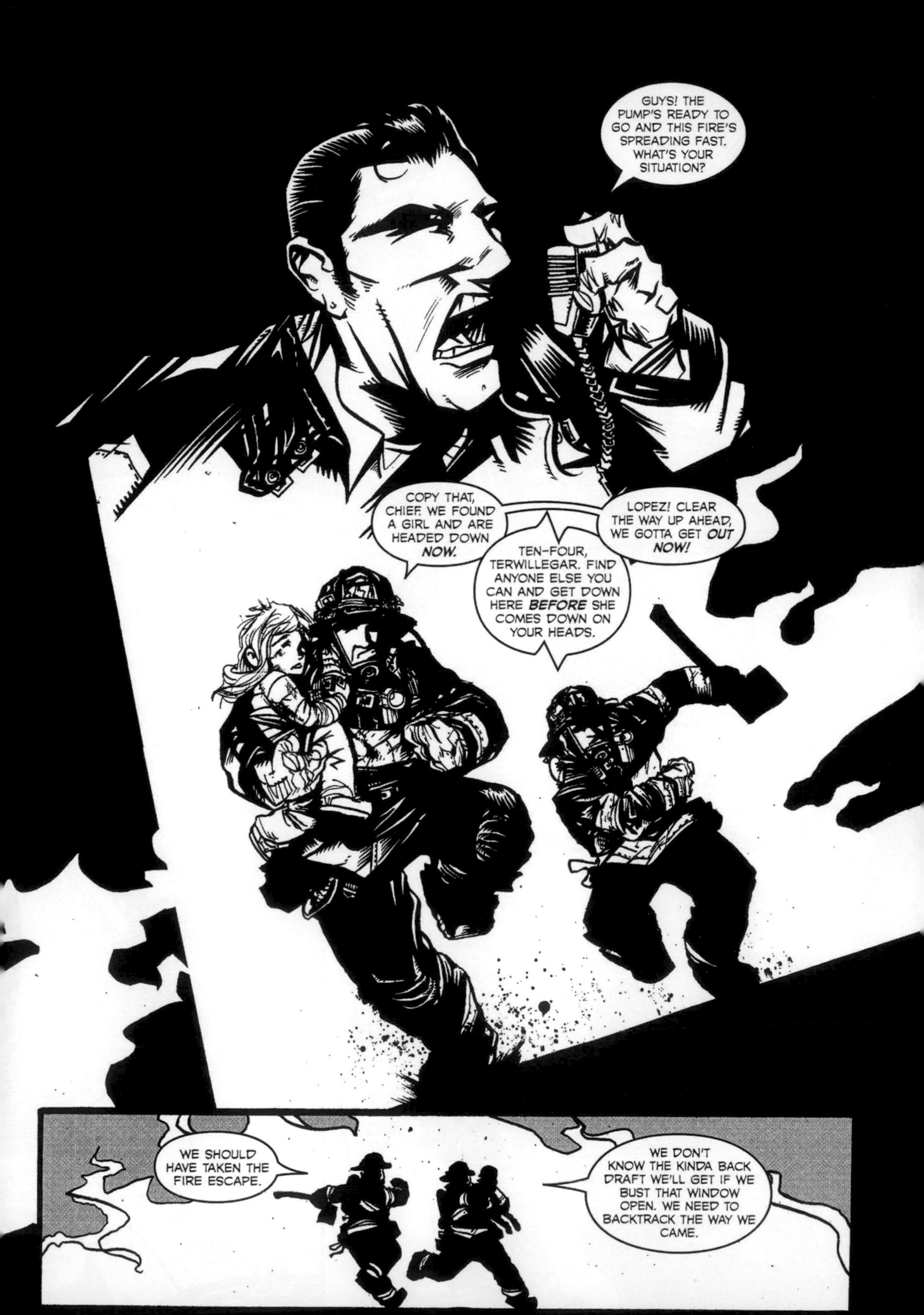
GUYS! THE PUMP'S READY TO GO AND THIS FIRE'S SPREADING FAST. WHAT'S YOUR SITUATION?
COPY THAT, CHIEF. WE FOUND A GIRL AND ARE HEADED DOWN NOW.
LOPEZ! CLEAR THE WAY UP AHEAD, WE GOTTA GET OUT NOW!
TEN-FOUR, TERWILLEGAR. FIND ANYONE ELSE YOU CAN AND GET DOWN HERE BEFORE SHE COMES DOWN ON YOUR HEADS.
WE SHOULD HAVE TAKEN THE FIRE ESCAPE.
WE DON'T KNOW THE KINDA BACK DRAFT WE'LL GET IF WE BUST THAT WINDOW OPEN. WE NEED TO BACKTRACK THE WAY WE CAME.

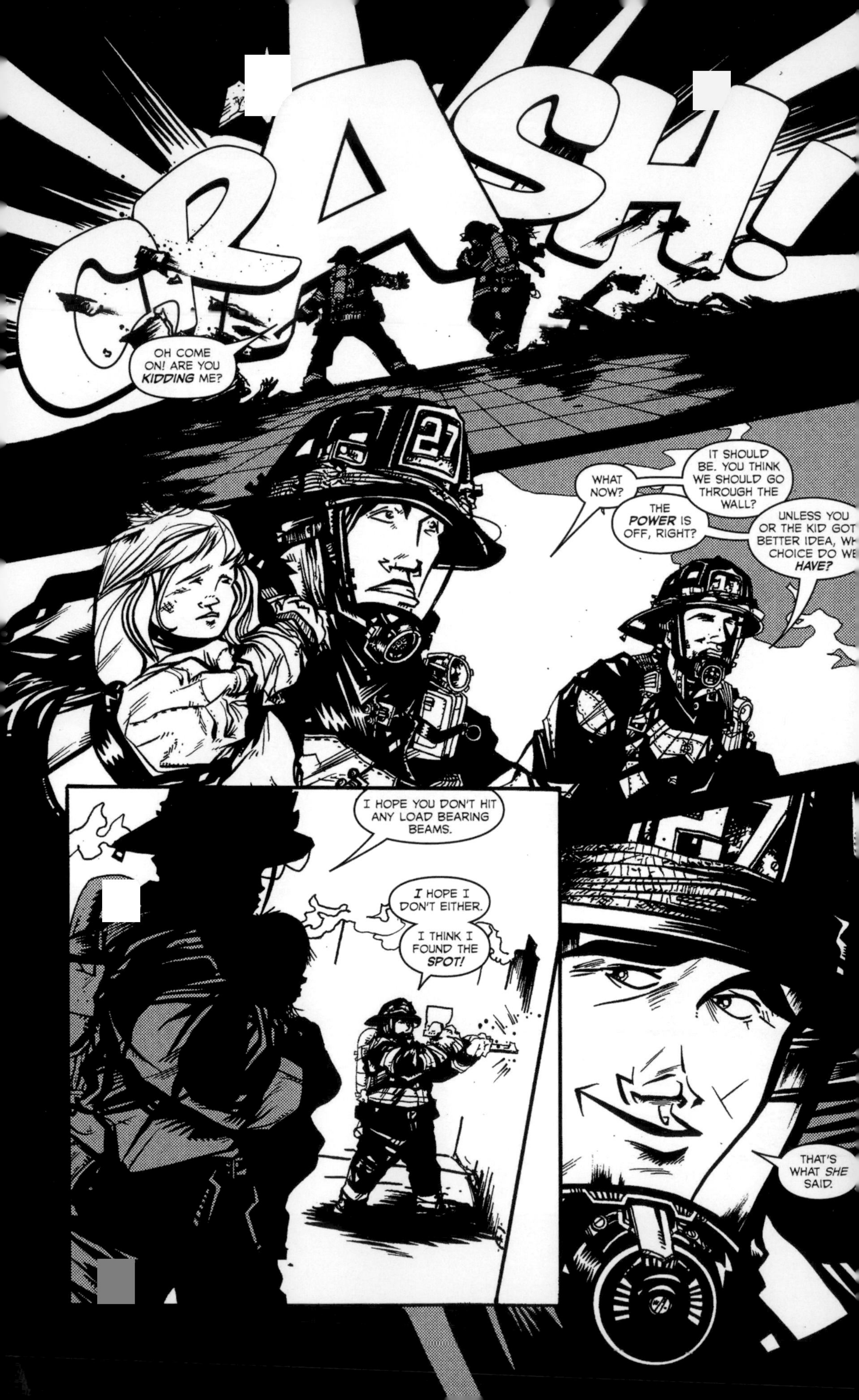
CRASH!
OH COME ON! ARE YOU KIDDING ME?
WHAT NOW?
IT SHOULD BE. YOU THINK WE SHOULD GO THROUGH THE WALL?
THE POWER IS OFF, RIGHT?
UNLESS YOU OR THE KID GOT BETTER IDEA, WH CHOICE DO WE HAVE?
I HOPE YOU DON'T HIT ANY LOAD BEARING BEAMS.
I HOPE I DON'T EITHER.
I THINK I FOUND THE SPOT!
THAT'S WHAT SHE SAID.

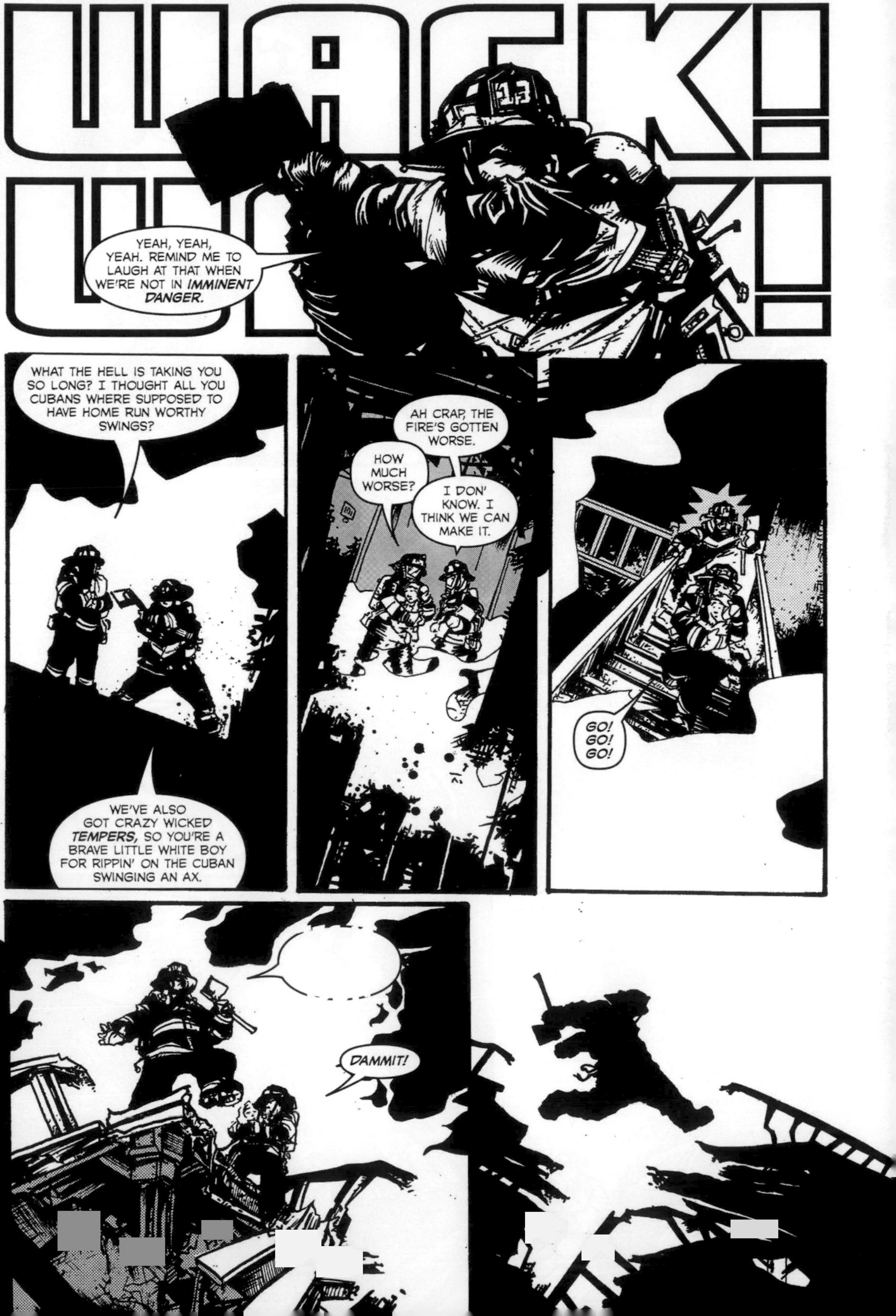
WACK!
WACK!
YEAH, YEAH, YEAH. REMIND ME TO LAUGH AT THAT WHEN WE'RE NOT IN *IMMINENT DANGER.*
WHAT THE HELL IS TAKING YOU SO LONG? I THOUGHT ALL YOU CUBANS WHERE SUPPOSED TO HAVE HOME RUN WORTHY SWINGS?
WE'VE ALSO GOT CRAZY WICKED *TEMPERS,* SO YOU'RE A BRAVE LITTLE WHITE BOY FOR RIPPIN' ON THE CUBAN SWINGING AN AX.
AH CRAP, THE FIRE'S GOTTEN WORSE.
HOW MUCH WORSE?
I DON' KNOW. I THINK WE CAN MAKE IT.
GO! GO! GO!
DAMMIT!

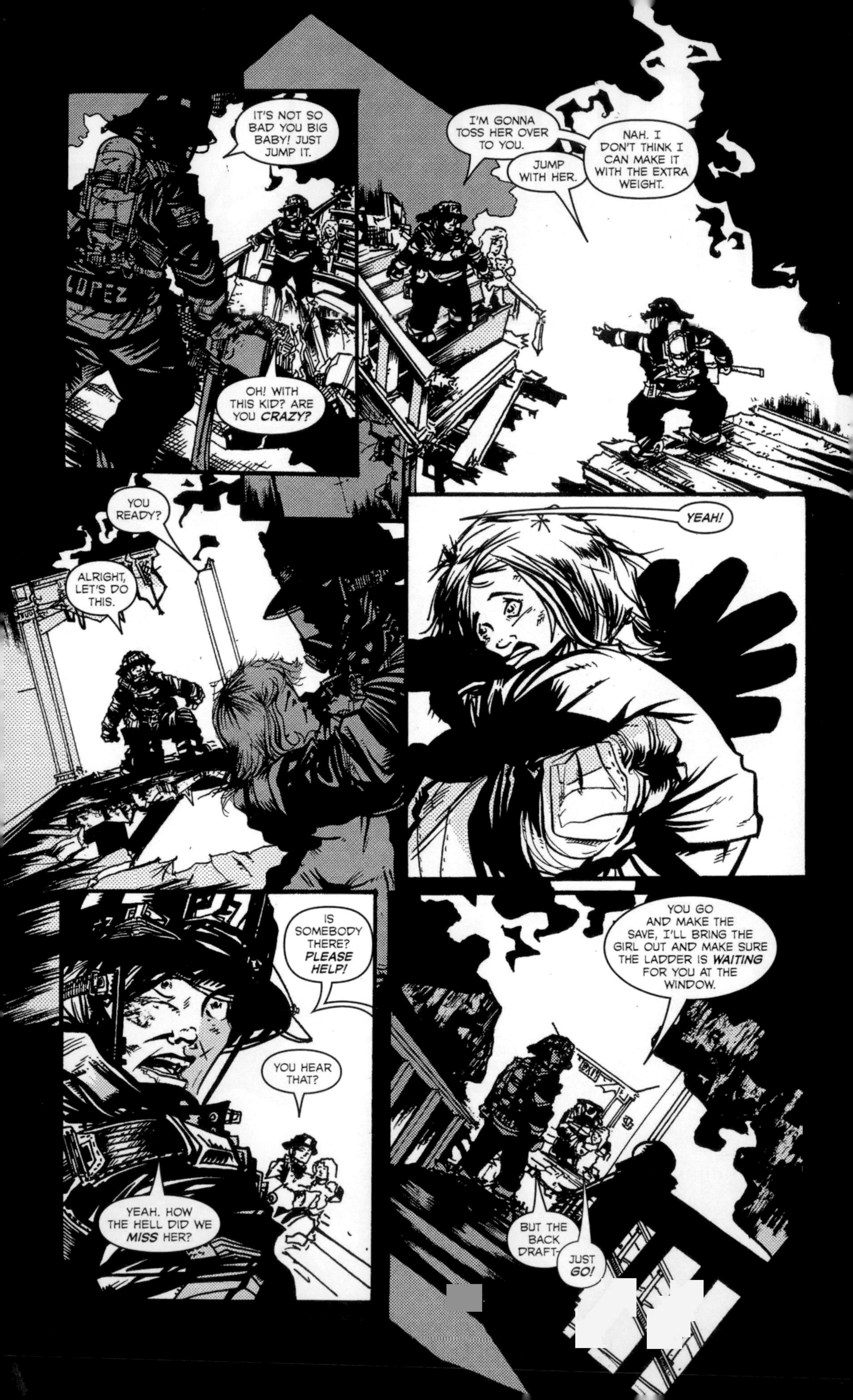

IT'S NOT SO BAD YOU BIG BABY! JUST JUMP IT.
OH! WITH THIS KID? ARE YOU *CRAZY?*
LOPEZ
I'M GONNA TOSS HER OVER TO YOU.
JUMP WITH HER.
NAH. I DON'T THINK I CAN MAKE IT WITH THE EXTRA WEIGHT.
YOU READY?
ALRIGHT, LET'S DO THIS.
YEAH!
IS SOMEBODY THERE? *PLEASE HELP!*
YOU HEAR THAT?
YEAH. HOW THE HELL DID WE *MISS* HER?
YOU GO AND MAKE THE SAVE, I'LL BRING THE GIRL OUT AND MAKE SURE THE LADDER IS *WAITING* FOR YOU AT THE WINDOW.
EXIT
BUT THE BACK DRAFT-
JUST *GO!*

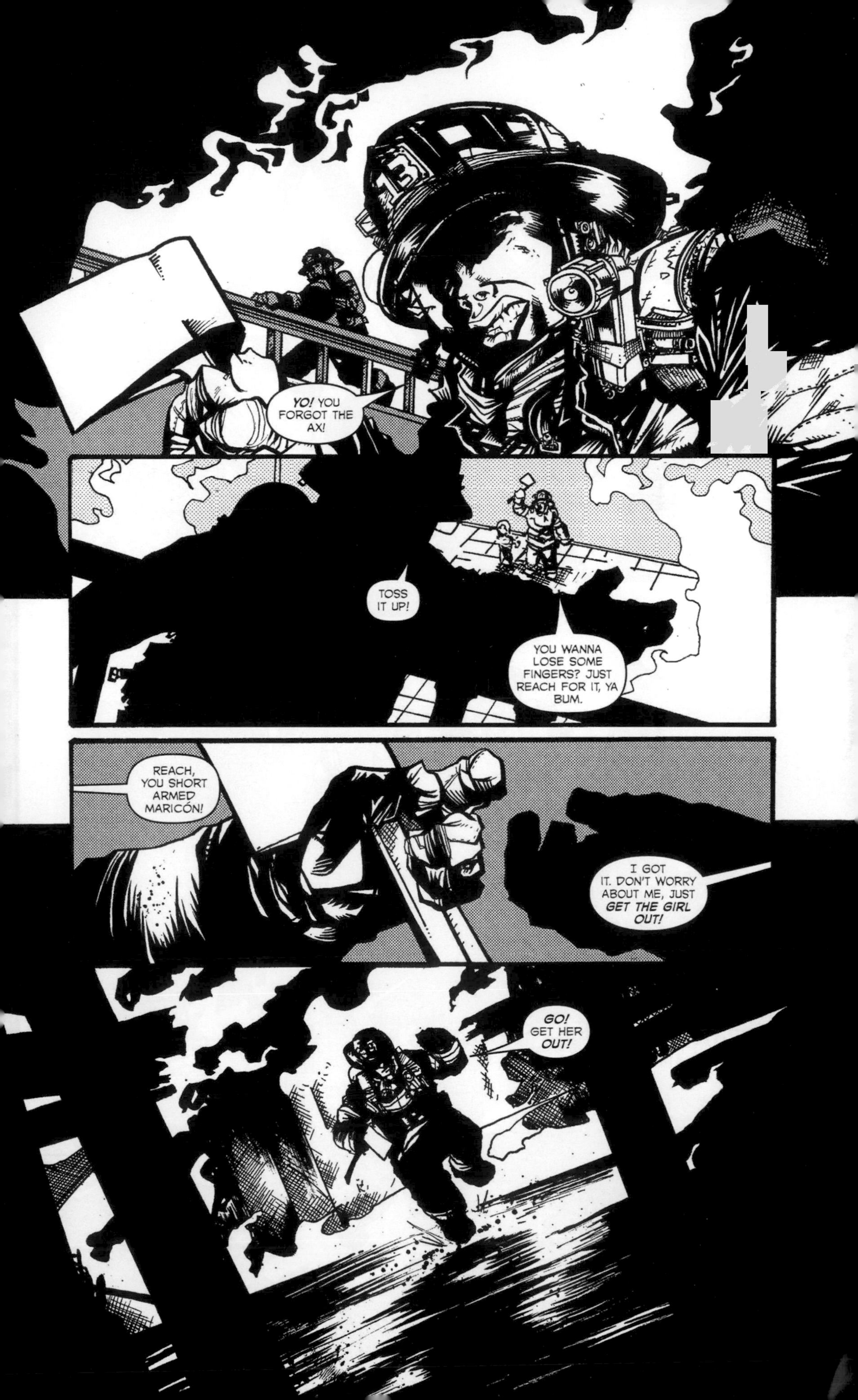
YO! YOU FORGOT THE AX!
TOSS IT UP!
YOU WANNA LOSE SOME FINGERS? JUST REACH FOR IT, YA BUM.
REACH, YOU SHORT ARMED MARICÓN!
I GOT IT. DON'T WORRY ABOUT ME, JUST GET THE GIRL OUT!
GO! GET HER OUT!

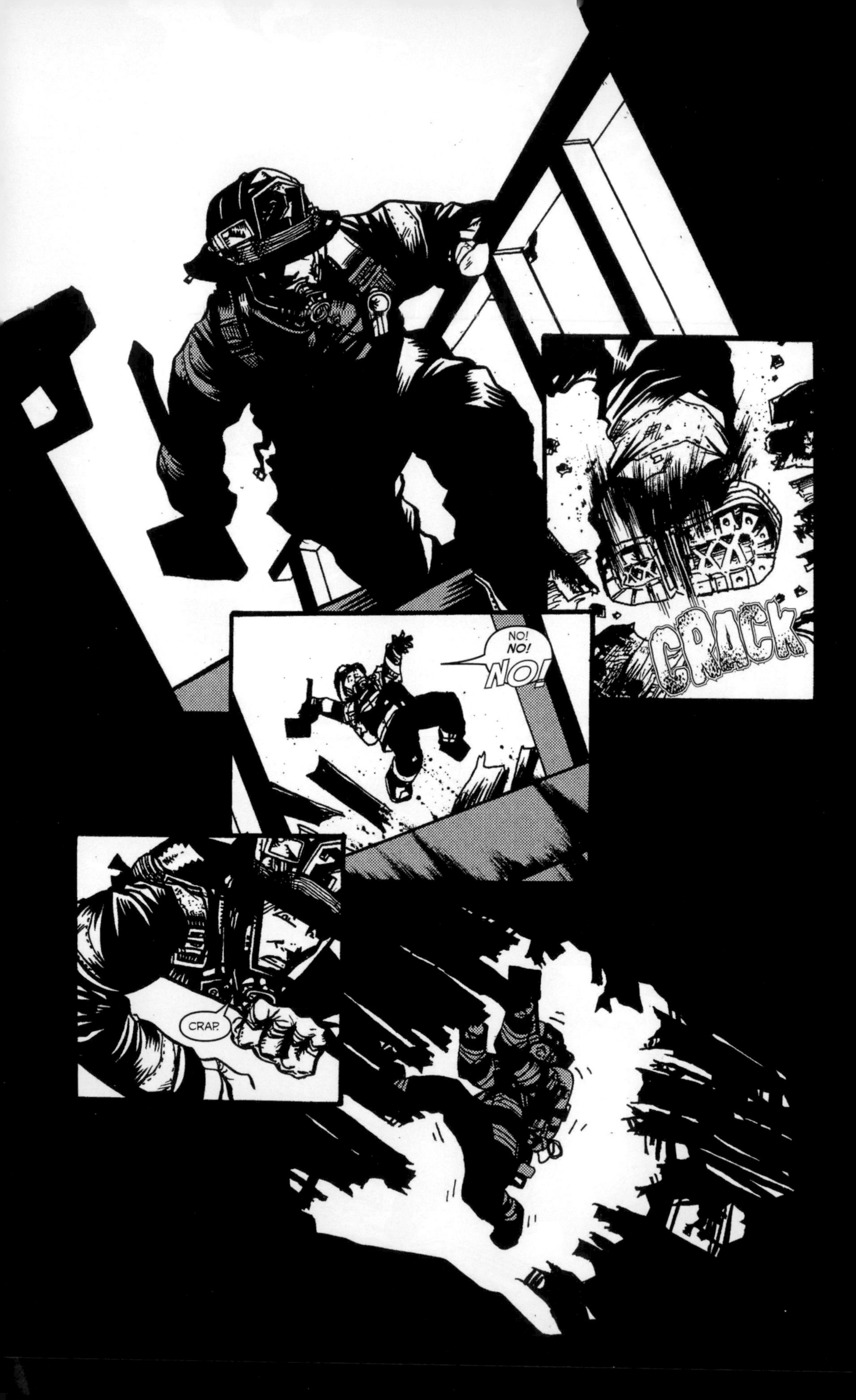
CRACK
NO! NO! NO!
CRAP.

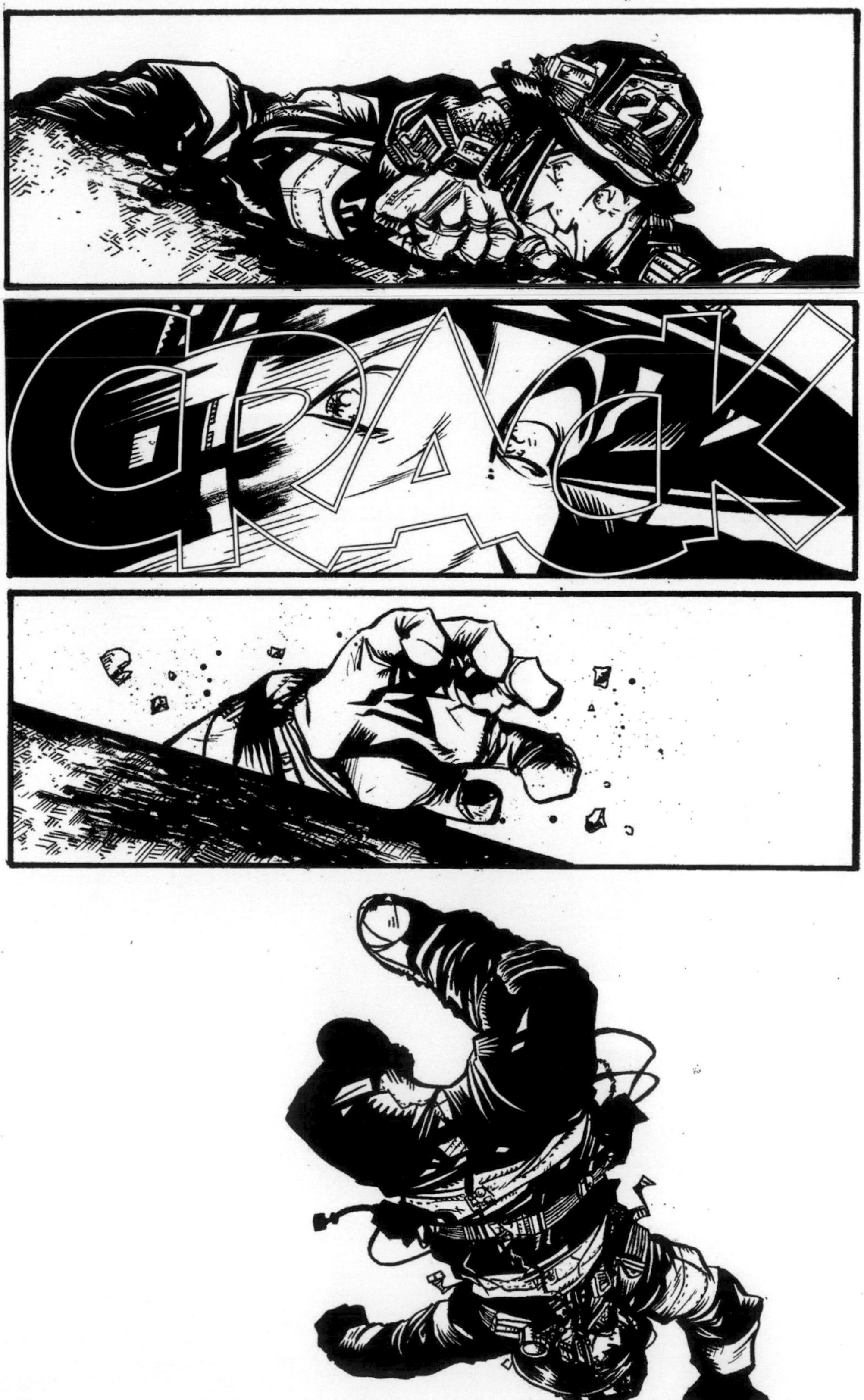
CRACK

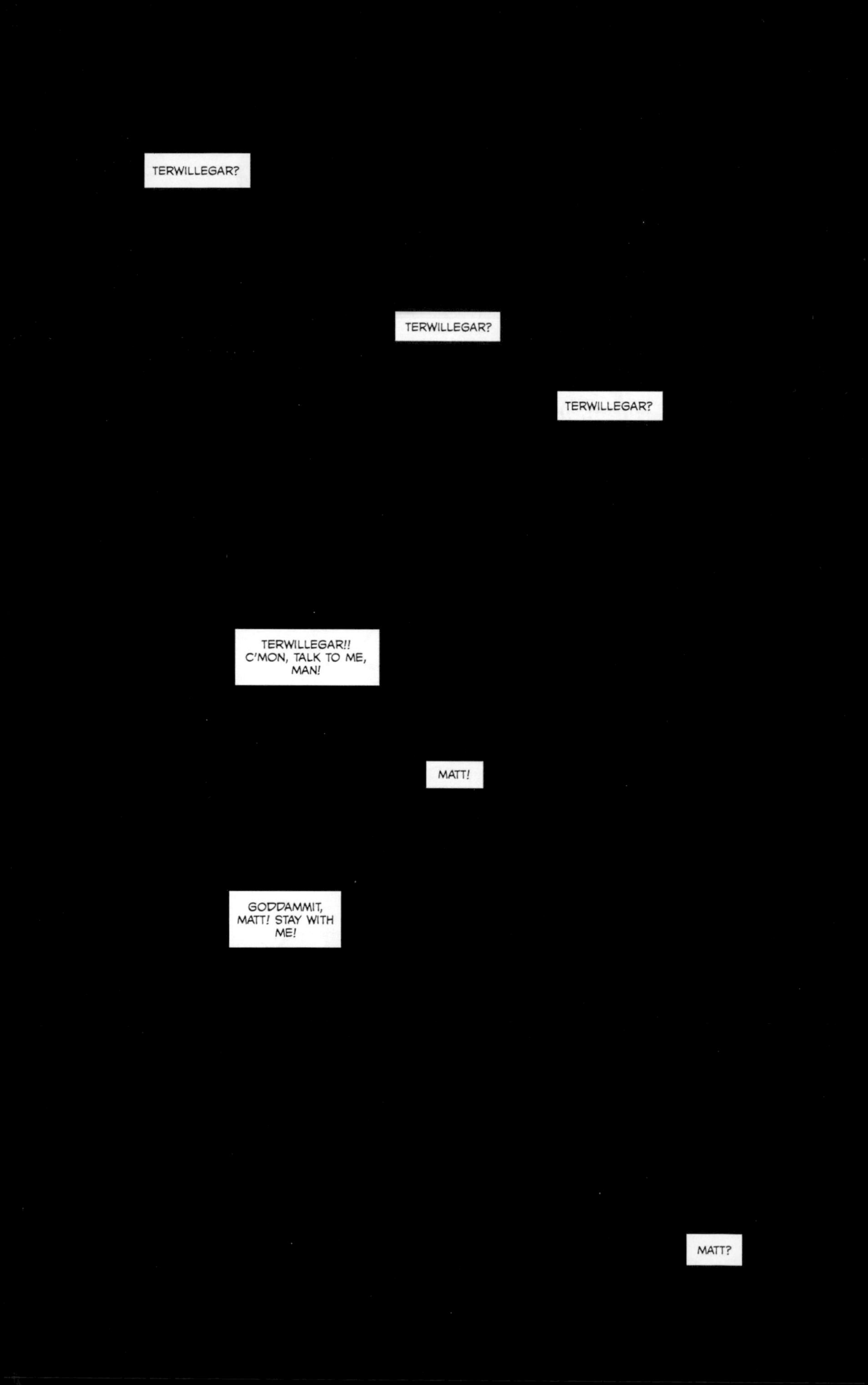
TERWILLEGAR?
TERWILLEGAR?
TERWILLEGAR?
TERWILLEGAR!! C'MON, TALK TO ME, MAN!
MATT!
GODDAMMIT, MATT! STAY WITH ME!
MATT?

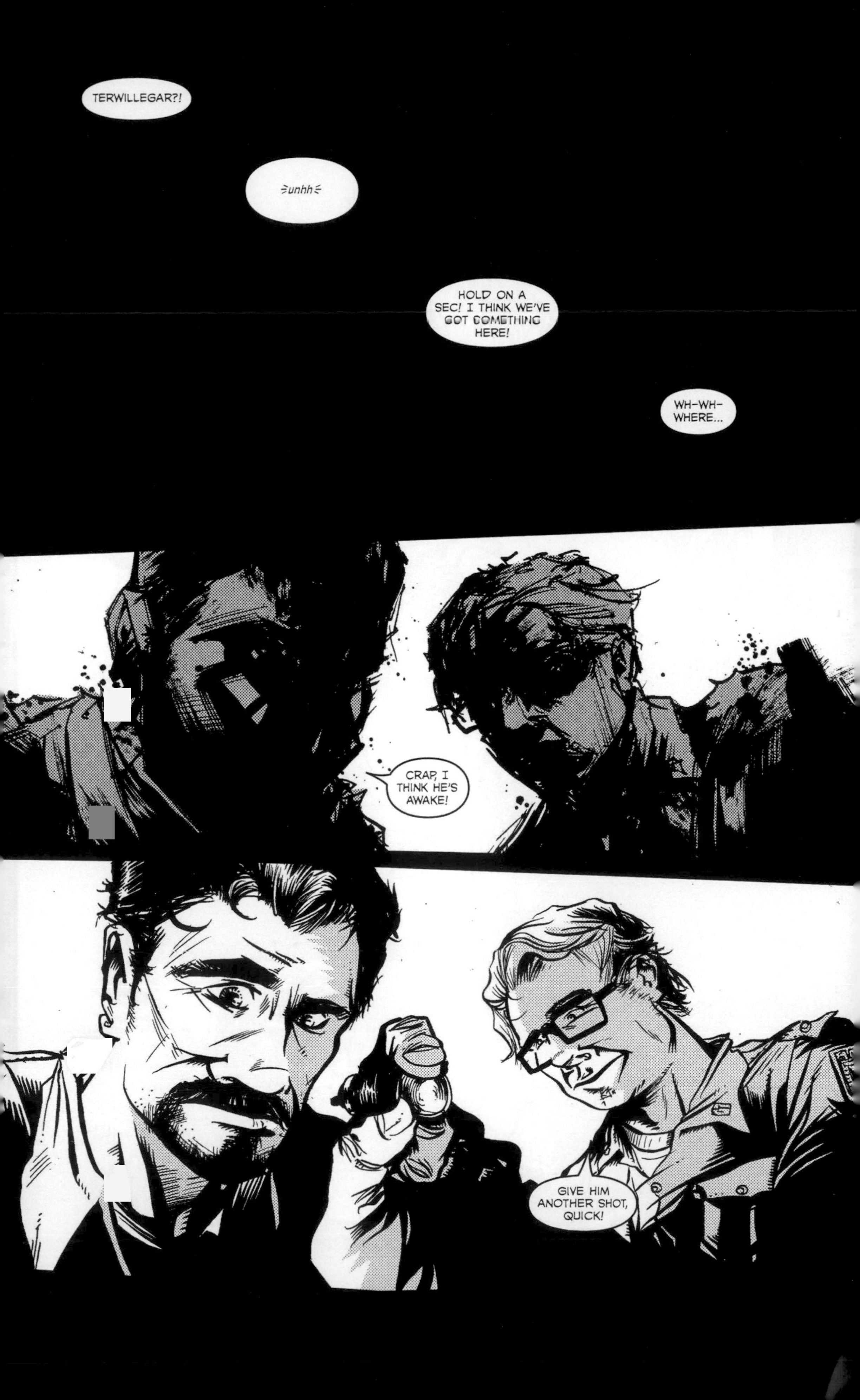
TERWILLEGAR?!
unhh
HOLD ON A SEC! I THINK WE'VE GOT SOMETHING HERE!
WH-WH- WHERE...
CRAP, I THINK HE'S AWAKE!
GIVE HIM ANOTHER SHOT, QUICK!

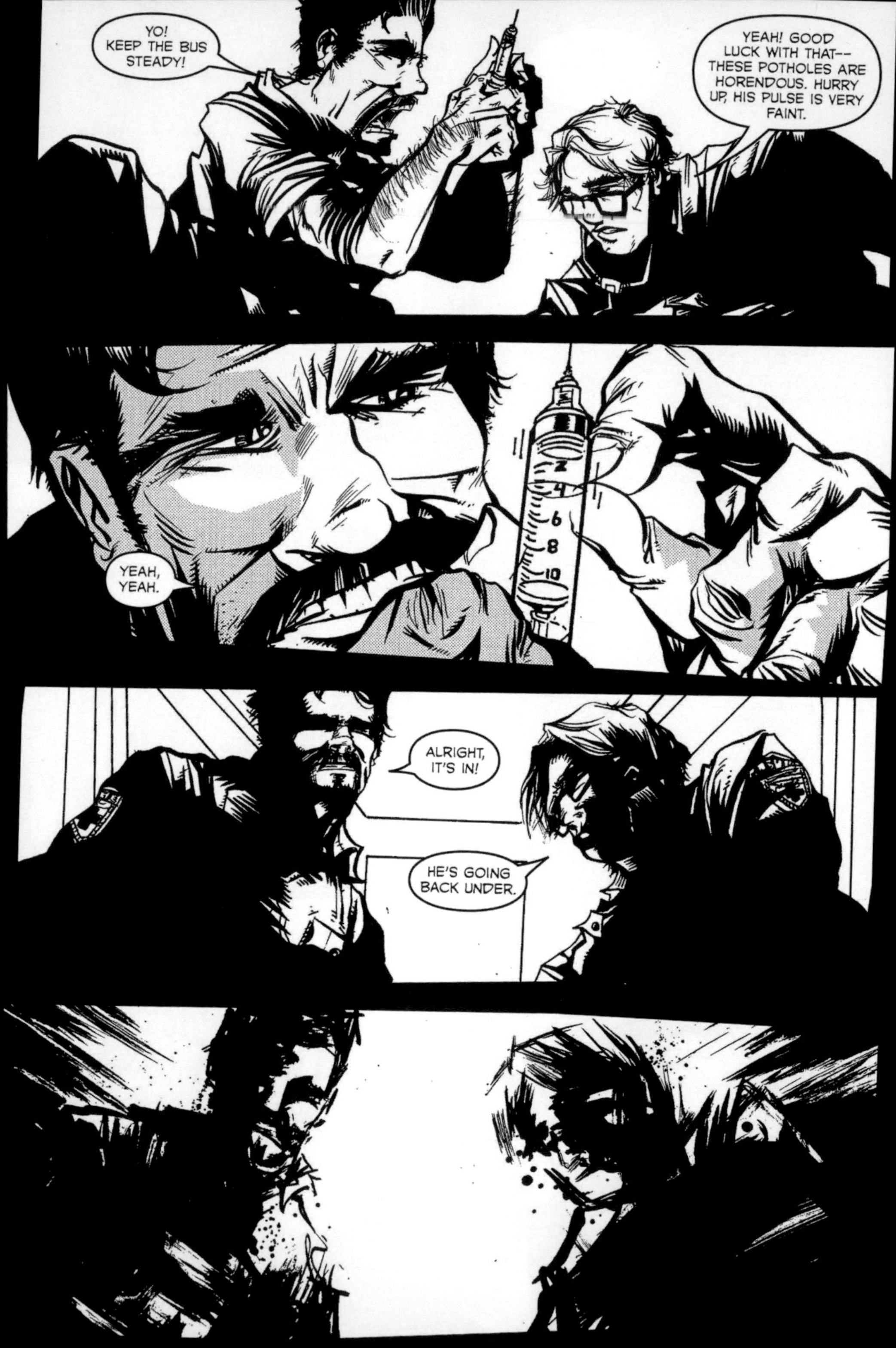
YO! KEEP THE BUS STEADY!
YEAH! GOOD LUCK WITH THAT-- THESE POTHOLES ARE HORENDOUS. HURRY UP, HIS PULSE IS VERY FAINT.
YEAH, YEAH.
2
4
6
8
10
ALRIGHT, IT'S IN!
HE'S GOING BACK UNDER.

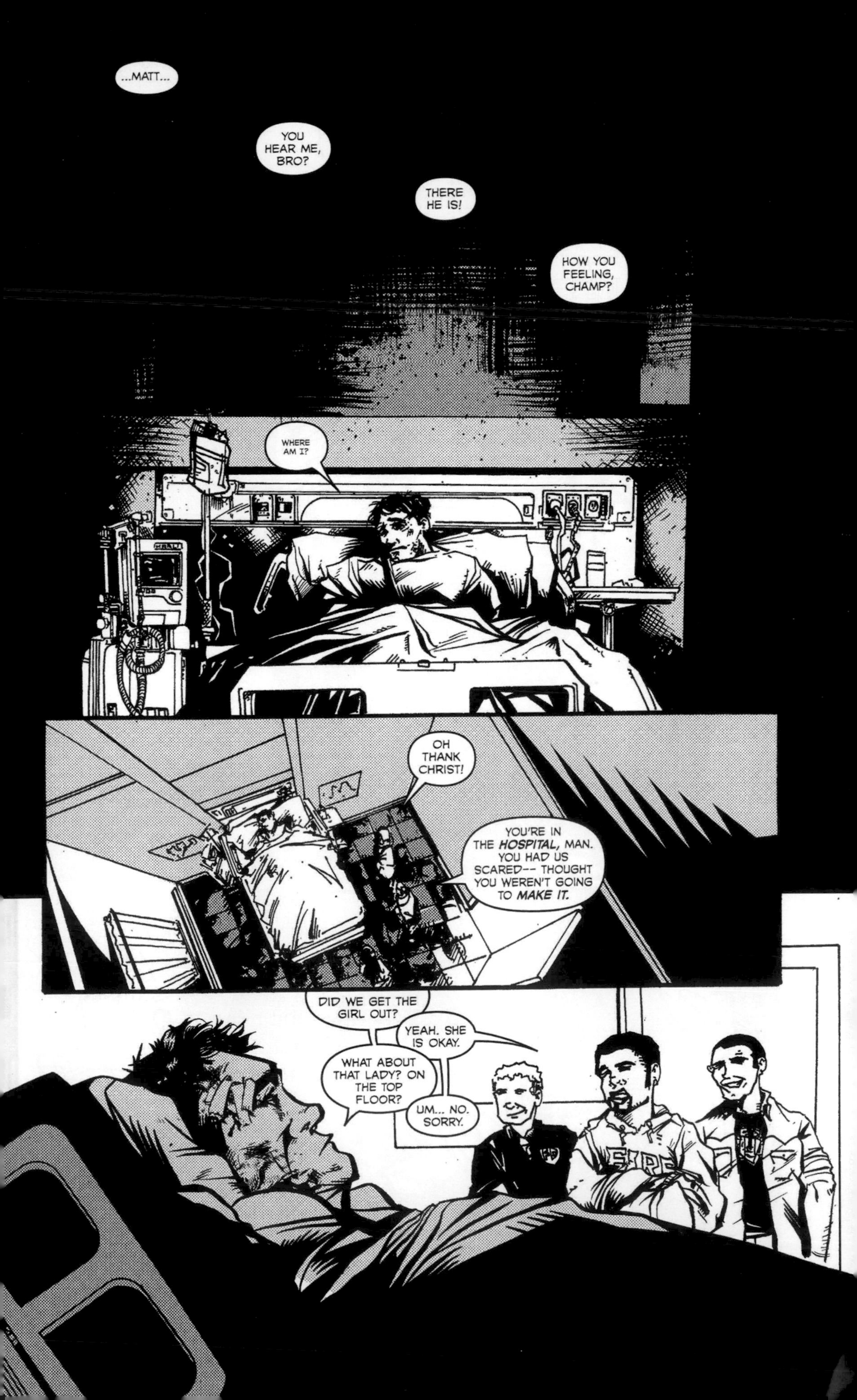
...MATT...
YOU HEAR ME, BRO?
THERE HE IS!
HOW YOU FEELING, CHAMP?
WHERE AM I?
OH THANK CHRIST!
YOU'RE IN THE HOSPITAL, MAN. YOU HAD US SCARED-- THOUGHT YOU WEREN'T GOING TO MAKE IT.
DID WE GET THE GIRL OUT?
YEAH. SHE IS OKAY.
WHAT ABOUT THAT LADY? ON THE TOP FLOOR?
UM... NO. SORRY.

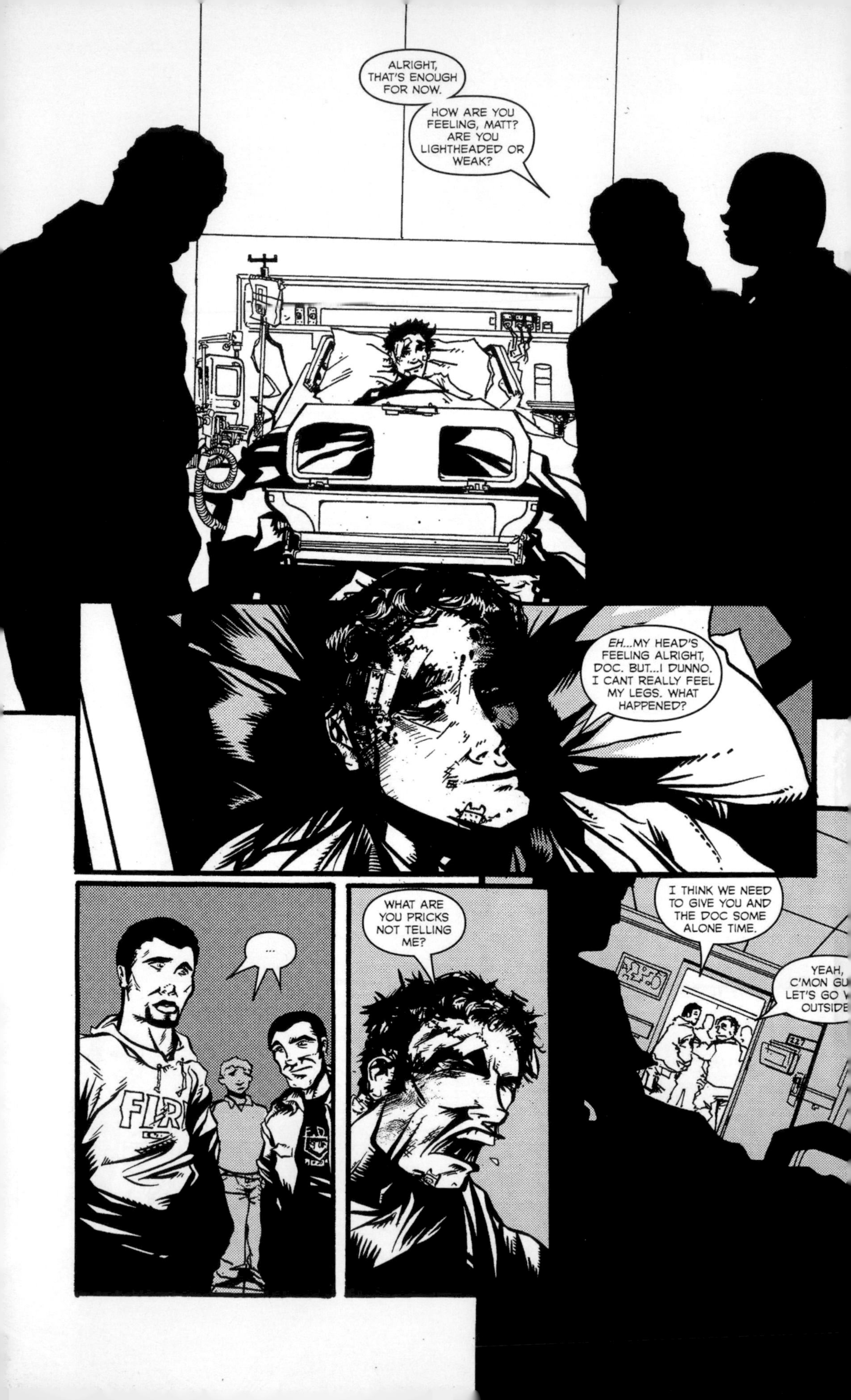
ALRIGHT, THAT'S ENOUGH FOR NOW.
HOW ARE YOU FEELING, MATT? ARE YOU LIGHTHEADED OR WEAK?
EH...MY HEAD'S FEELING ALRIGHT, DOC. BUT...I DUNNO. I CANT REALLY FEEL MY LEGS. WHAT HAPPENED?
...
WHAT ARE YOU PRICKS NOT TELLING ME?
I THINK WE NEED TO GIVE YOU AND THE DOC SOME ALONE TIME.
YEAH,
C'MON GU
LET'S GO
OUTSIDE

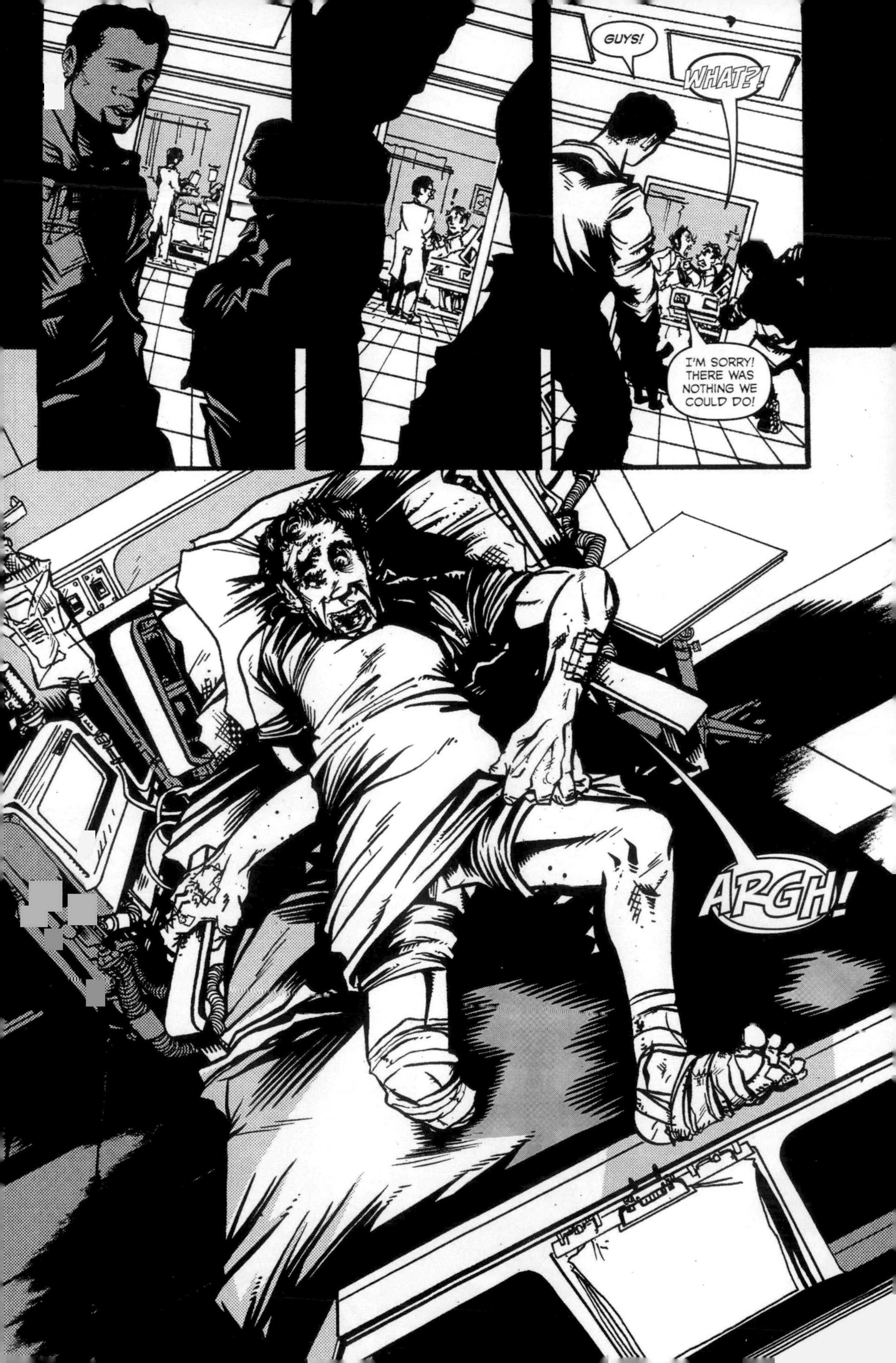
GUYS!
WHAT?!
I'M SORRY! THERE WAS NOTHING WE COULD DO!
ARGH!

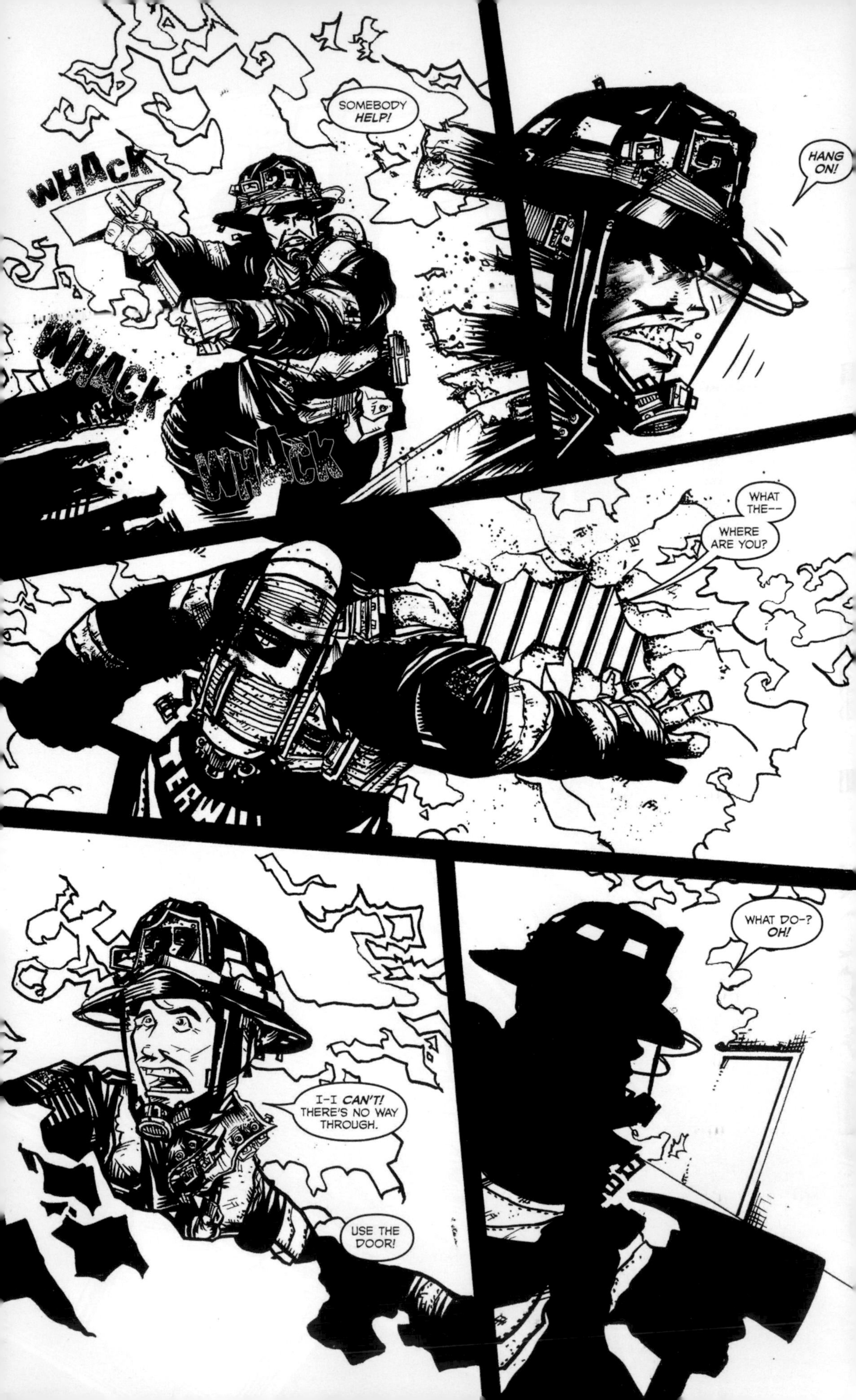
SOMEBODY HELP!
WHACK
WHACK
WHACK
HANG ON!
WHAT THE--
WHERE ARE YOU?
I-I CAN'T! THERE'S NO WAY THROUGH.
USE THE DOOR!
WHAT DO-? OH!

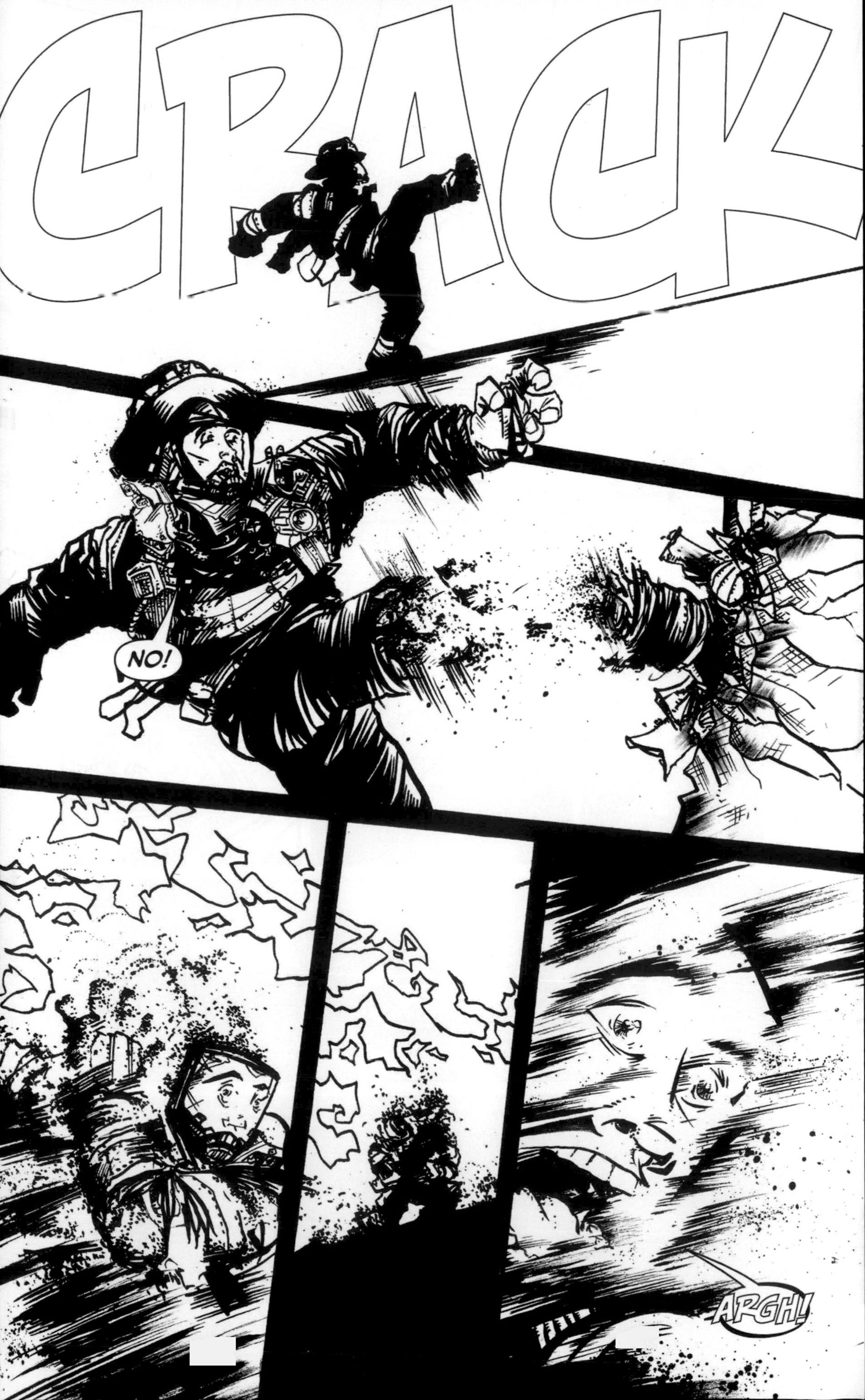
CRACK
NO!
ARGH!

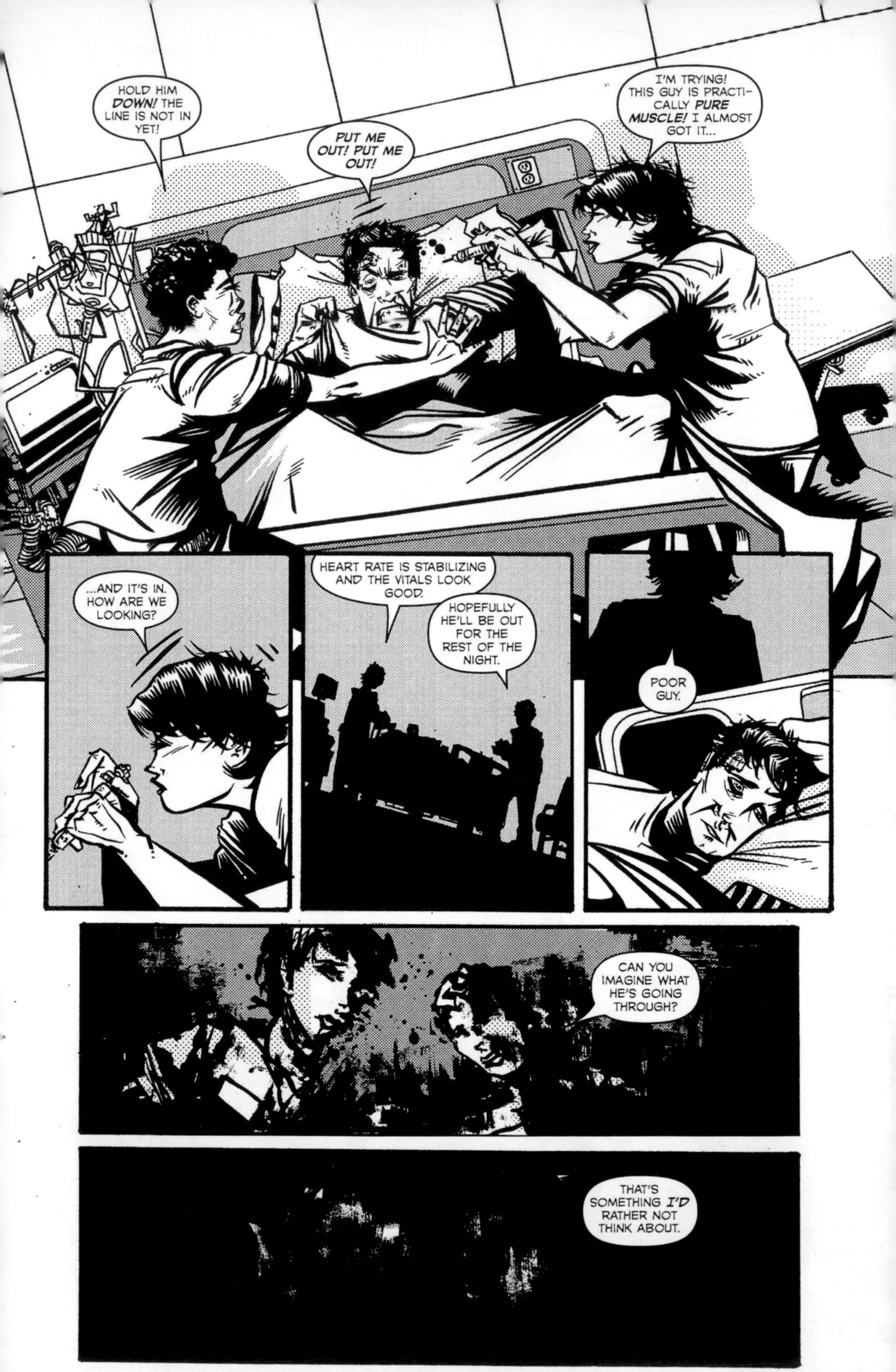
HOLD HIM DOWN! THE LINE IS NOT IN YET!
PUT ME OUT! PUT ME OUT!
I'M TRYING! THIS GUY IS PRACTI-CALLY PURE MUSCLE! I ALMOST GOT IT...
...AND IT'S IN. HOW ARE WE LOOKING?
HEART RATE IS STABILIZING AND THE VITALS LOOK GOOD.
HOPEFULLY HE'LL BE OUT FOR THE REST OF THE NIGHT.
POOR GUY.
CAN YOU IMAGINE WHAT HE'S GOING THROUGH?
THAT'S SOMETHING I'D RATHER NOT THINK ABOUT.

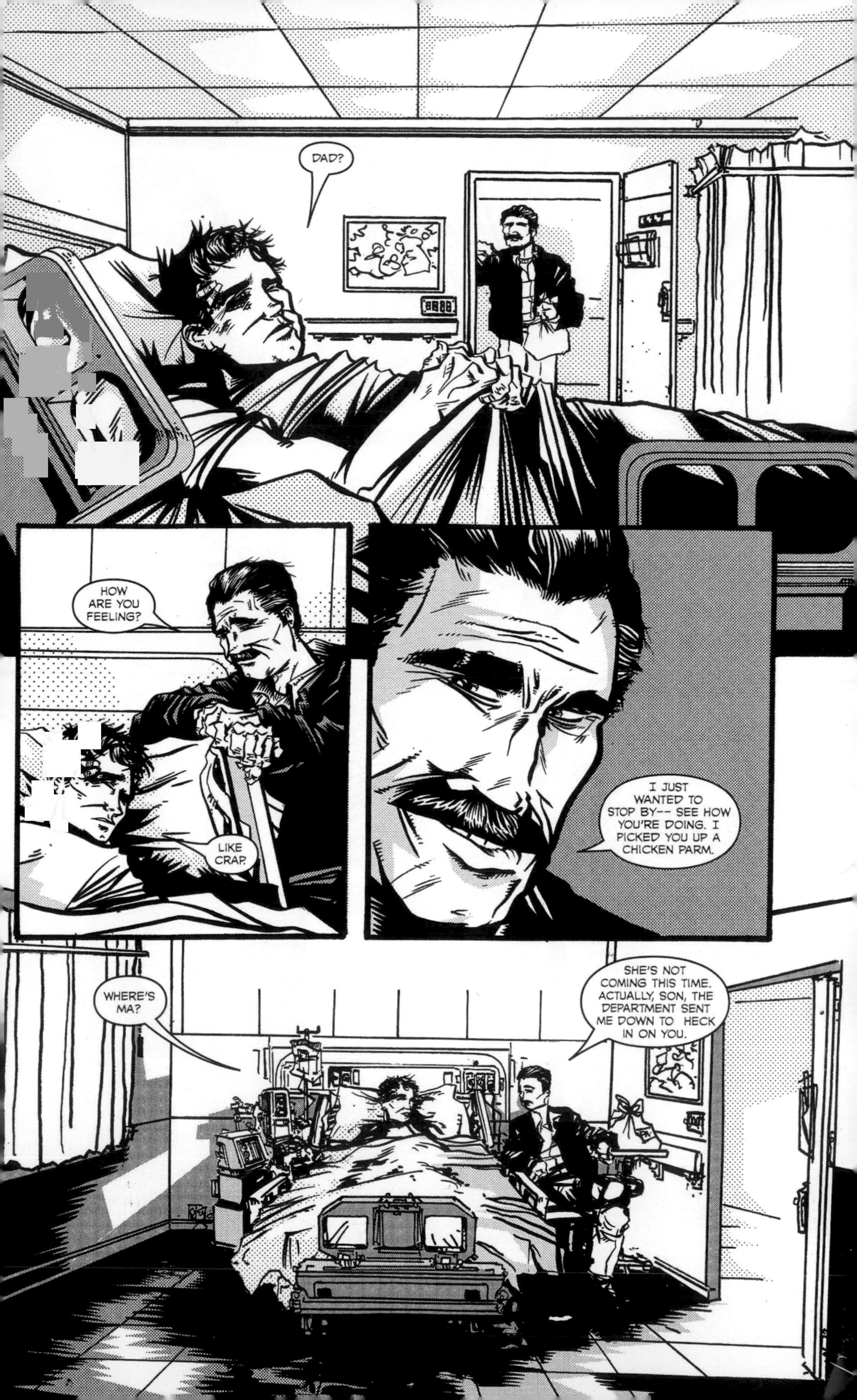
DAD?
HOW ARE YOU FEELING?
LIKE CRAP.
I JUST WANTED TO STOP BY-- SEE HOW YOU'RE DOING. I PICKED YOU UP A CHICKEN PARM.
WHERE'S MA?
SHE'S NOT COMING THIS TIME. ACTUALLY, SON, THE DEPARTMENT SENT ME DOWN TO HECK IN ON YOU.

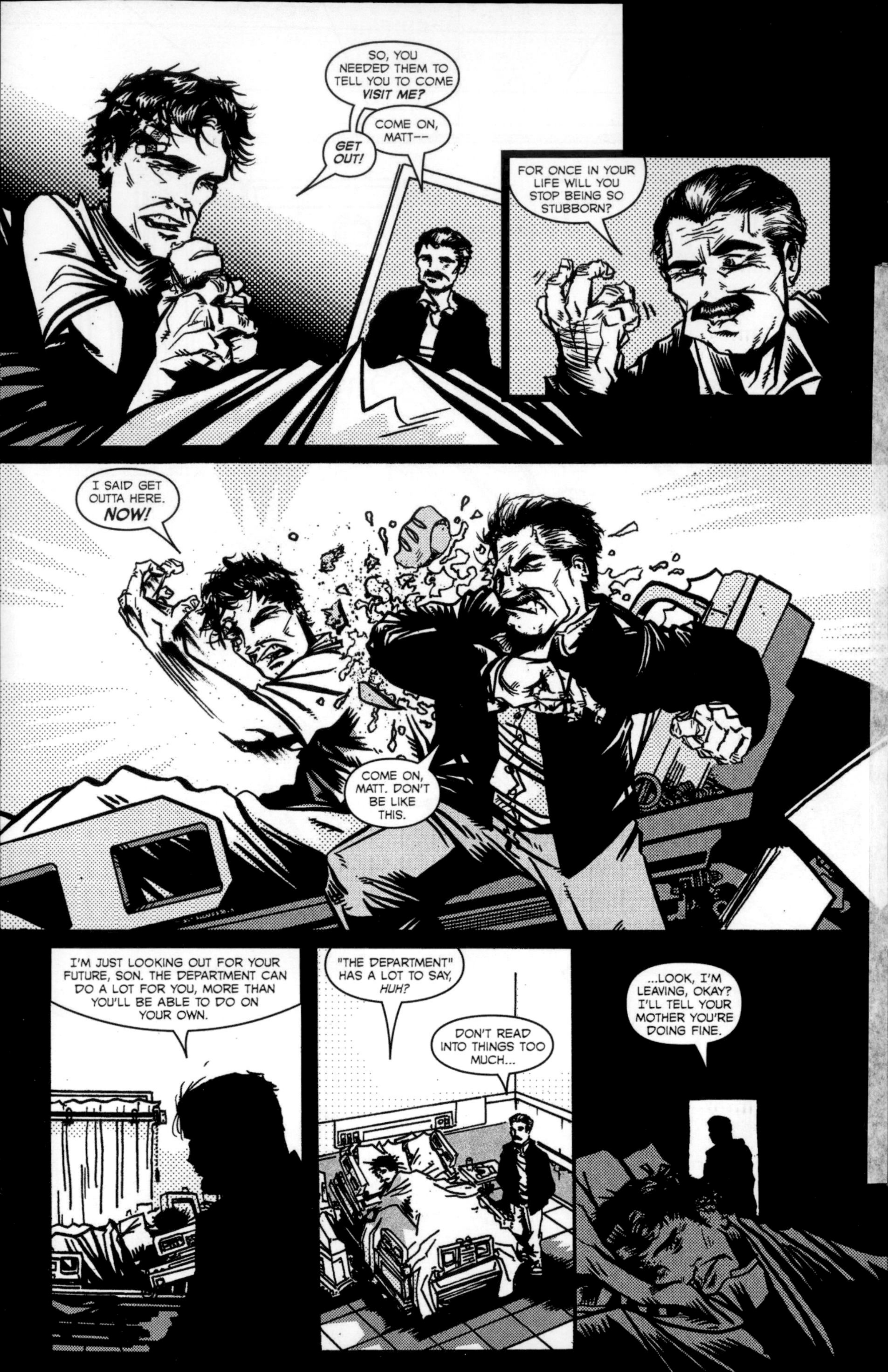
SO, YOU NEEDED THEM TO TELL YOU TO COME *VISIT ME?*
COME ON, MATT--
GET OUT!
FOR ONCE IN YOUR LIFE WILL YOU STOP BEING SO STUBBORN?
I SAID GET OUTTA HERE. *NOW!*
COME ON, MATT. DON'T BE LIKE THIS.
I'M JUST LOOKING OUT FOR YOUR FUTURE, SON. THE DEPARTMENT CAN DO A LOT FOR YOU, MORE THAN YOU'LL BE ABLE TO DO ON YOUR OWN.
"THE DEPARTMENT" HAS A LOT TO SAY, *HUH?*
DON'T READ INTO THINGS TOO MUCH...
...LOOK, I'M LEAVING, OKAY? I'LL TELL YOUR MOTHER YOU'RE DOING FINE.

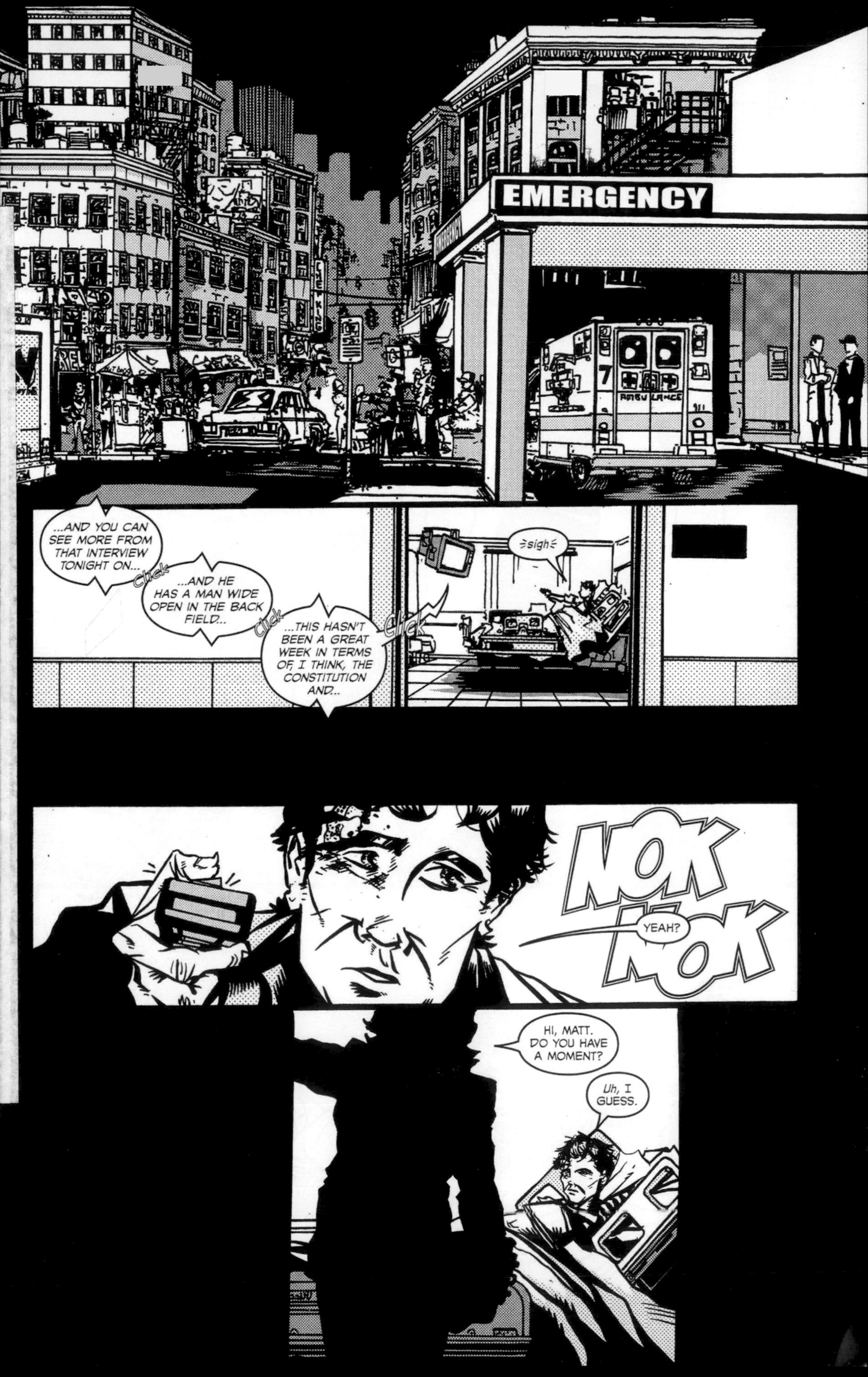
EMERGENCY
...AND YOU CAN SEE MORE FROM THAT INTERVIEW TONIGHT ON...
Click
...AND HE HAS A MAN WIDE OPEN IN THE BACK FIELD...
Click
...THIS HASN'T BEEN A GREAT WEEK IN TERMS OF, I THINK, THE CONSTITUTION AND...
Click
sigh
NOK NOK
YEAH?
HI, MATT. DO YOU HAVE A MOMENT?
Uh, I GUESS.

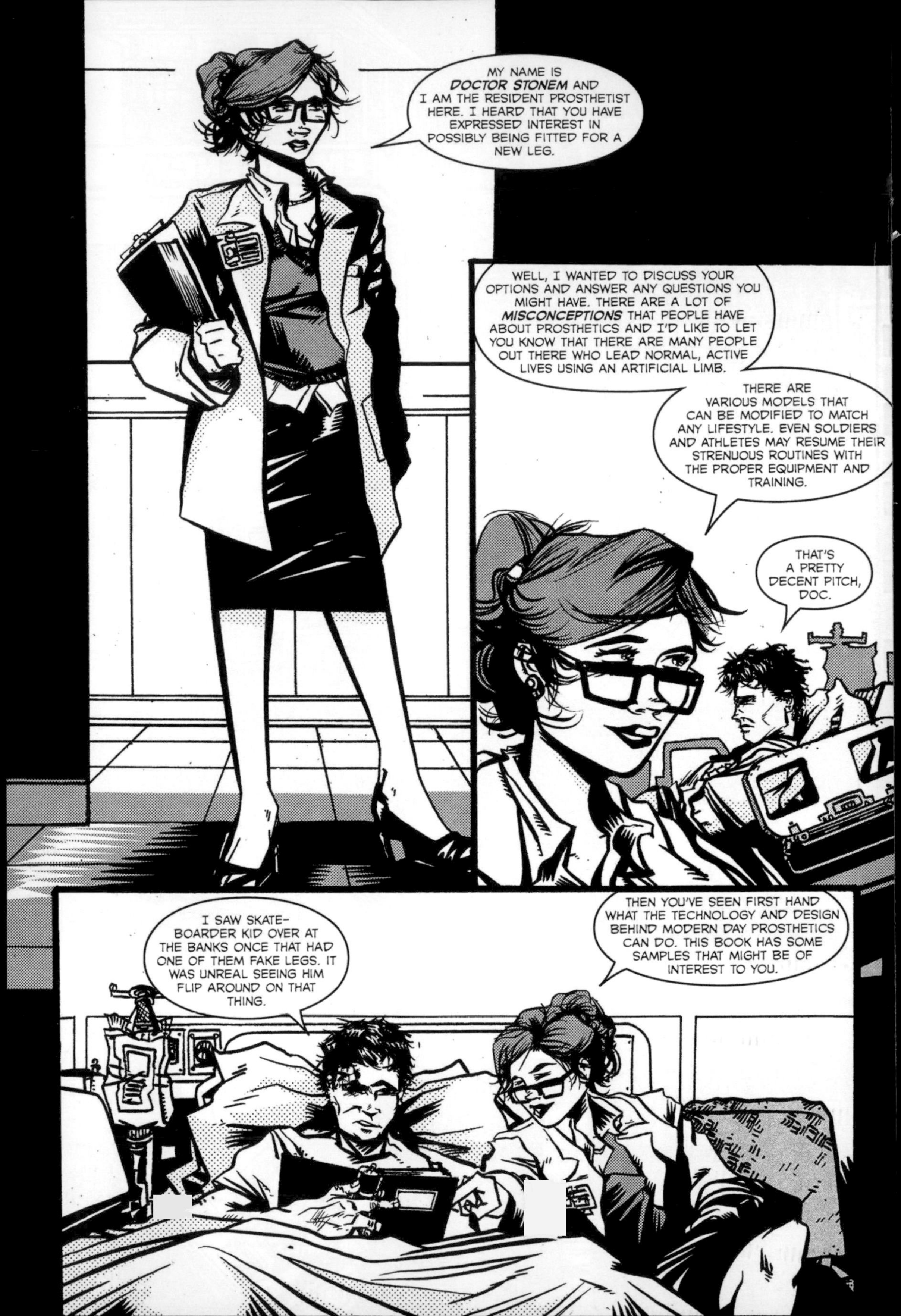
MY NAME IS DOCTOR STONEM AND I AM THE RESIDENT PROSTHETIST HERE. I HEARD THAT YOU HAVE EXPRESSED INTEREST IN POSSIBLY BEING FITTED FOR A NEW LEG.
WELL, I WANTED TO DISCUSS YOUR OPTIONS AND ANSWER ANY QUESTIONS YOU MIGHT HAVE. THERE ARE A LOT OF MISCONCEPTIONS THAT PEOPLE HAVE ABOUT PROSTHETICS AND I'D LIKE TO LET YOU KNOW THAT THERE ARE MANY PEOPLE OUT THERE WHO LEAD NORMAL, ACTIVE LIVES USING AN ARTIFICIAL LIMB.
THERE ARE VARIOUS MODELS THAT CAN BE MODIFIED TO MATCH ANY LIFESTYLE. EVEN SOLDIERS AND ATHLETES MAY RESUME THEIR STRENUOUS ROUTINES WITH THE PROPER EQUIPMENT AND TRAINING.
THAT'S A PRETTY DECENT PITCH, DOC.
I SAW SKATE-BOARDER KID OVER AT THE BANKS ONCE THAT HAD ONE OF THEM FAKE LEGS. IT WAS UNREAL SEEING HIM FLIP AROUND ON THAT THING.
THEN YOU'VE SEEN FIRST HAND WHAT THE TECHNOLOGY AND DESIGN BEHIND MODERN DAY PROSTHETICS CAN DO. THIS BOOK HAS SOME SAMPLES THAT MIGHT BE OF INTEREST TO YOU.

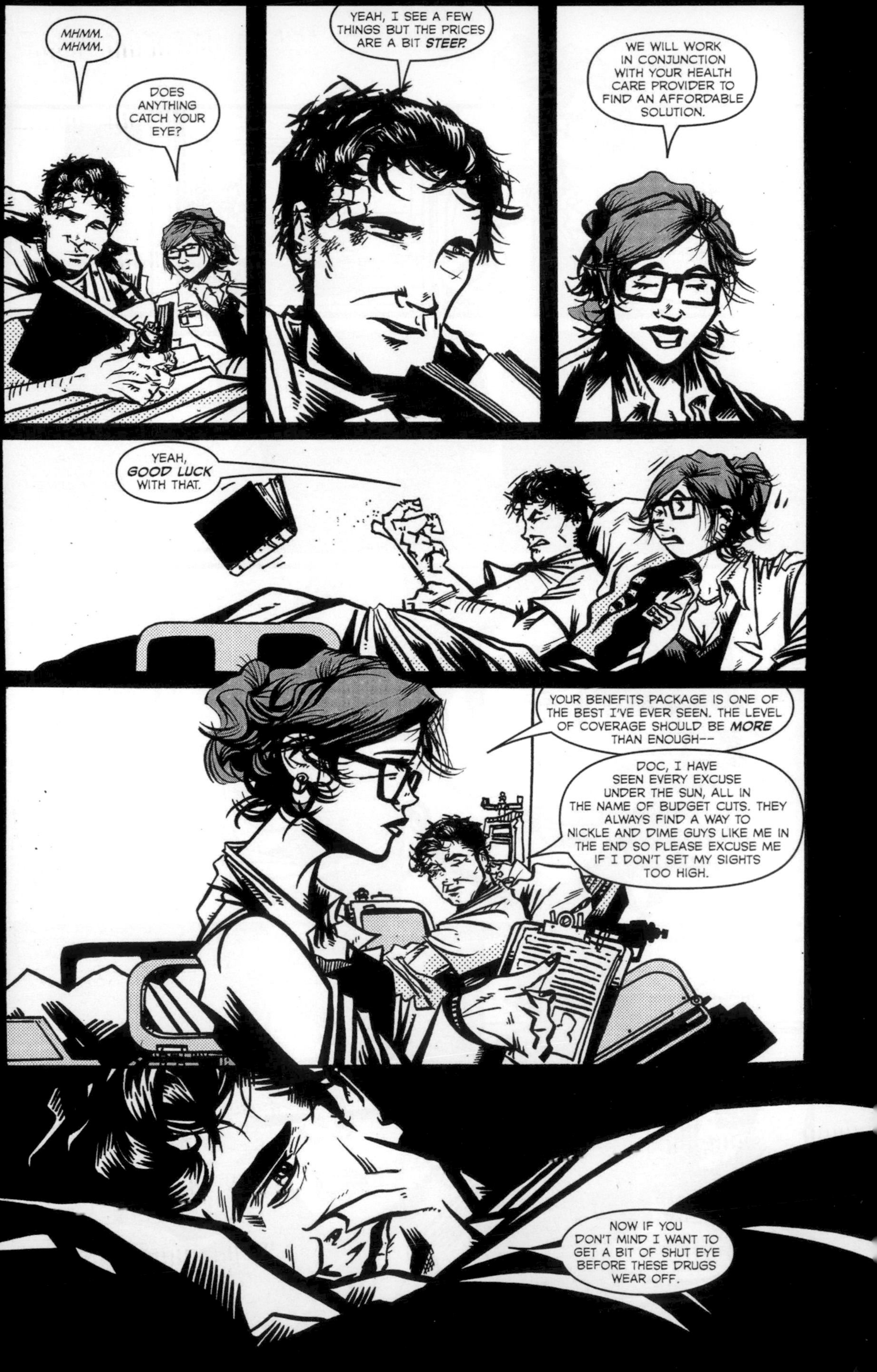
MHMM. MHMM.
DOES ANYTHING CATCH YOUR EYE?
YEAH, I SEE A FEW THINGS BUT THE PRICES ARE A BIT *STEEP.*
WE WILL WORK IN CONJUNCTION WITH YOUR HEALTH CARE PROVIDER TO FIND AN AFFORDABLE SOLUTION.
YEAH, *GOOD LUCK* WITH THAT.
YOUR BENEFITS PACKAGE IS ONE OF THE BEST I'VE EVER SEEN. THE LEVEL OF COVERAGE SHOULD BE *MORE* THAN ENOUGH--
DOC, I HAVE SEEN EVERY EXCUSE UNDER THE SUN, ALL IN THE NAME OF BUDGET CUTS. THEY ALWAYS FIND A WAY TO NICKLE AND DIME GUYS LIKE ME IN THE END SO PLEASE EXCUSE ME IF I DON'T SET MY SIGHTS TOO HIGH.
NOW IF YOU DON'T MIND I WANT TO GET A BIT OF SHUT EYE BEFORE THESE DRUGS WEAR OFF.

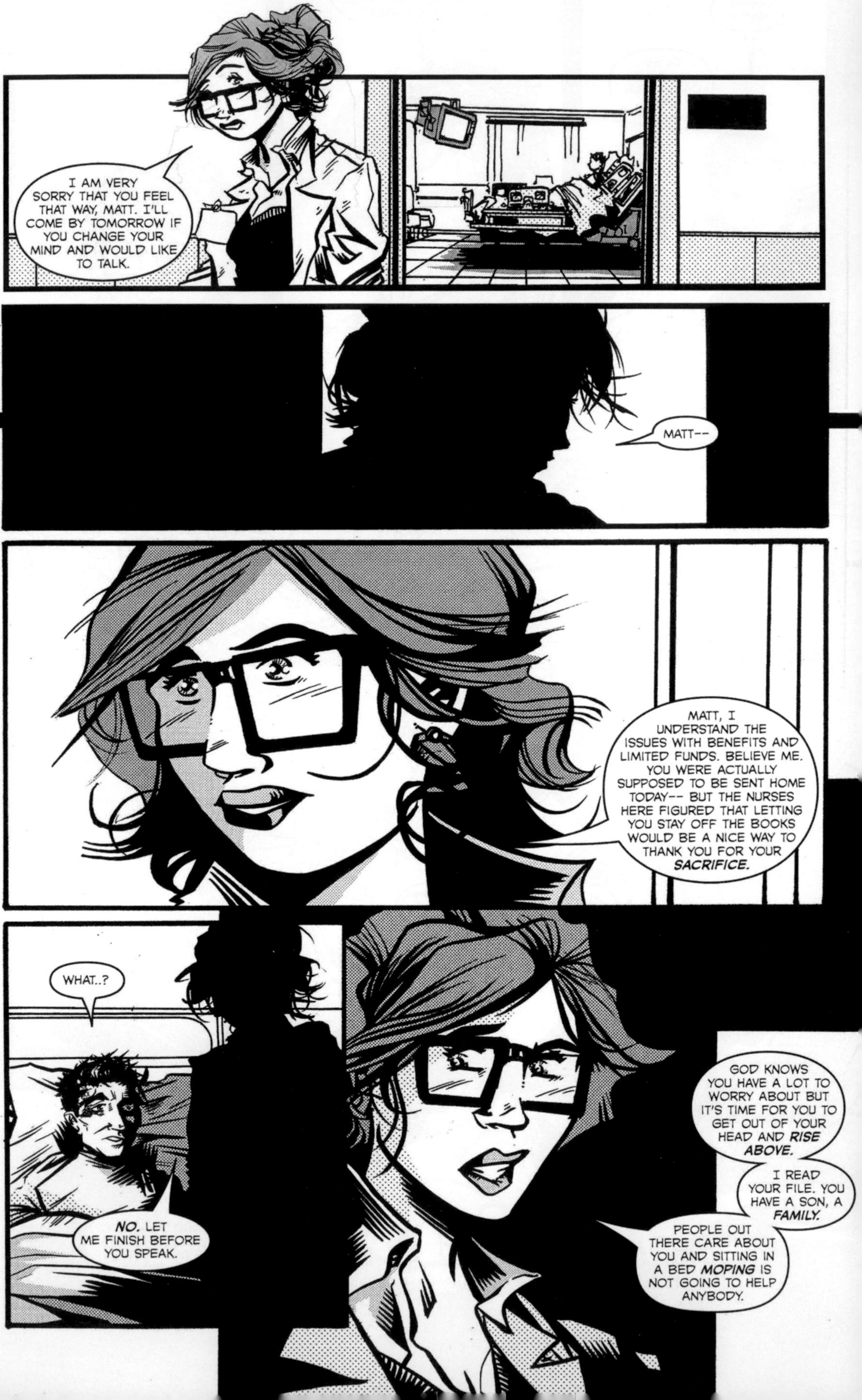

I AM VERY SORRY THAT YOU FEEL THAT WAY, MATT. I'LL COME BY TOMORROW IF YOU CHANGE YOUR MIND AND WOULD LIKE TO TALK.
MATT--
MATT, I UNDERSTAND THE ISSUES WITH BENEFITS AND LIMITED FUNDS. BELIEVE ME. YOU WERE ACTUALLY SUPPOSED TO BE SENT HOME TODAY-- BUT THE NURSES HERE FIGURED THAT LETTING YOU STAY OFF THE BOOKS WOULD BE A NICE WAY TO THANK YOU FOR YOUR ***SACRIFICE.***
WHAT..?
NO. LET ME FINISH BEFORE YOU SPEAK.
PEOPLE OUT THERE CARE ABOUT YOU AND SITTING IN A BED ***MOPING*** IS NOT GOING TO HELP ANYBODY.
I READ YOUR FILE. YOU HAVE A SON, A ***FAMILY.***
GOD KNOWS YOU HAVE A LOT TO WORRY ABOUT BUT IT'S TIME FOR YOU TO GET OUT OF YOUR HEAD AND ***RISE ABOVE.***

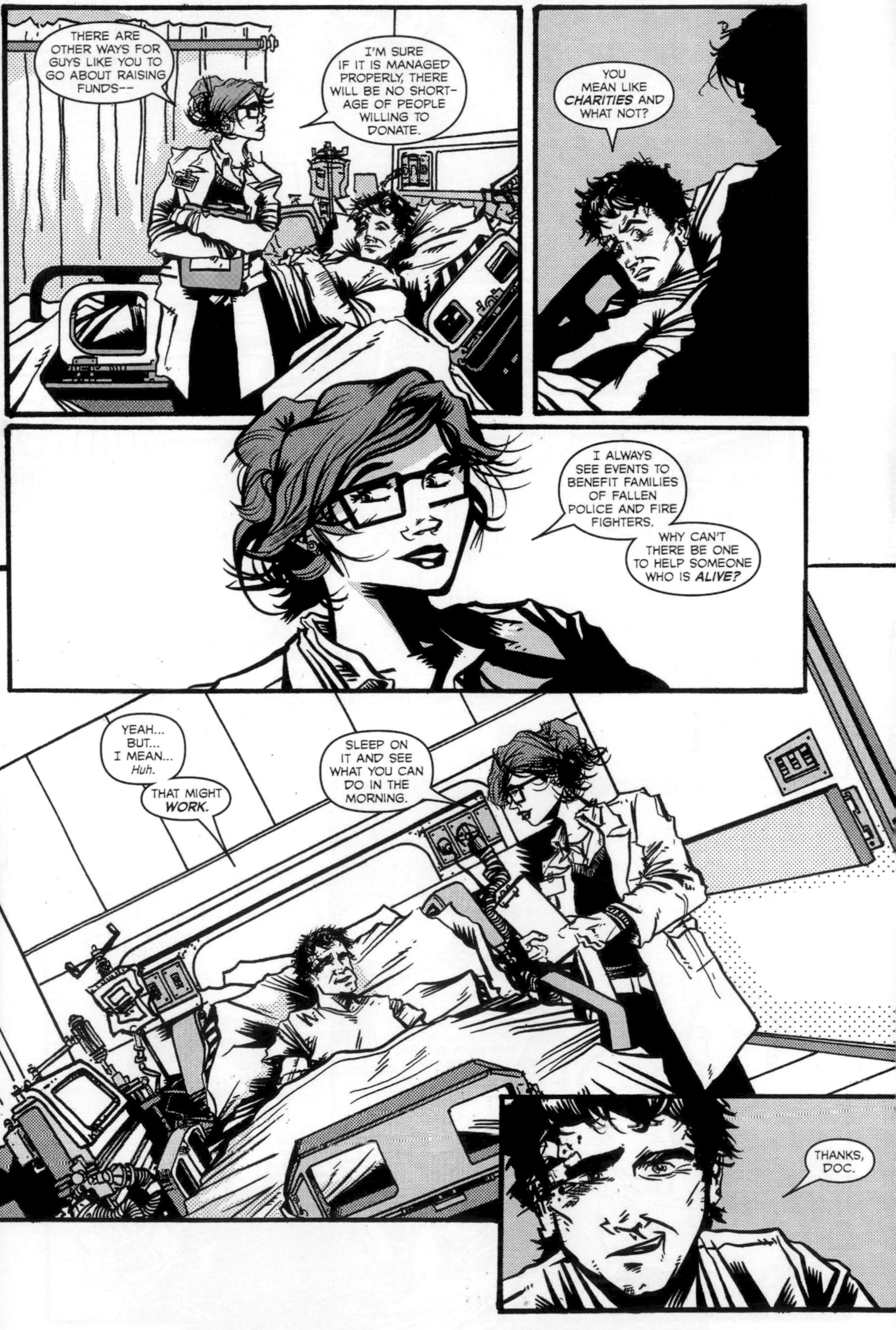
THERE ARE OTHER WAYS FOR GUYS LIKE YOU TO GO ABOUT RAISING FUNDS--
I'M SURE IF IT IS MANAGED PROPERLY, THERE WILL BE NO SHORTAGE OF PEOPLE WILLING TO DONATE.
YOU MEAN LIKE *CHARITIES* AND WHAT NOT?
I ALWAYS SEE EVENTS TO BENEFIT FAMILIES OF FALLEN POLICE AND FIRE FIGHTERS.
WHY CAN'T THERE BE ONE TO HELP SOMEONE WHO IS *ALIVE?*
YEAH... BUT... I MEAN... *Huh.*
THAT MIGHT *WORK.*
SLEEP ON IT AND SEE WHAT YOU CAN DO IN THE MORNING.
THANKS, DOC.

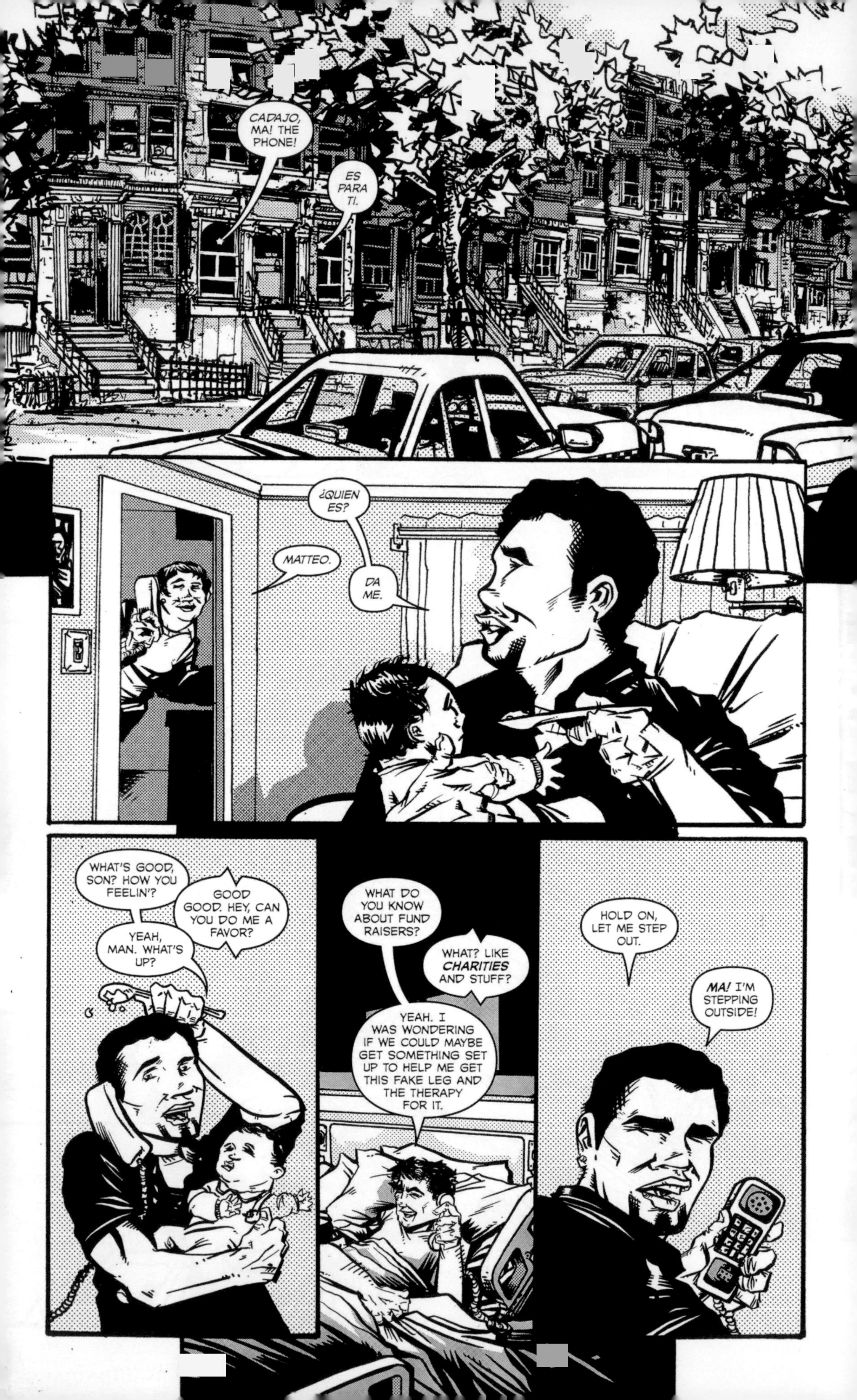
CADAJO, MA! THE PHONE!
ES PARA TI.
¿QUIEN ES?
MATTEO.
DA ME.
WHAT'S GOOD, SON? HOW YOU FEELIN'?
GOOD GOOD. HEY, CAN YOU DO ME A FAVOR?
YEAH, MAN. WHAT'S UP?
WHAT DO YOU KNOW ABOUT FUND RAISERS?
WHAT? LIKE CHARITIES AND STUFF?
YEAH. I WAS WONDERING IF WE COULD MAYBE GET SOMETHING SET UP TO HELP ME GET THIS FAKE LEG AND THE THERAPY FOR IT.
HOLD ON, LET ME STEP OUT.
MA! I'M STEPPING OUTSIDE!

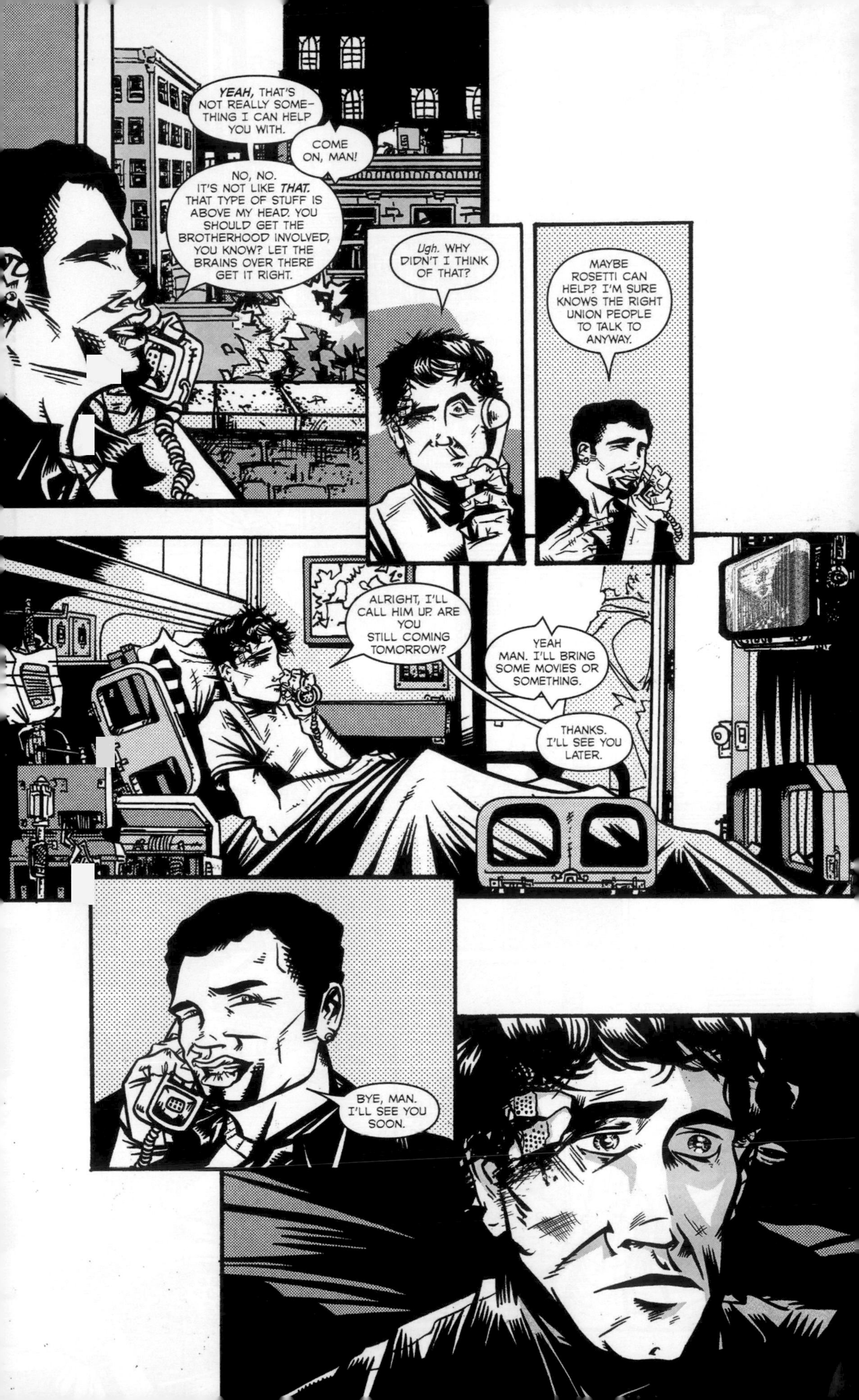

YEAH, THAT'S NOT REALLY SOMETHING I CAN HELP YOU WITH.
COME ON, MAN!
NO, NO. IT'S NOT LIKE THAT. THAT TYPE OF STUFF IS ABOVE MY HEAD. YOU SHOULD GET THE BROTHERHOOD INVOLVED, YOU KNOW? LET THE BRAINS OVER THERE GET IT RIGHT.
Ugh. WHY DIDN'T I THINK OF THAT?
MAYBE ROSETTI CAN HELP? I'M SURE KNOWS THE RIGHT UNION PEOPLE TO TALK TO ANYWAY.
ALRIGHT, I'LL CALL HIM UP. ARE YOU STILL COMING TOMORROW?
YEAH MAN. I'LL BRING SOME MOVIES OR SOMETHING.
THANKS. I'LL SEE YOU LATER.
BYE, MAN. I'LL SEE YOU SOON.

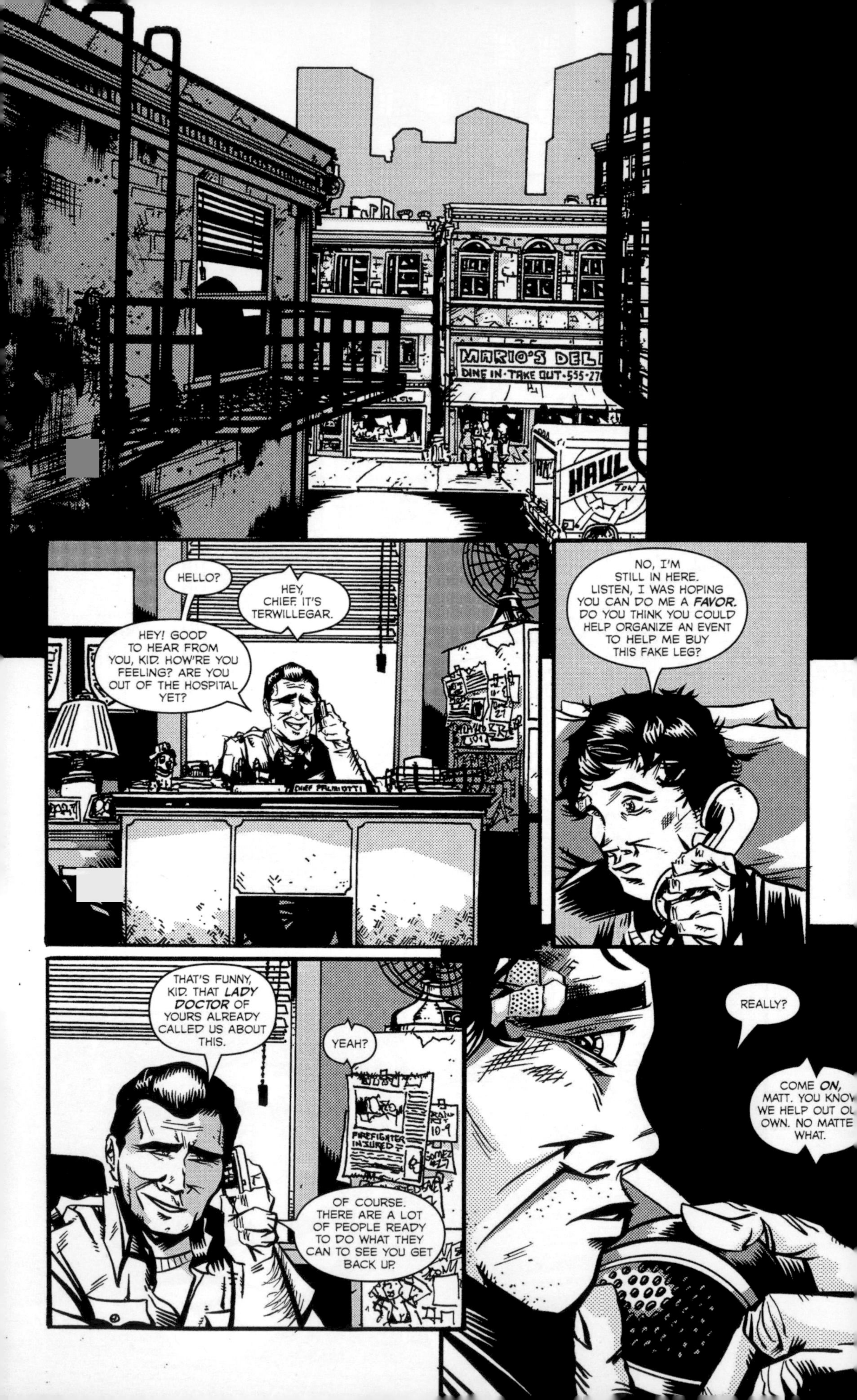
MARIO'S DELI
DINE IN · TAKE OUT · 555-27
HAUL
HELLO?
HEY, CHIEF. IT'S TERWILLEGAR.
HEY! GOOD TO HEAR FROM YOU, KID. HOW'RE YOU FEELING? ARE YOU OUT OF THE HOSPITAL YET?
NO, I'M STILL IN HERE. LISTEN, I WAS HOPING YOU CAN DO ME A *FAVOR.* DO YOU THINK YOU COULD HELP ORGANIZE AN EVENT TO HELP ME BUY THIS FAKE LEG?
THAT'S FUNNY, KID. THAT *LADY DOCTOR* OF YOURS ALREADY CALLED US ABOUT THIS.
YEAH?
REALLY?
FIREFIGHTER INJURED
OF COURSE. THERE ARE A LOT OF PEOPLE READY TO DO WHAT THEY CAN TO SEE YOU GET BACK UP.
COME *ON,* MATT. YOU KNOW WE HELP OUT OUR OWN. NO MATTER WHAT.

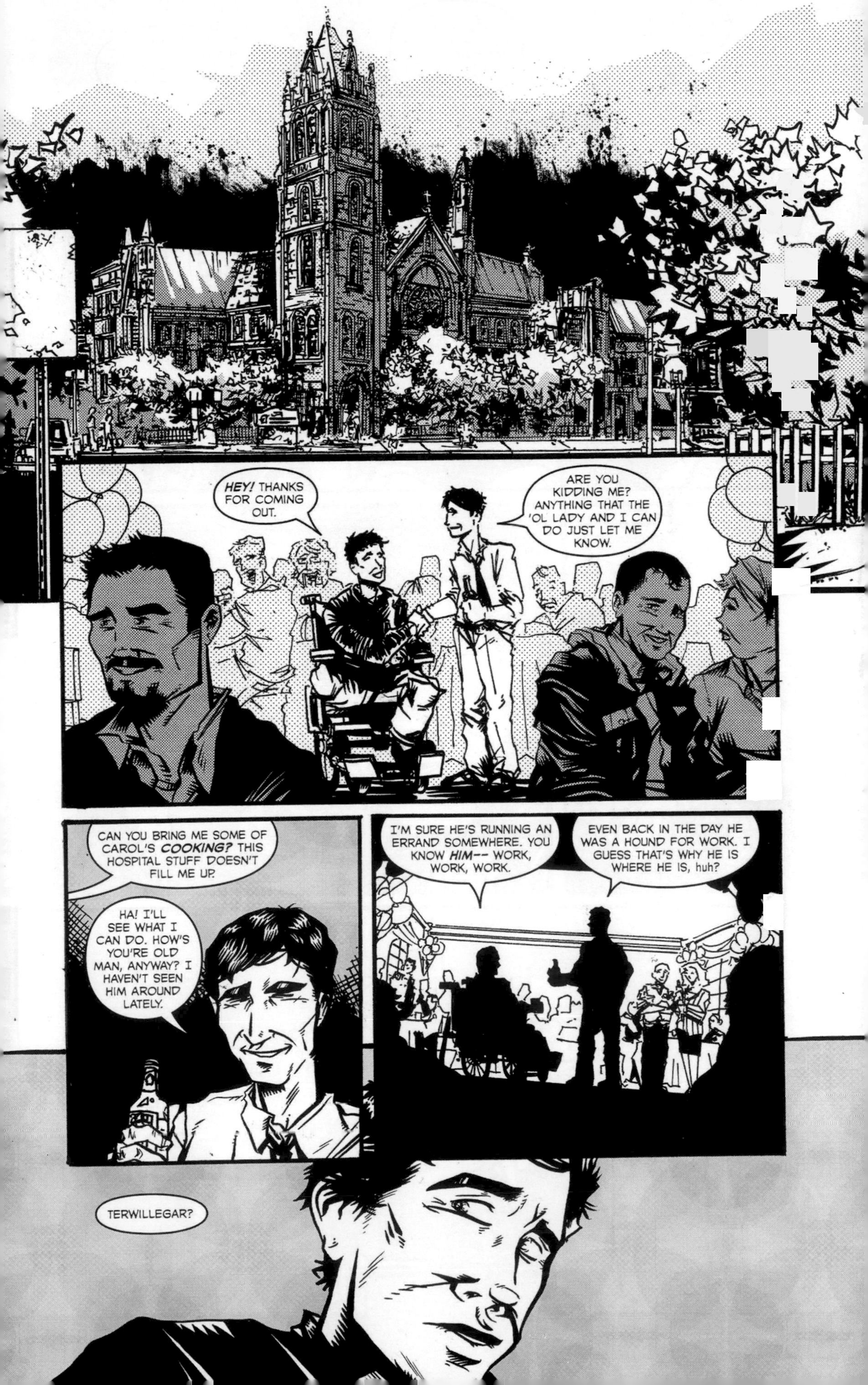
HEY! THANKS FOR COMING OUT.
ARE YOU KIDDING ME? ANYTHING THAT THE 'OL LADY AND I CAN DO JUST LET ME KNOW.
CAN YOU BRING ME SOME OF CAROL'S COOKING? THIS HOSPITAL STUFF DOESN'T FILL ME UP.
HA! I'LL SEE WHAT I CAN DO. HOW'S YOU'RE OLD MAN, ANYWAY? I HAVEN'T SEEN HIM AROUND LATELY.
I'M SURE HE'S RUNNING AN ERRAND SOMEWHERE. YOU KNOW HIM-- WORK, WORK, WORK.
EVEN BACK IN THE DAY HE WAS A HOUND FOR WORK. I GUESS THAT'S WHY HE IS WHERE HE IS, huh?
TERWILLEGAR?

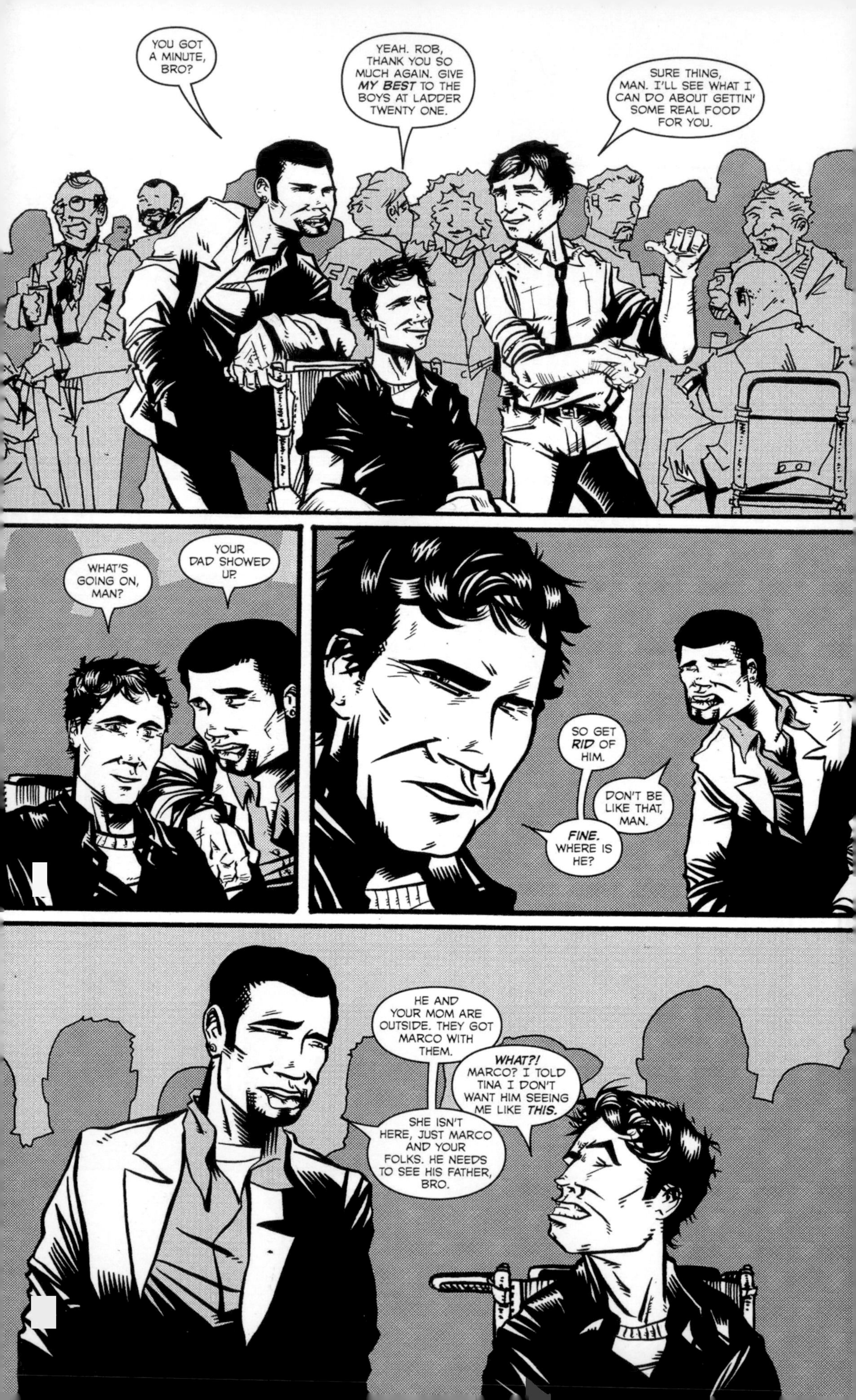
YOU GOT A MINUTE, BRO?
YEAH. ROB, THANK YOU SO MUCH AGAIN. GIVE MY BEST TO THE BOYS AT LADDER TWENTY ONE.
SURE THING, MAN. I'LL SEE WHAT I CAN DO ABOUT GETTIN' SOME REAL FOOD FOR YOU.
WHAT'S GOING ON, MAN?
YOUR DAD SHOWED UP.
SO GET RID OF HIM.
DON'T BE LIKE THAT, MAN.
FINE. WHERE IS HE?
HE AND YOUR MOM ARE OUTSIDE. THEY GOT MARCO WITH THEM.
WHAT?! MARCO? I TOLD TINA I DON'T WANT HIM SEEING ME LIKE THIS.
SHE ISN'T HERE, JUST MARCO AND YOUR FOLKS. HE NEEDS TO SEE HIS FATHER, BRO.

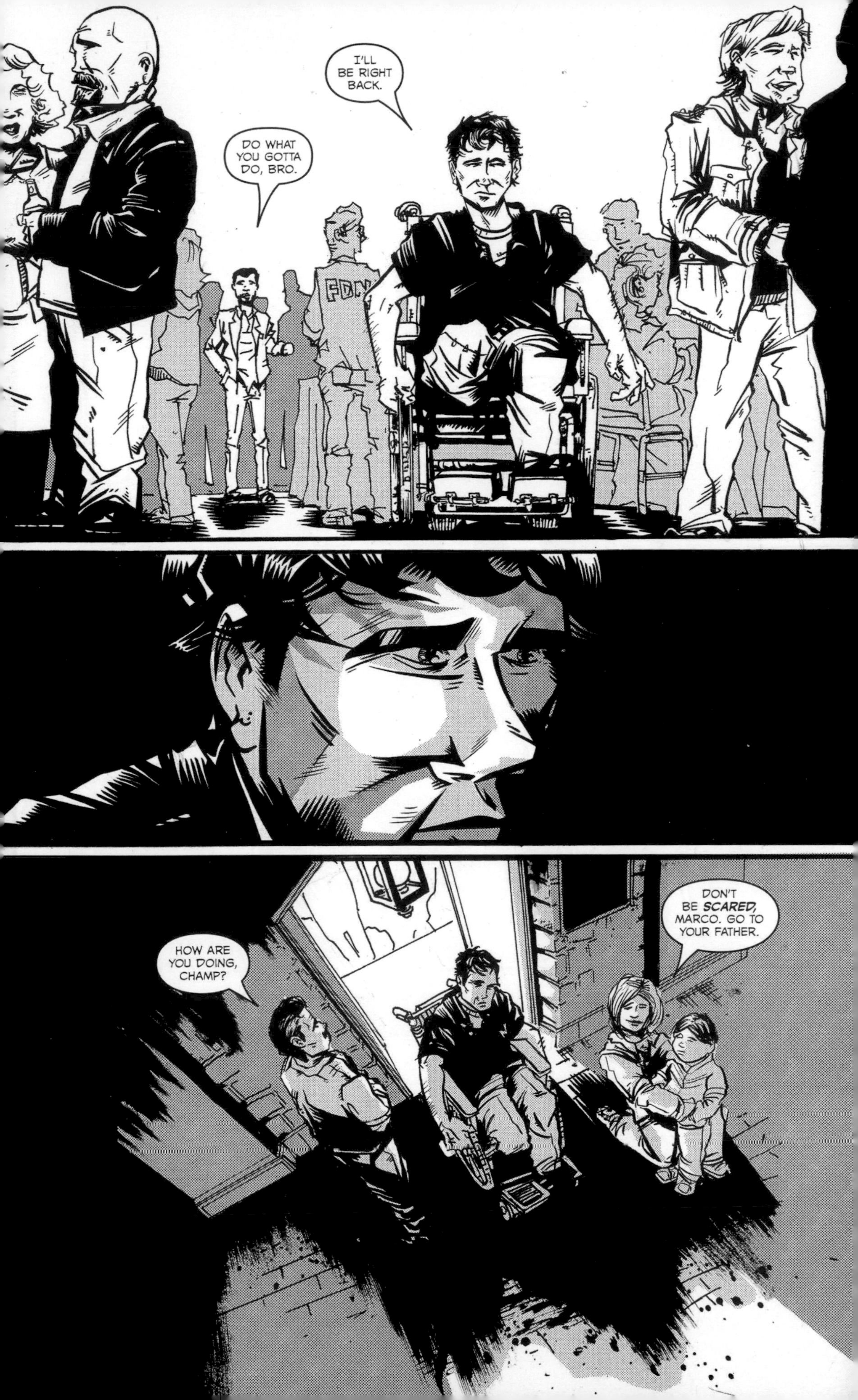
I'LL BE RIGHT BACK.
DO WHAT YOU GOTTA DO, BRO.
FDNY
HOW ARE YOU DOING, CHAMP?
DON'T BE SCARED, MARCO. GO TO YOUR FATHER.

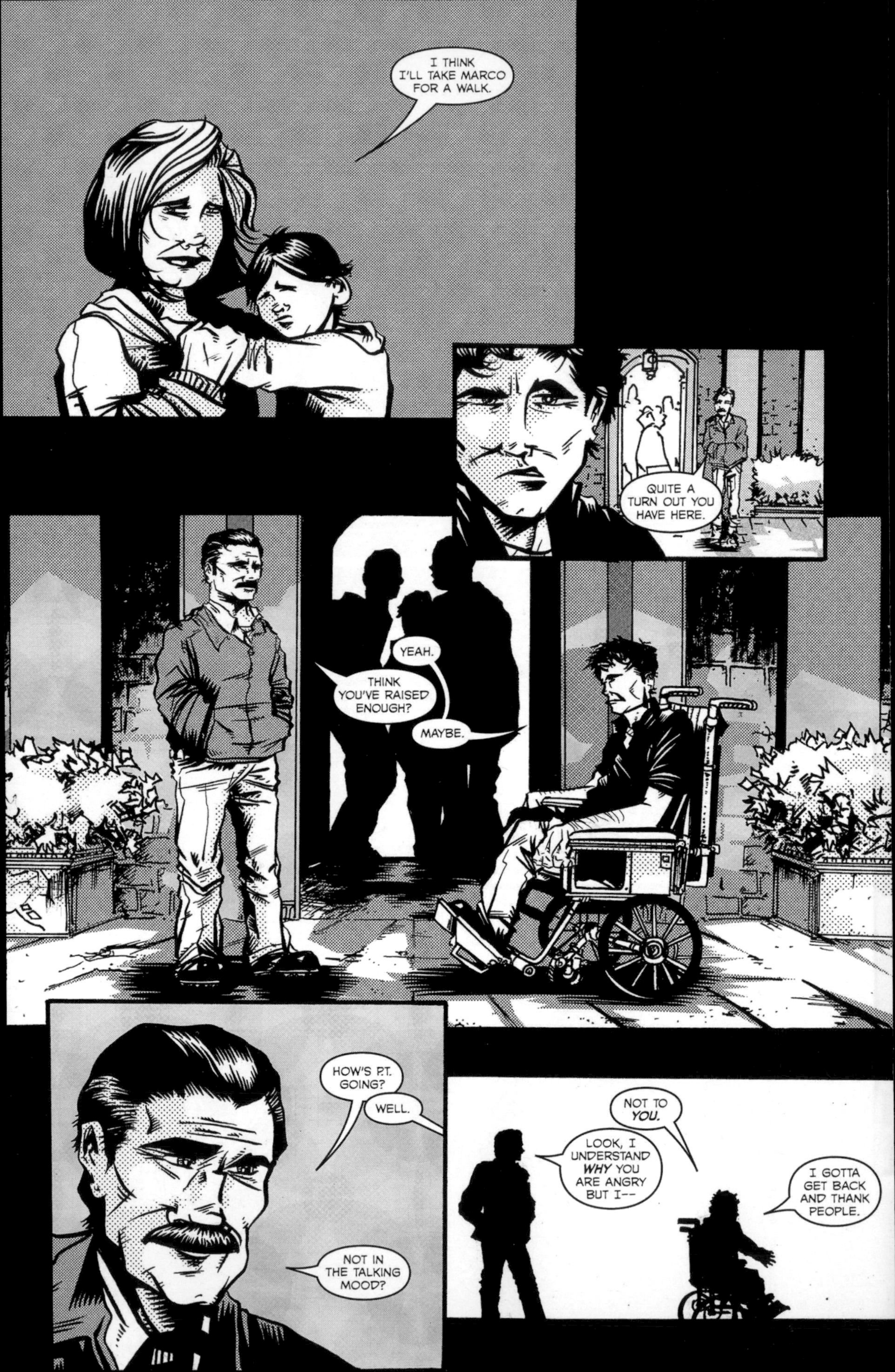

I THINK I'LL TAKE MARCO FOR A WALK.
QUITE A TURN OUT YOU HAVE HERE.
YEAH.
THINK YOU'VE RAISED ENOUGH?
MAYBE.
HOW'S P.T. GOING?
WELL.
NOT IN THE TALKING MOOD?
NOT TO *YOU.*
LOOK, I UNDERSTAND *WHY* YOU ARE ANGRY BUT I--
I GOTTA GET BACK AND THANK PEOPLE.

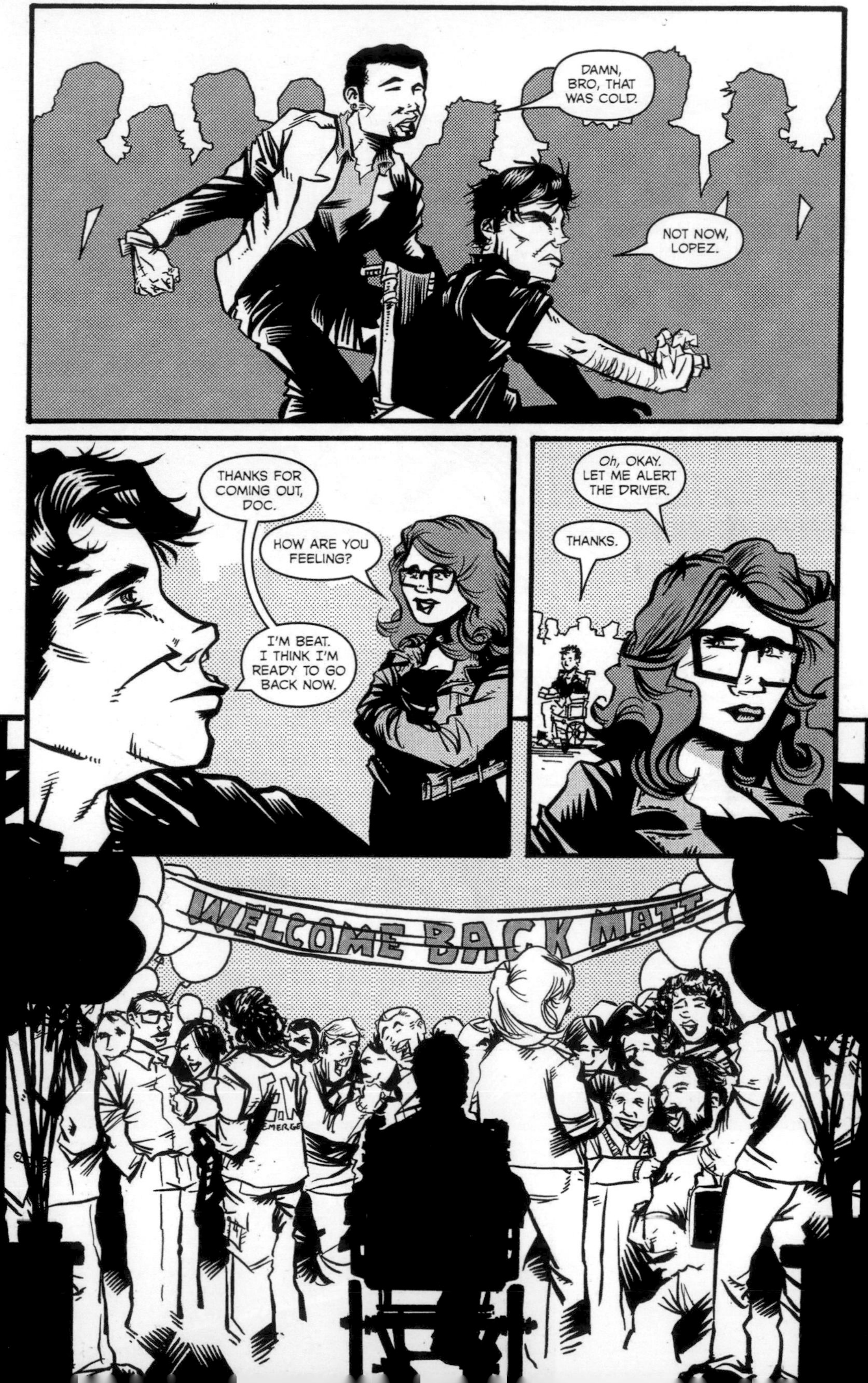
DAMN, BRO, THAT WAS COLD.
NOT NOW, LOPEZ.
THANKS FOR COMING OUT, DOC.
HOW ARE YOU FEELING?
I'M BEAT. I THINK I'M READY TO GO BACK NOW.
Oh, OKAY. LET ME ALERT THE DRIVER.
THANKS.
WELCOME BACK MATT

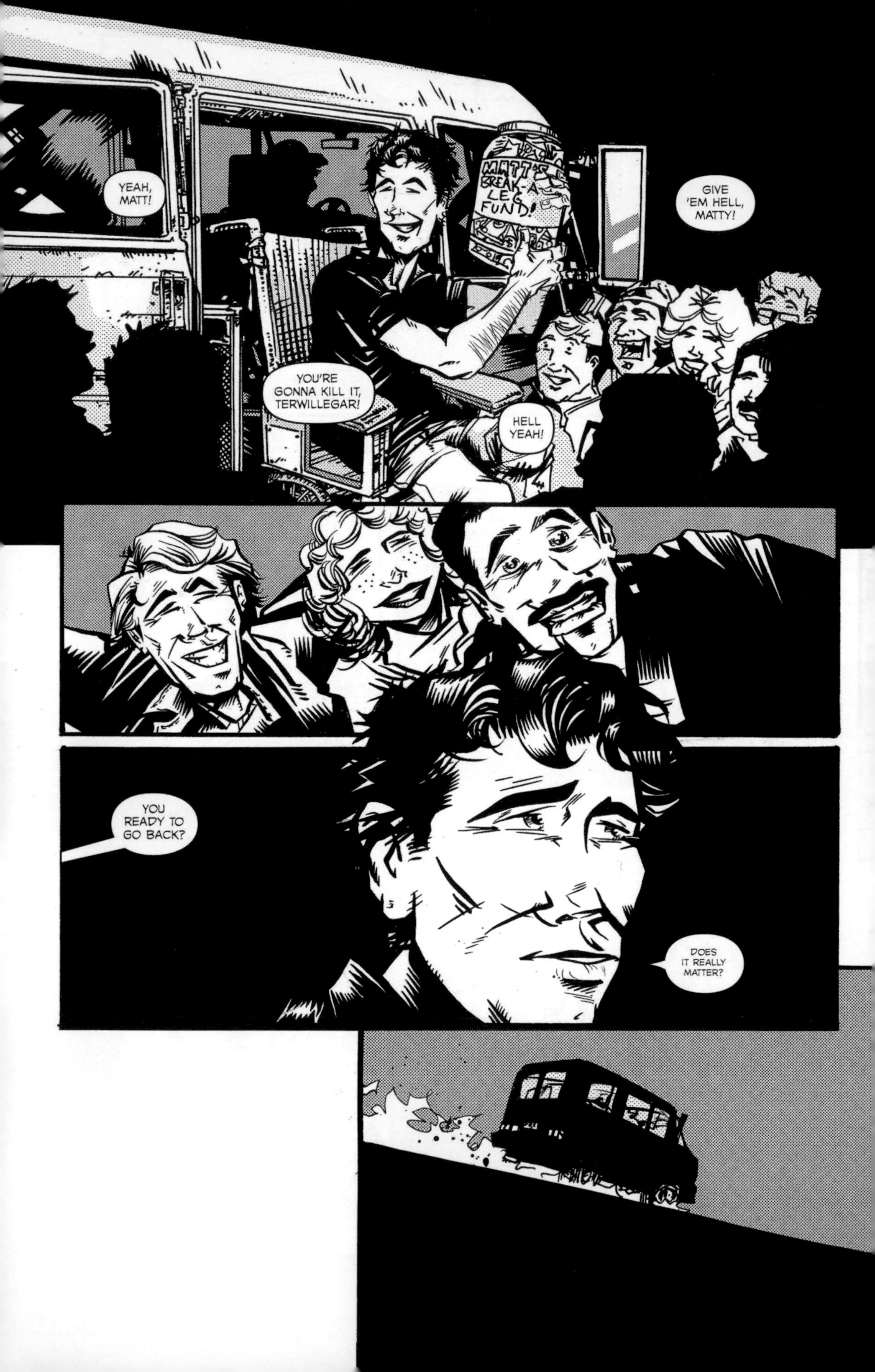
YEAH, MATT!
MATT'S BREAK-A-LEG FUND!
GIVE 'EM HELL, MATTY!
YOU'RE GONNA KILL IT, TERWILLEGAR!
HELL YEAH!
YOU READY TO GO BACK?
DOES IT REALLY MATTER?

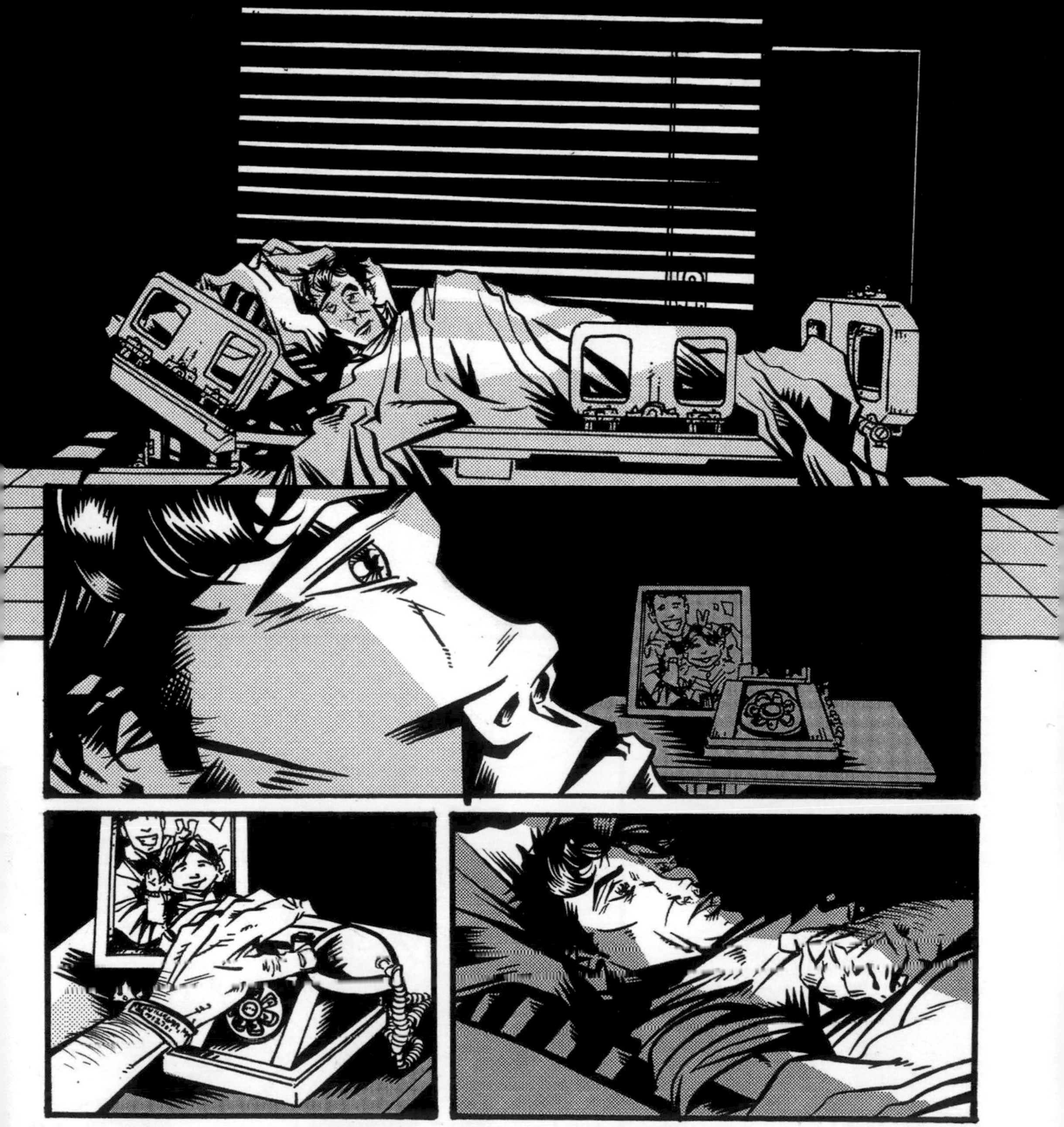

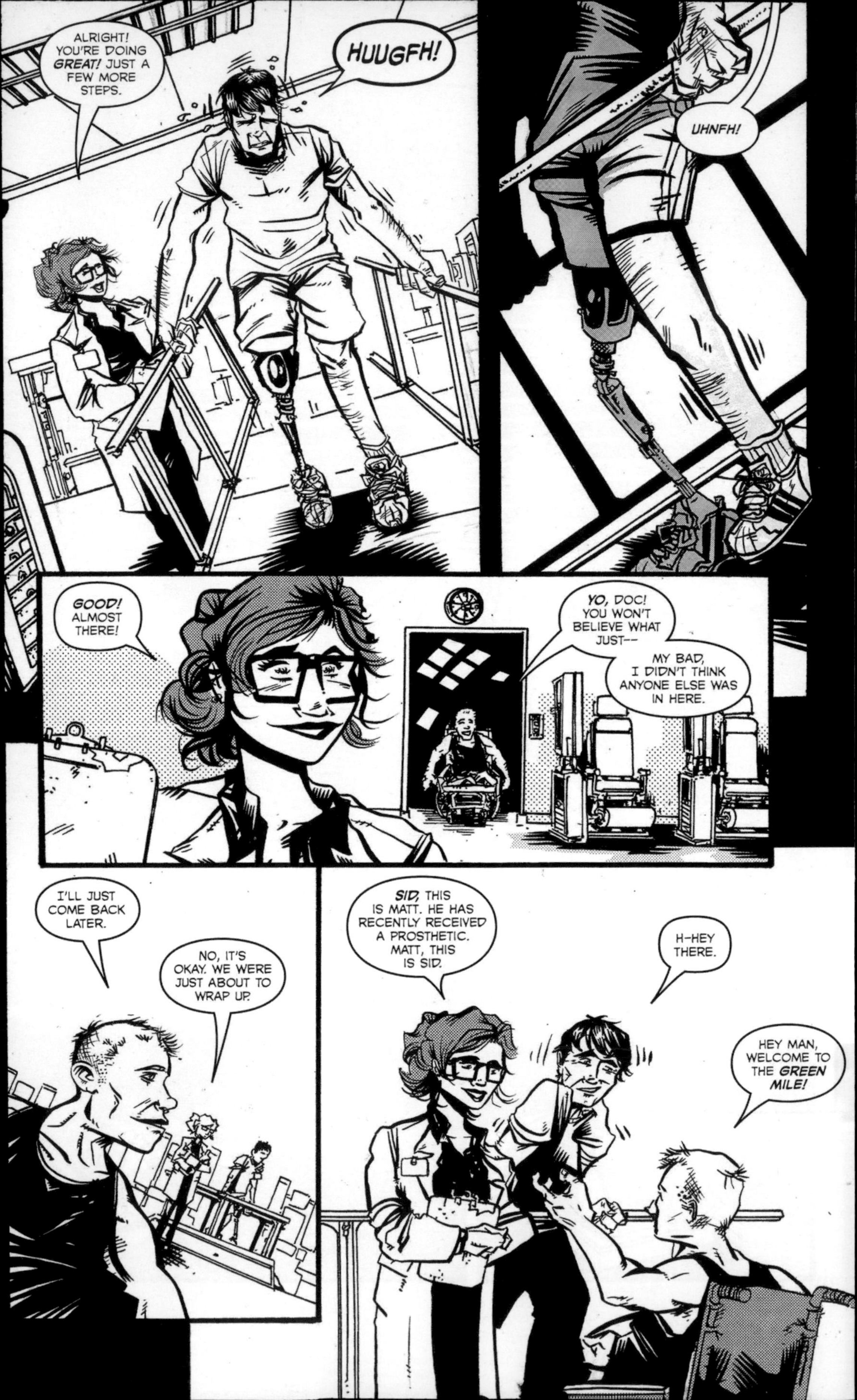

ALRIGHT! YOU'RE DOING GREAT! JUST A FEW MORE STEPS.
HUUGFH!
UHNFH!
GOOD! ALMOST THERE!
YO, DOC! YOU WON'T BELIEVE WHAT JUST--
MY BAD, I DIDN'T THINK ANYONE ELSE WAS IN HERE.
I'LL JUST COME BACK LATER.
NO, IT'S OKAY. WE WERE JUST ABOUT TO WRAP UP.
SID, THIS IS MATT. HE HAS RECENTLY RECEIVED A PROSTHETIC. MATT, THIS IS SID.
H-HEY THERE.
HEY MAN, WELCOME TO THE GREEN MILE!

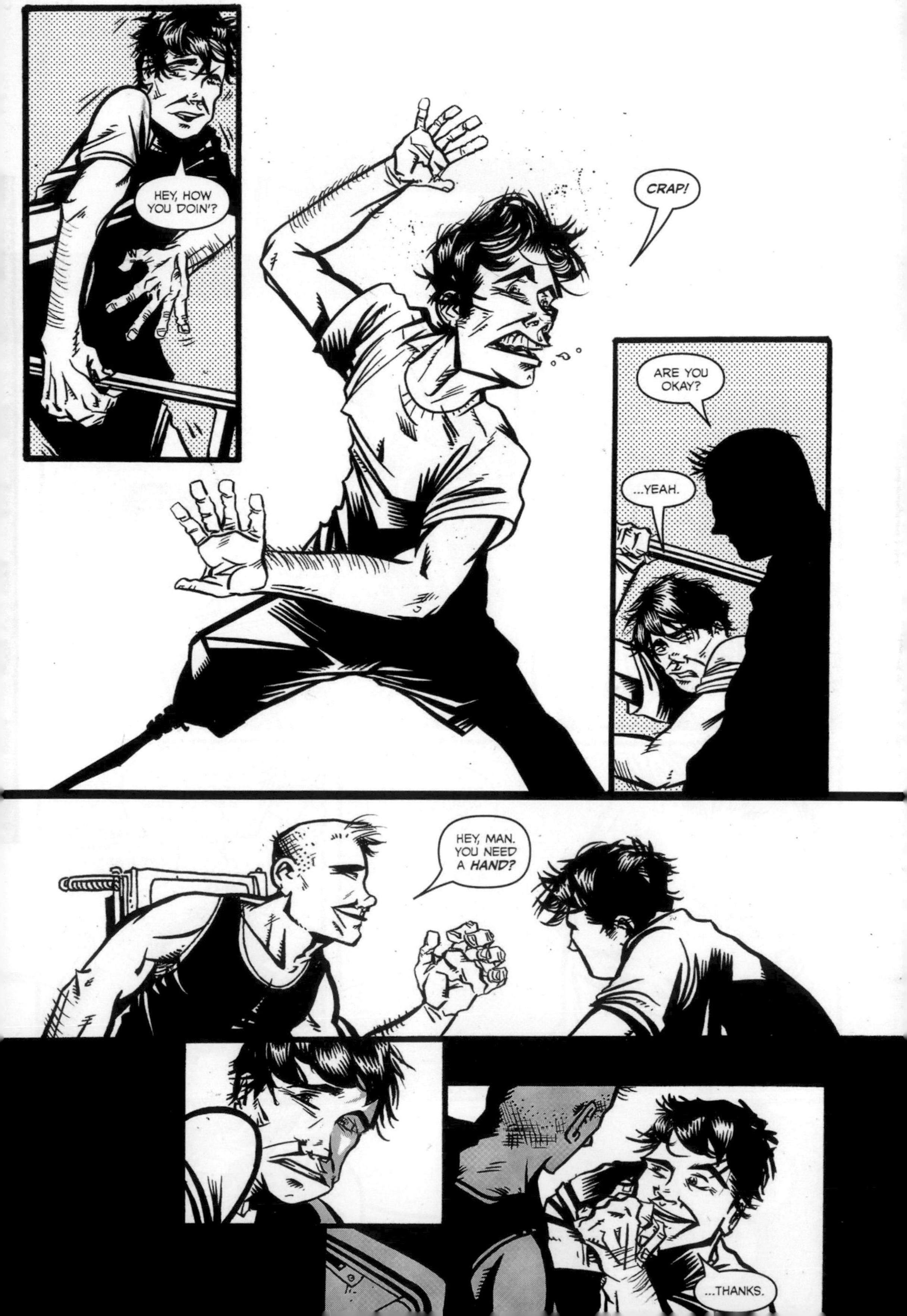
HEY, HOW YOU DOIN'?
CRAP!
ARE YOU OKAY?
...YEAH.
HEY, MAN. YOU NEED A HAND?
...THANKS.

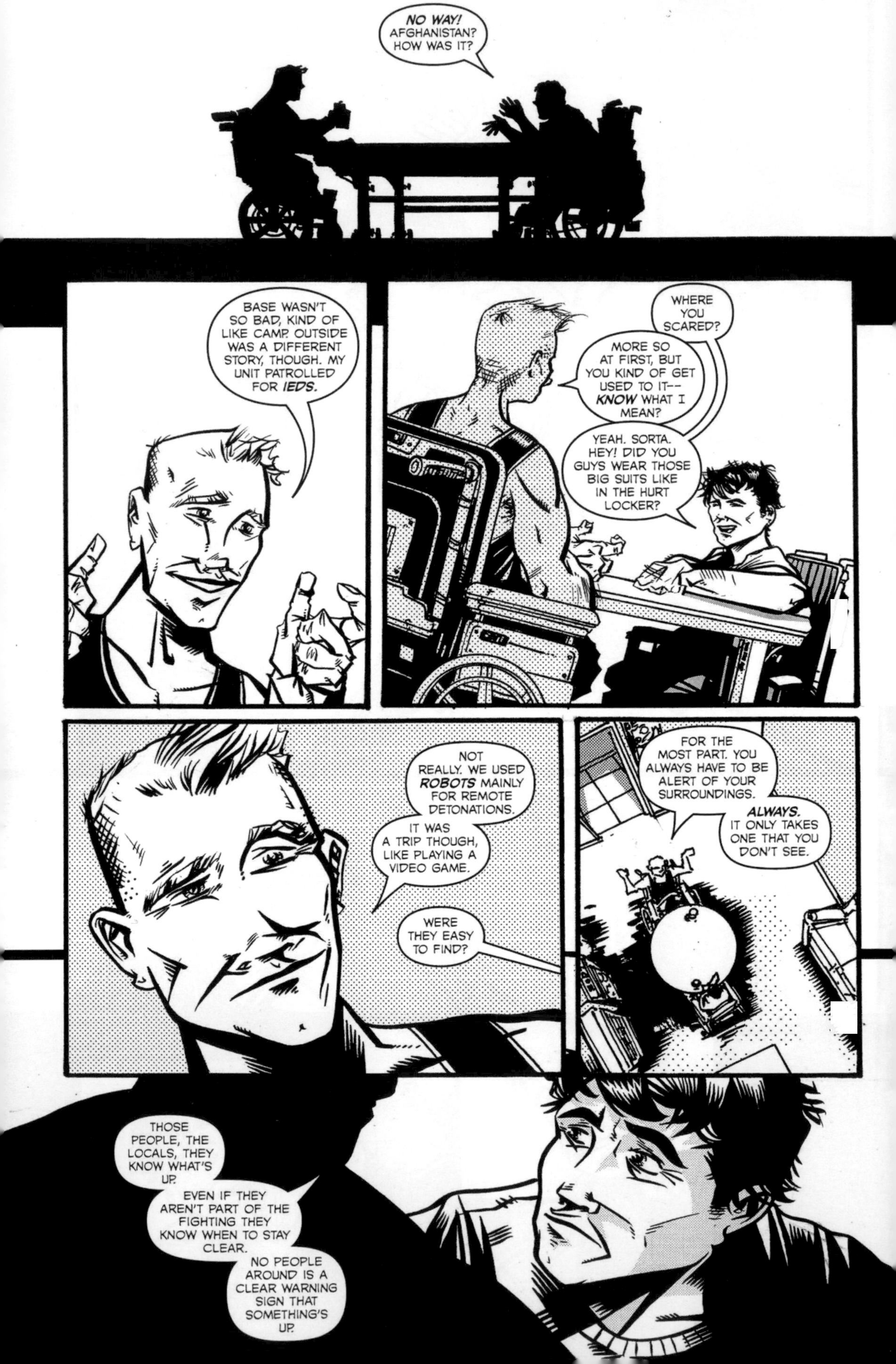

NO WAY! AFGHANISTAN? HOW WAS IT?
BASE WASN'T SO BAD, KIND OF LIKE CAMP. OUTSIDE WAS A DIFFERENT STORY, THOUGH. MY UNIT PATROLLED FOR IEDS.
WHERE YOU SCARED?
MORE SO AT FIRST, BUT YOU KIND OF GET USED TO IT-- KNOW WHAT I MEAN?
YEAH. SORTA. HEY! DID YOU GUYS WEAR THOSE BIG SUITS LIKE IN THE HURT LOCKER?
NOT REALLY. WE USED ROBOTS MAINLY FOR REMOTE DETONATIONS.
IT WAS A TRIP THOUGH, LIKE PLAYING A VIDEO GAME.
WERE THEY EASY TO FIND?
FOR THE MOST PART. YOU ALWAYS HAVE TO BE ALERT OF YOUR SURROUNDINGS.
ALWAYS. IT ONLY TAKES ONE THAT YOU DON'T SEE.
THOSE PEOPLE, THE LOCALS, THEY KNOW WHAT'S UP.
EVEN IF THEY AREN'T PART OF THE FIGHTING THEY KNOW WHEN TO STAY CLEAR.
NO PEOPLE AROUND IS A CLEAR WARNING SIGN THAT SOMETHING'S UP.

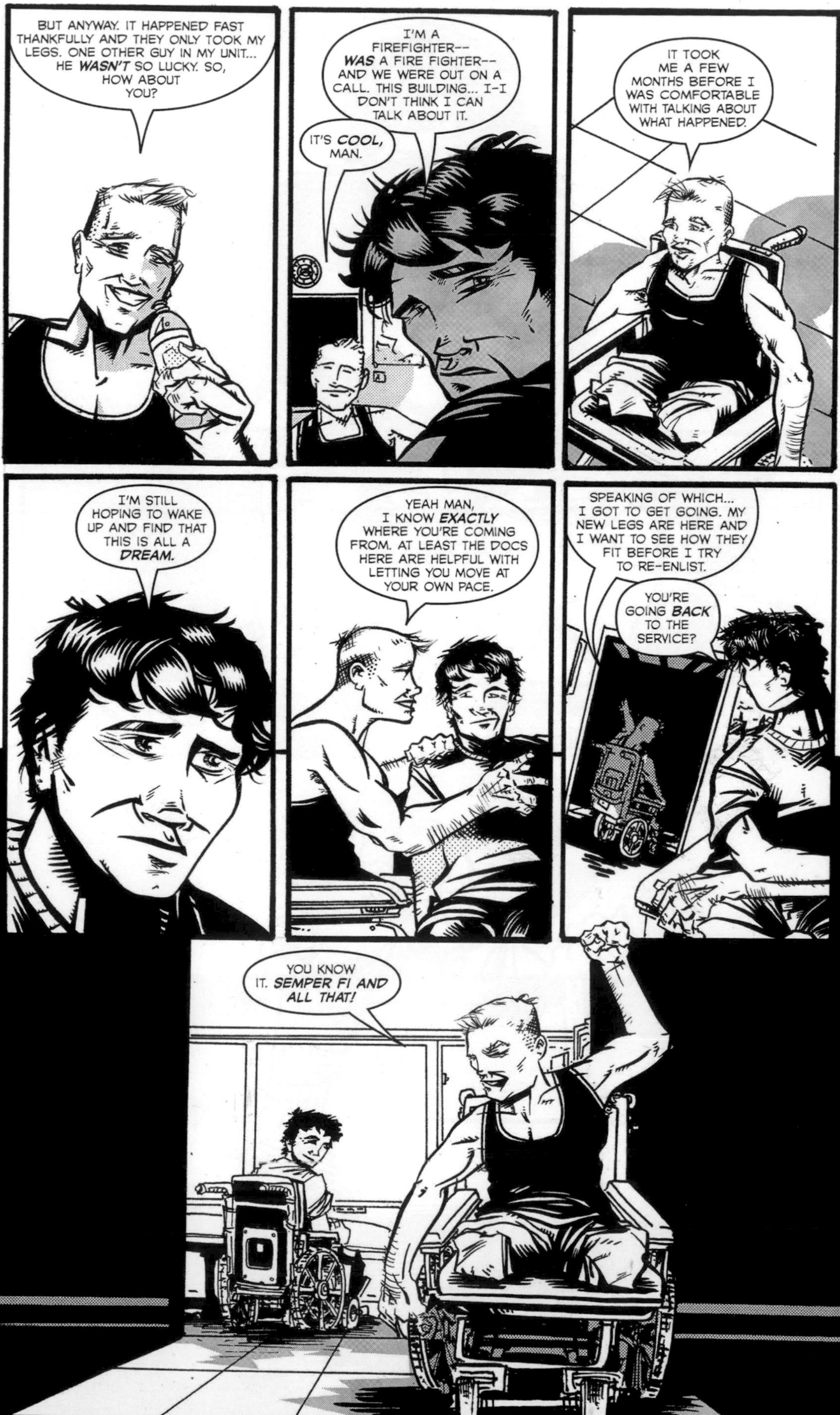
BUT ANYWAY. IT HAPPENED FAST THANKFULLY AND THEY ONLY TOOK MY LEGS. ONE OTHER GUY IN MY UNIT... HE WASN'T SO LUCKY. SO, HOW ABOUT YOU?
I'M A FIREFIGHTER-- WAS A FIRE FIGHTER-- AND WE WERE OUT ON A CALL. THIS BUILDING... I-I DON'T THINK I CAN TALK ABOUT IT.
IT'S COOL, MAN.
IT TOOK ME A FEW MONTHS BEFORE I WAS COMFORTABLE WITH TALKING ABOUT WHAT HAPPENED.
I'M STILL HOPING TO WAKE UP AND FIND THAT THIS IS ALL A DREAM.
YEAH MAN, I KNOW EXACTLY WHERE YOU'RE COMING FROM. AT LEAST THE DOCS HERE ARE HELPFUL WITH LETTING YOU MOVE AT YOUR OWN PACE.
SPEAKING OF WHICH... I GOT TO GET GOING. MY NEW LEGS ARE HERE AND I WANT TO SEE HOW THEY FIT BEFORE I TRY TO RE-ENLIST.
YOU'RE GOING BACK TO THE SERVICE?
YOU KNOW IT. SEMPER FI AND ALL THAT!

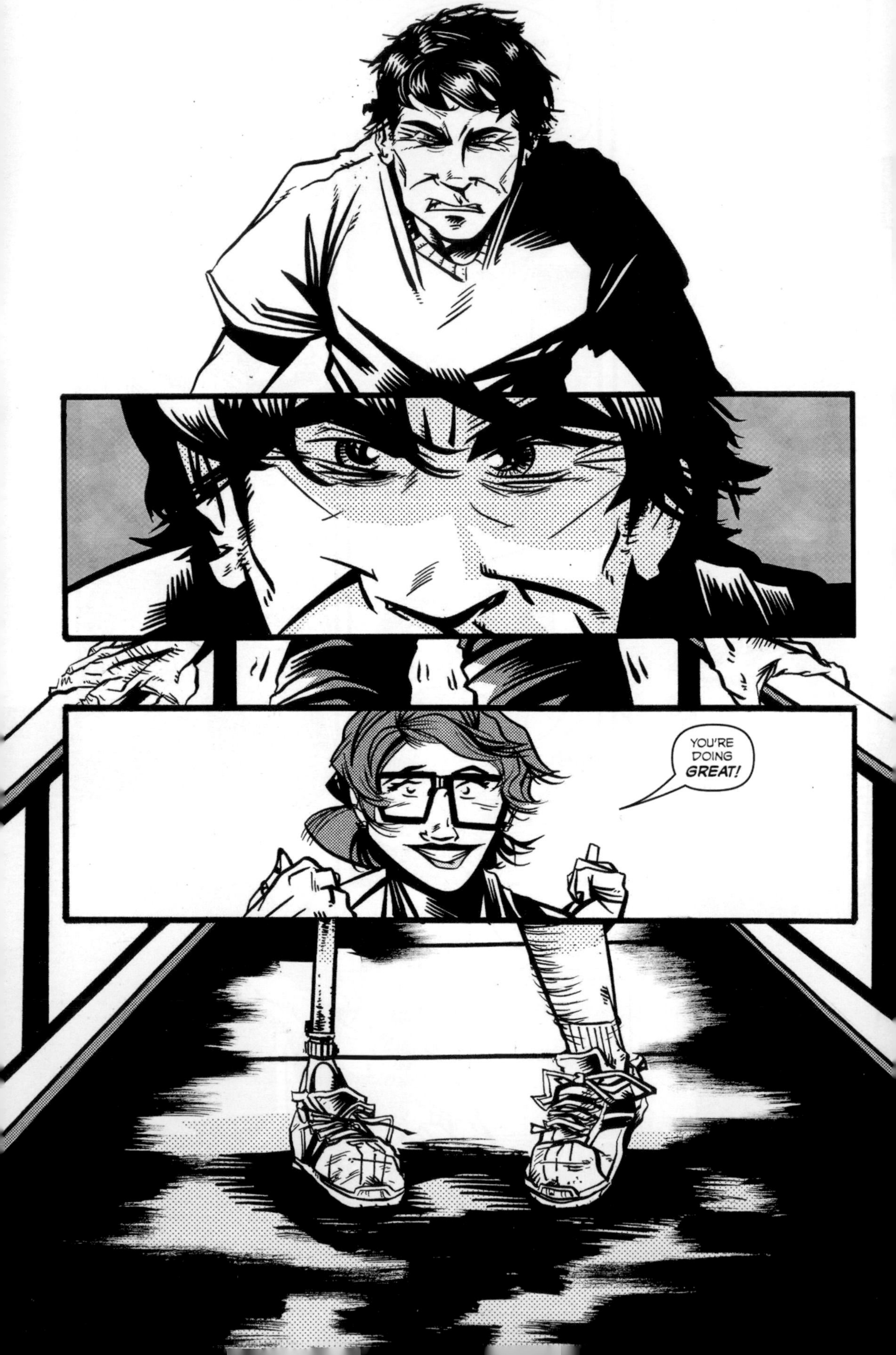
YOU'RE DOING GREAT!

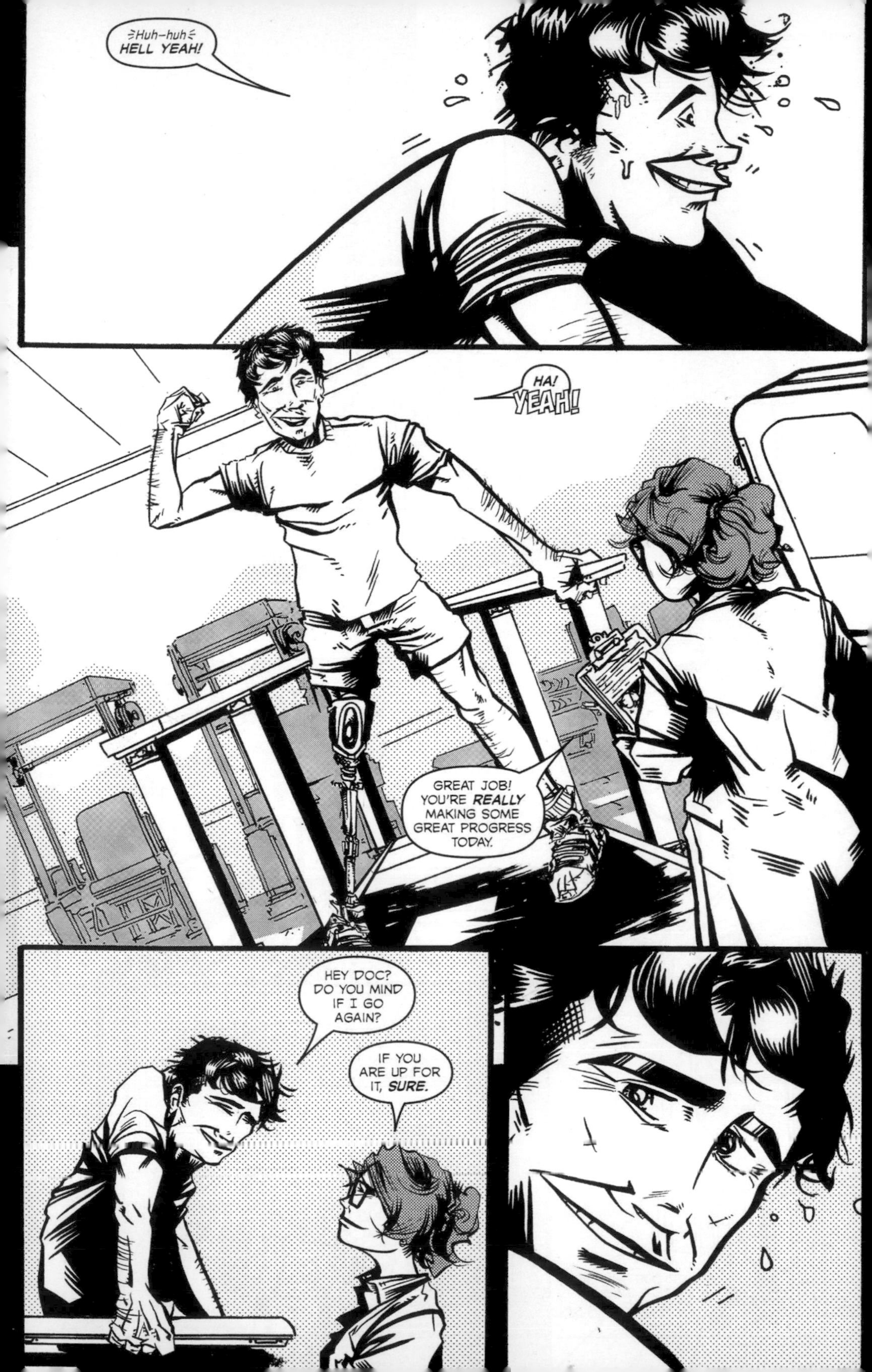
Huh-huh
HELL YEAH!
HA!
YEAH!
GREAT JOB! YOU'RE *REALLY* MAKING SOME GREAT PROGRESS TODAY.
HEY DOC? DO YOU MIND IF I GO AGAIN?
IF YOU ARE UP FOR IT, *SURE*.

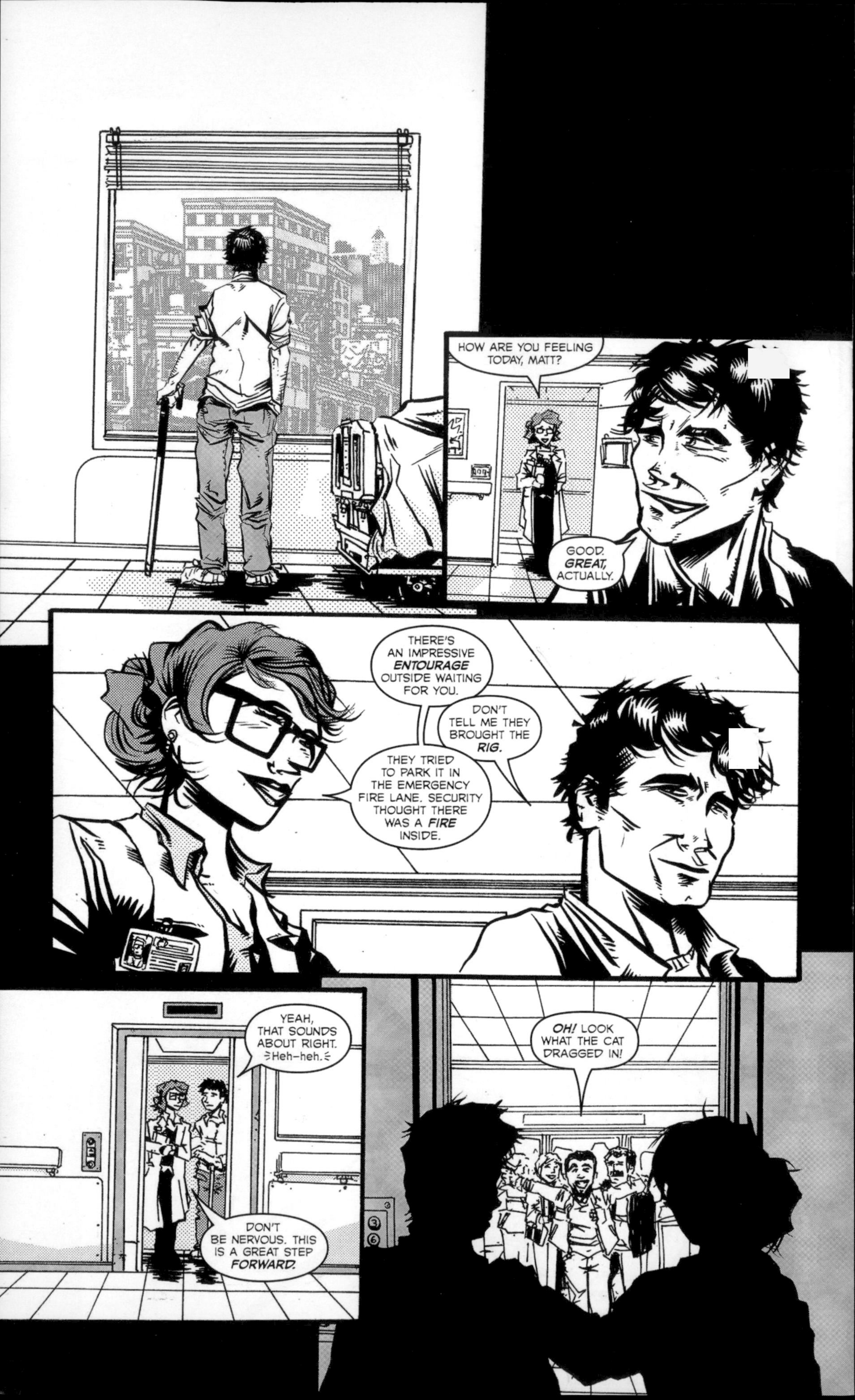

HOW ARE YOU FEELING TODAY, MATT?
GOOD. GREAT, ACTUALLY.
THERE'S AN IMPRESSIVE ENTOURAGE OUTSIDE WAITING FOR YOU.
DON'T TELL ME THEY BROUGHT THE RIG.
THEY TRIED TO PARK IT IN THE EMERGENCY FIRE LANE. SECURITY THOUGHT THERE WAS A FIRE INSIDE.
YEAH, THAT SOUNDS ABOUT RIGHT. Heh-heh.
DON'T BE NERVOUS. THIS IS A GREAT STEP FORWARD.
OH! LOOK WHAT THE CAT DRAGGED IN!

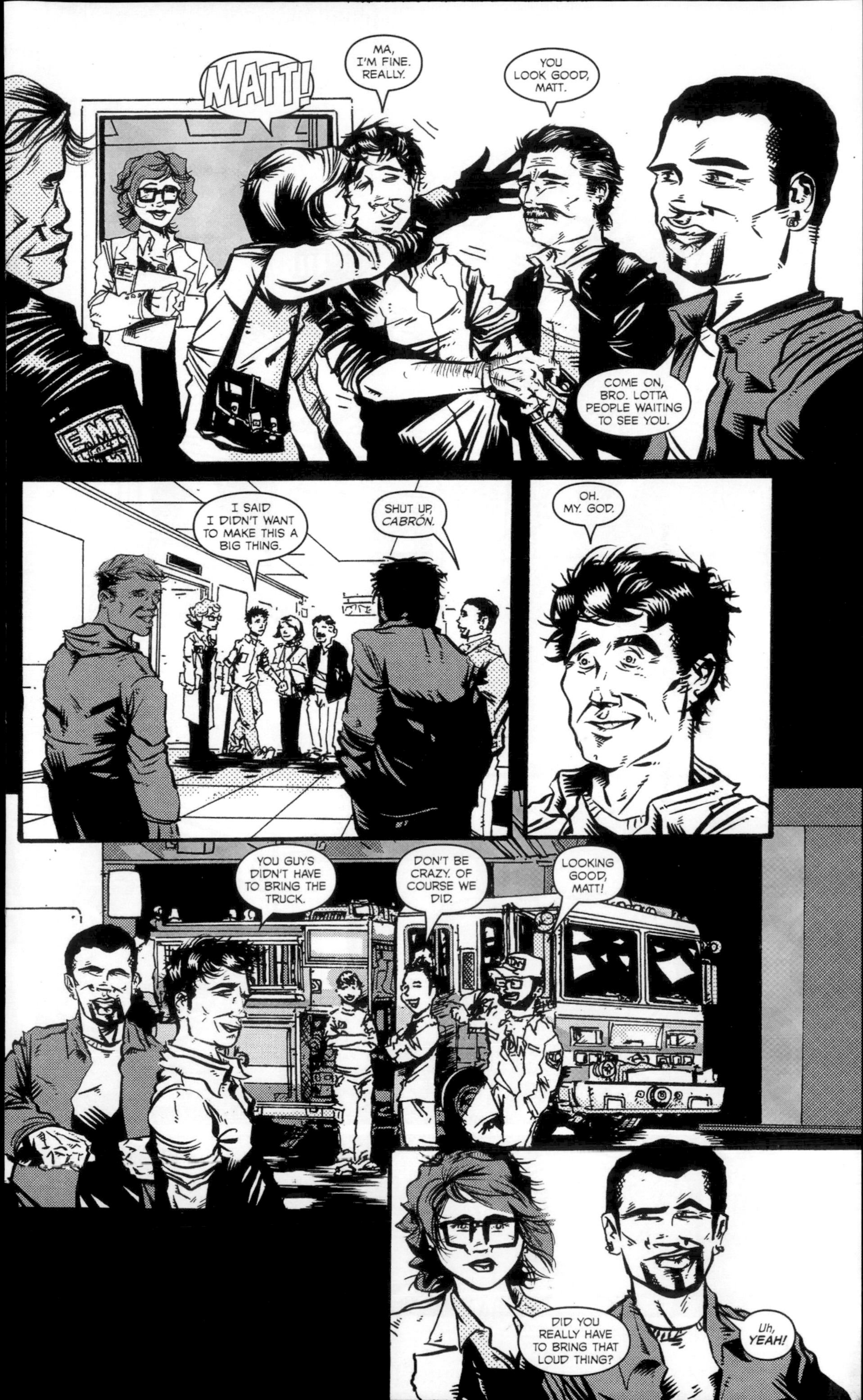
MATT!
MA, I'M FINE. REALLY.
YOU LOOK GOOD, MATT.
COME ON, BRO. LOTTA PEOPLE WAITING TO SEE YOU.
E.M.T.
I SAID I DIDN'T WANT TO MAKE THIS A BIG THING.
SHUT UP, *CABRÓN.*
OH. MY. GOD.
YOU GUYS DIDN'T HAVE TO BRING THE TRUCK.
DON'T BE CRAZY. OF COURSE WE DID.
LOOKING GOOD, MATT!
DID YOU REALLY HAVE TO BRING THAT LOUD THING?
Uh, ***YEAH!***

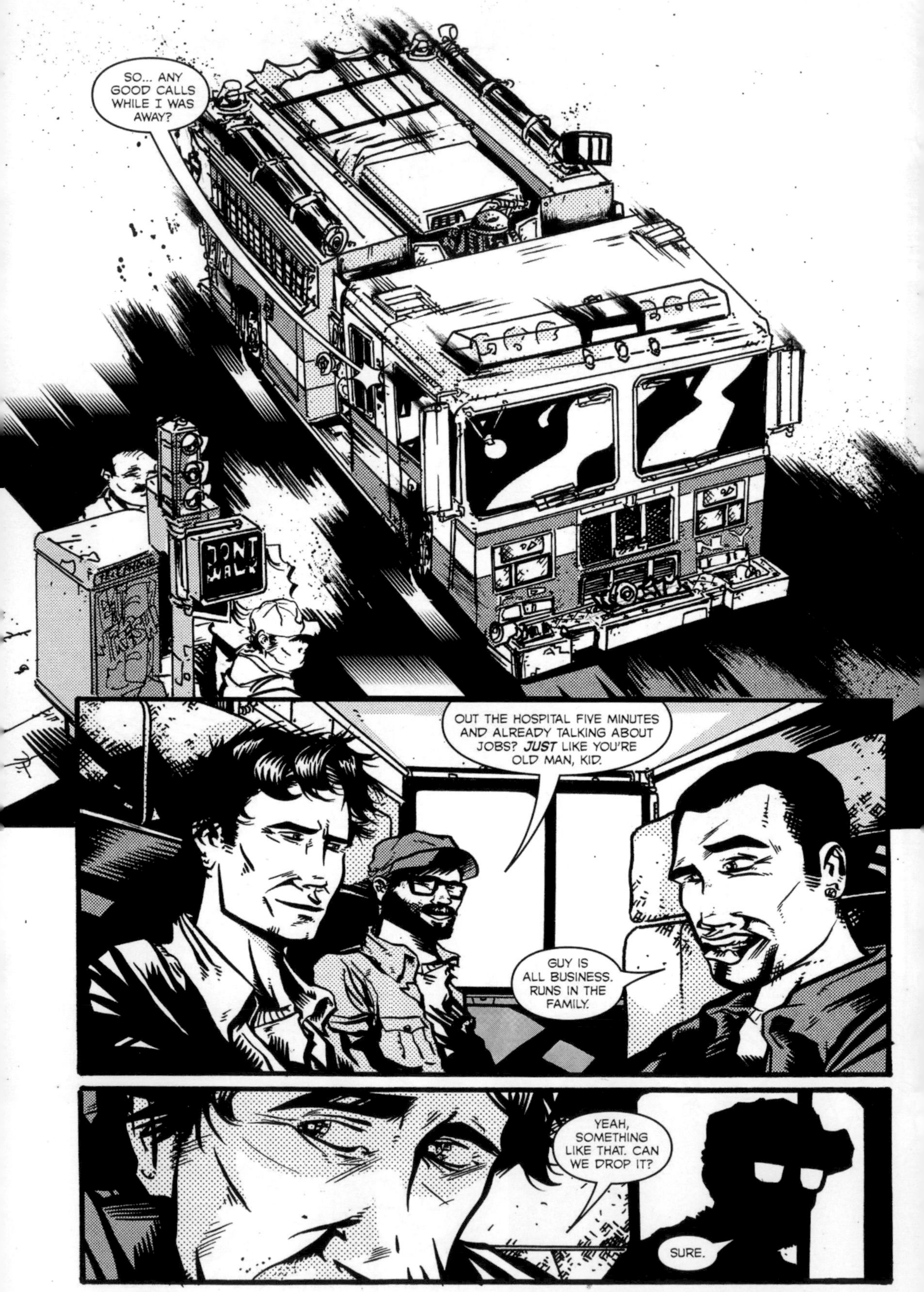
SO... ANY GOOD CALLS WHILE I WAS AWAY?
DONT WALK
OUT THE HOSPITAL FIVE MINUTES AND ALREADY TALKING ABOUT JOBS? JUST LIKE YOU'RE OLD MAN, KID.
GUY IS ALL BUSINESS. RUNS IN THE FAMILY.
YEAH, SOMETHING LIKE THAT. CAN WE DROP IT?
SURE.

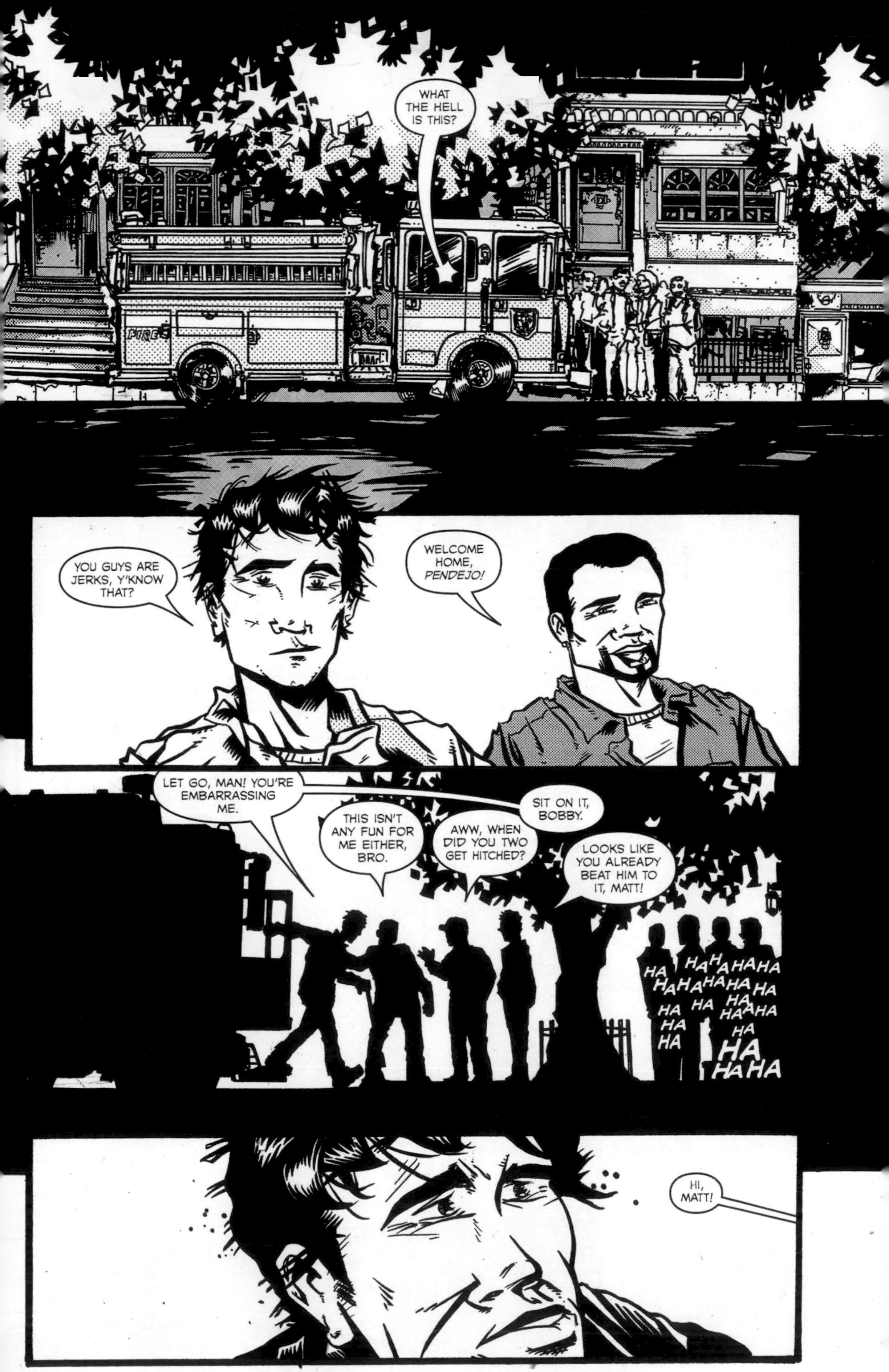
WHAT THE HELL IS THIS?
YOU GUYS ARE JERKS, Y'KNOW THAT?
WELCOME HOME, *PENDEJO!*
LET GO, MAN! YOU'RE EMBARRASSING ME.
SIT ON IT, BOBBY.
THIS ISN'T ANY FUN FOR ME EITHER, BRO.
AWW, WHEN DID YOU TWO GET HITCHED?
LOOKS LIKE YOU ALREADY BEAT HIM TO IT, MATT!
HA HA HA HA HA HA HA HA HA HA HA HA HA HA HA HA HA HA HA HA HA HA HA
HI, MATT!

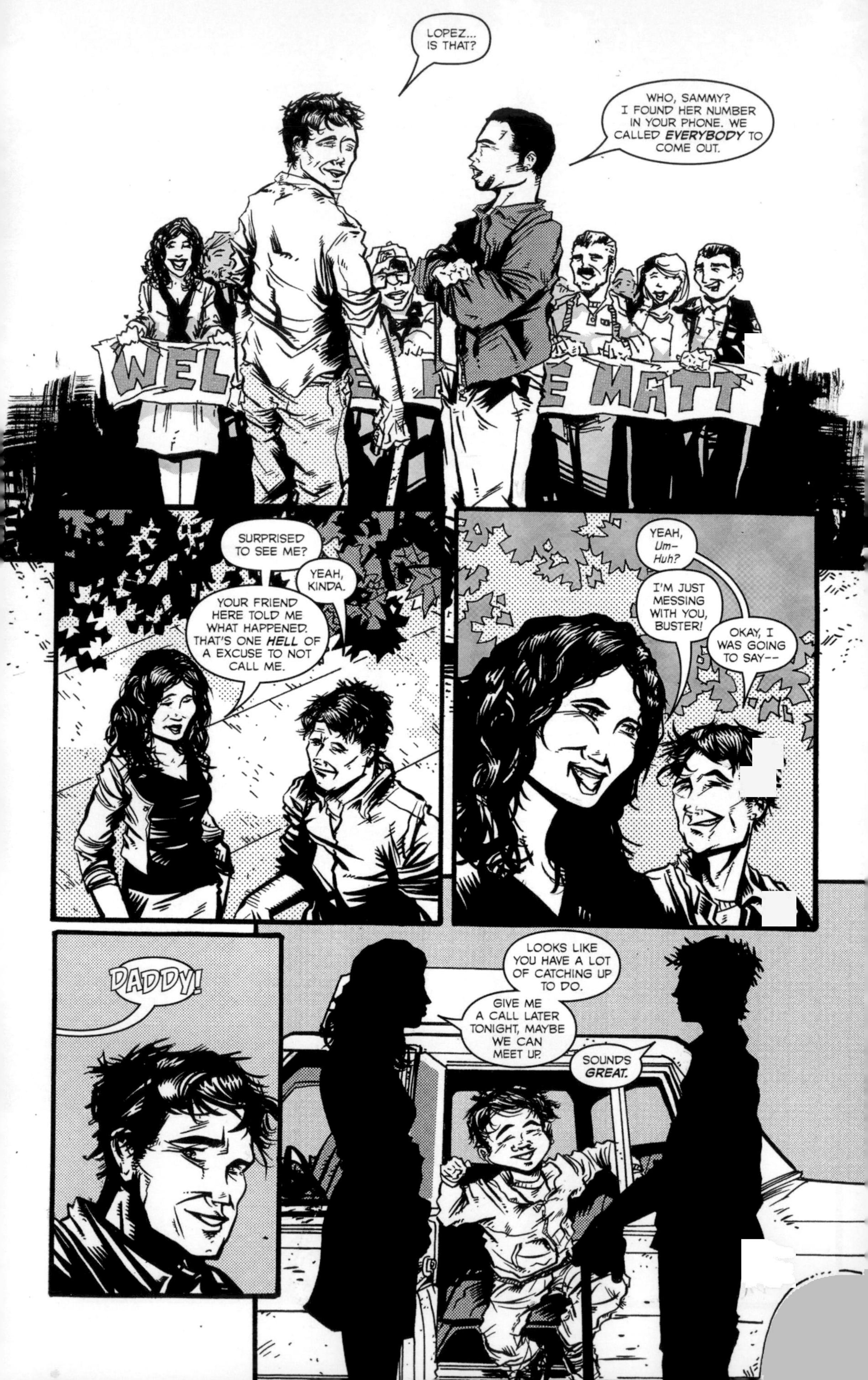

LOPEZ... IS THAT?
WHO, SAMMY? I FOUND HER NUMBER IN YOUR PHONE. WE CALLED **EVERYBODY** TO COME OUT.
WEL
E MATT
SURPRISED TO SEE ME?
YEAH, KINDA.
YOUR FRIEND HERE TOLD ME WHAT HAPPENED. THAT'S ONE **HELL** OF A EXCUSE TO NOT CALL ME.
YEAH, *Um-Huh?*
I'M JUST MESSING WITH YOU, BUSTER!
OKAY, I WAS GOING TO SAY--
DADDY!
LOOKS LIKE YOU HAVE A LOT OF CATCHING UP TO DO.
GIVE ME A CALL LATER TONIGHT, MAYBE WE CAN MEET UP.
SOUNDS *GREAT.*

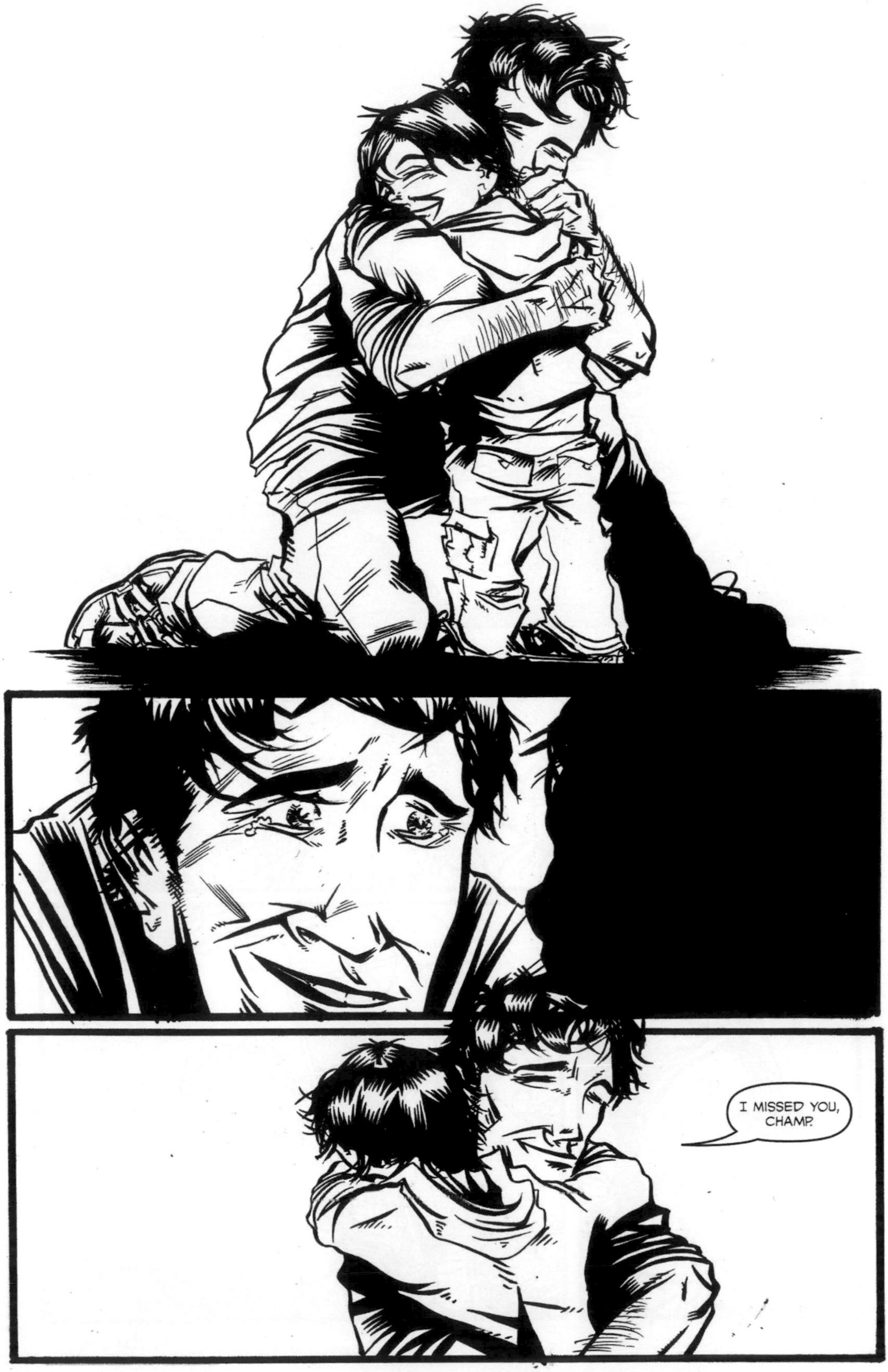
I MISSED YOU, CHAMP.

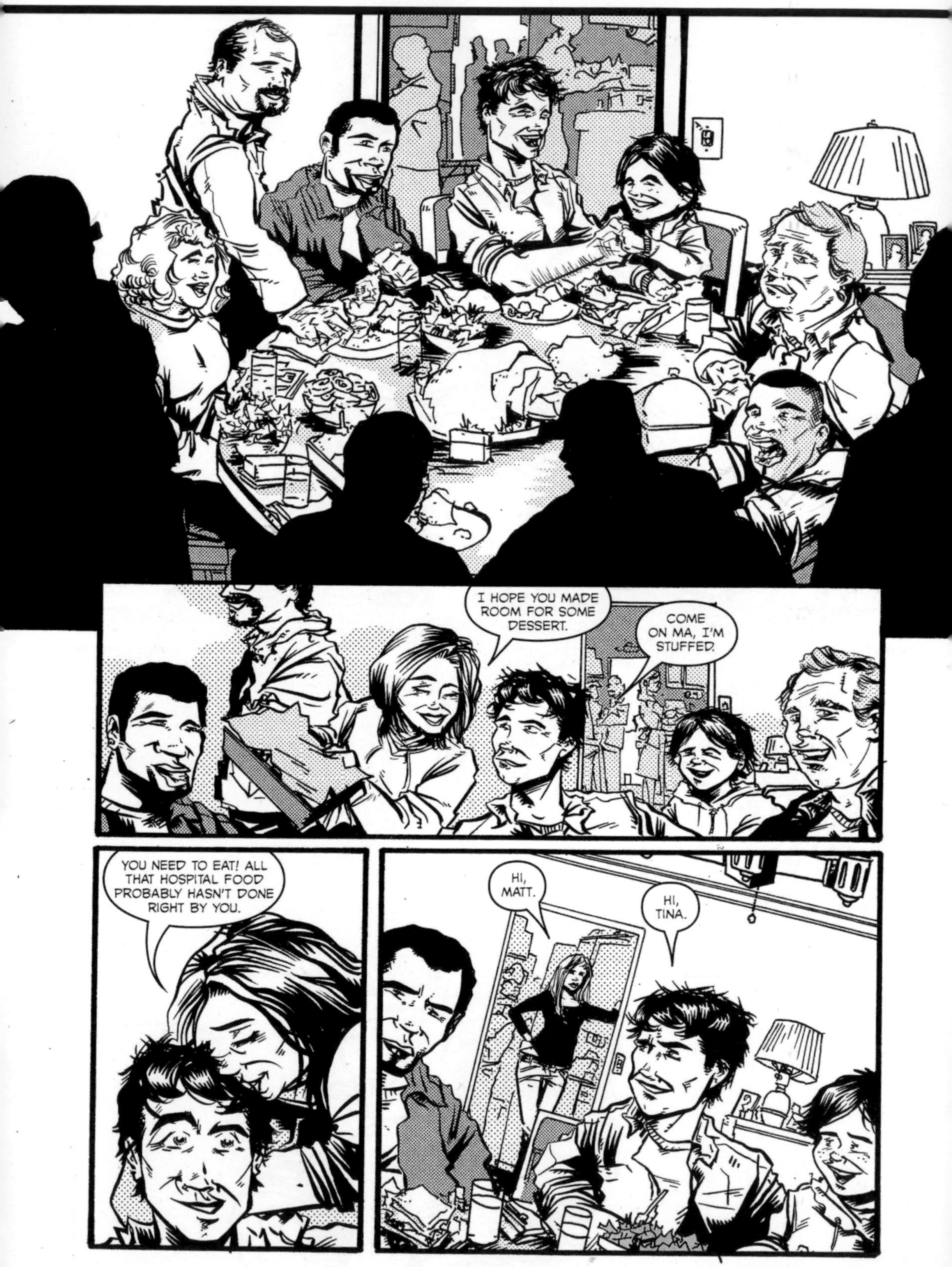
I HOPE YOU MADE ROOM FOR SOME DESSERT.
COME ON MA, I'M STUFFED.
YOU NEED TO EAT! ALL THAT HOSPITAL FOOD PROBABLY HASN'T DONE RIGHT BY YOU.
HI, MATT.
HI, TINA.

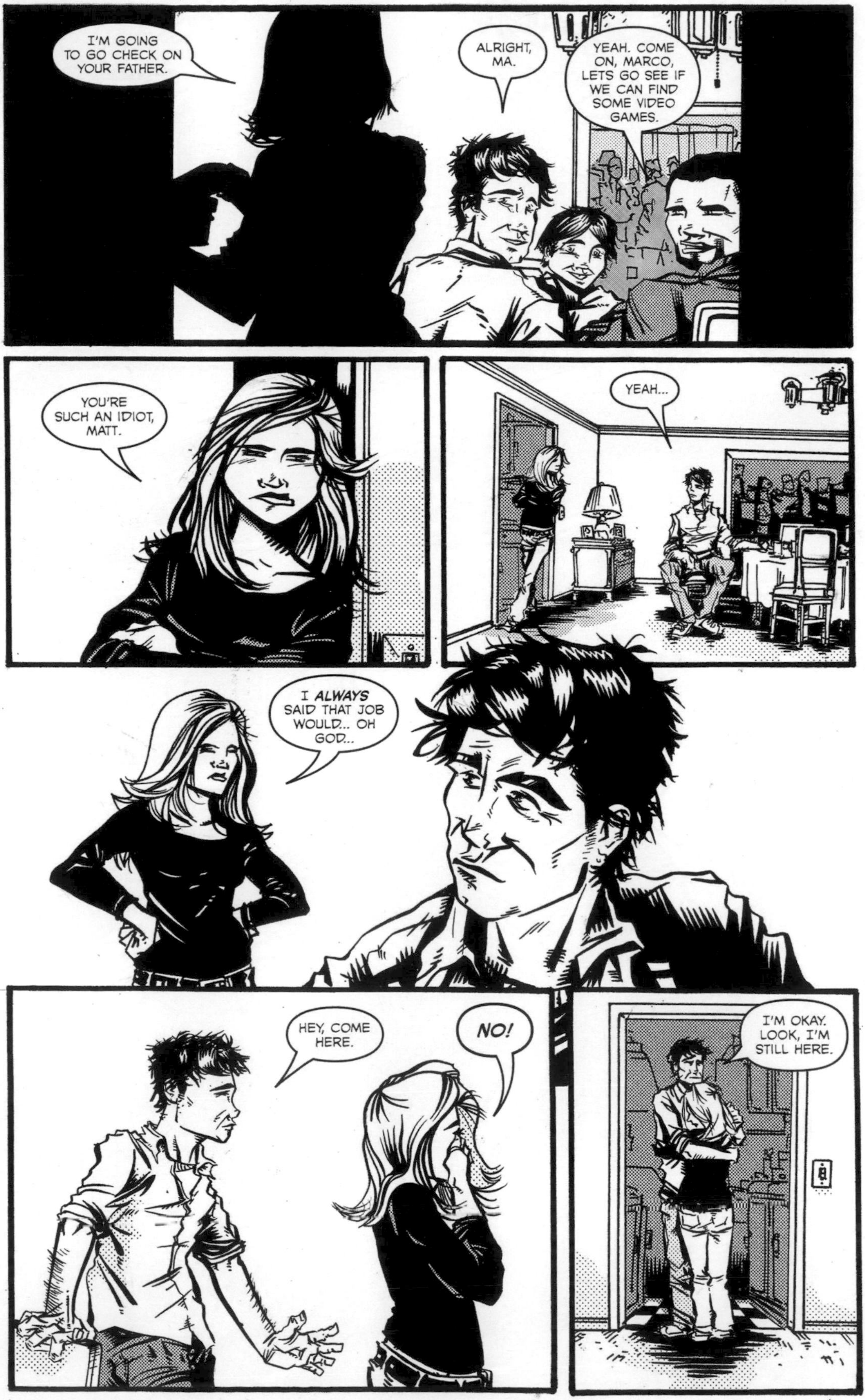
I'M GOING TO GO CHECK ON YOUR FATHER.
ALRIGHT, MA.
YEAH. COME ON, MARCO, LETS GO SEE IF WE CAN FIND SOME VIDEO GAMES.
YOU'RE SUCH AN IDIOT, MATT.
YEAH...
I ALWAYS SAID THAT JOB WOULD... OH GOD...
HEY, COME HERE.
NO!
I'M OKAY. LOOK, I'M STILL HERE.

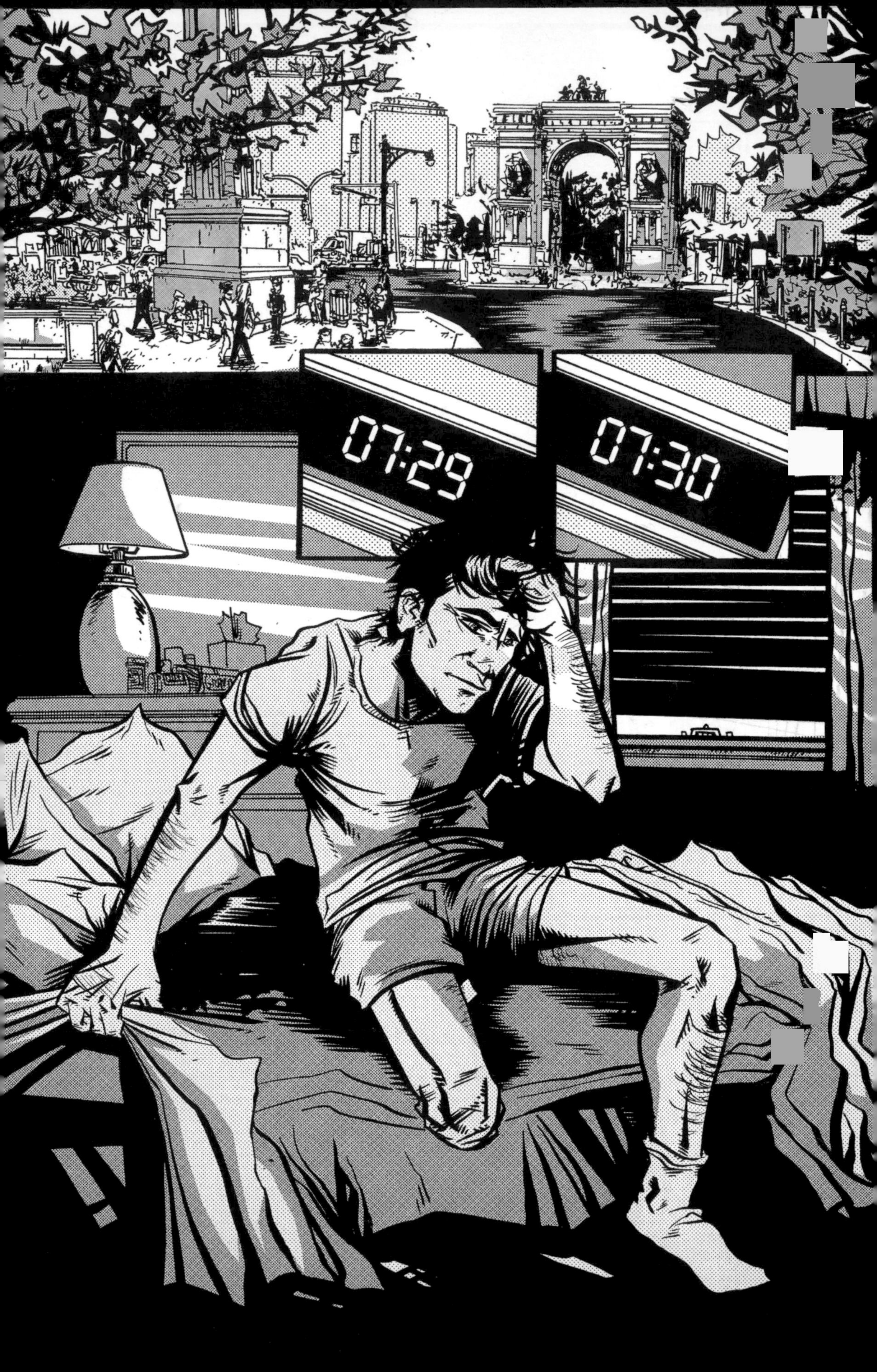
07:29
07:30

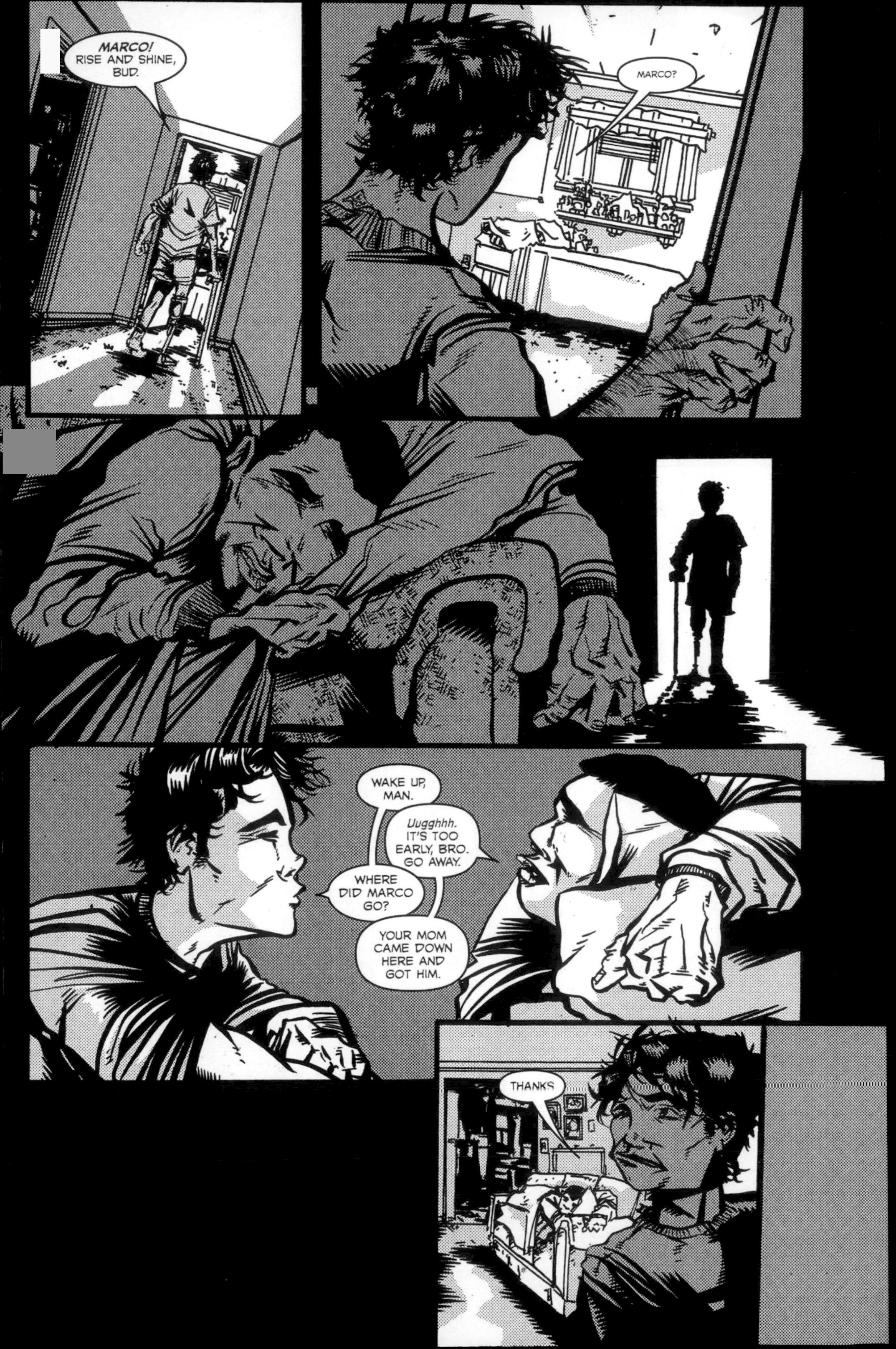
MARCO! RISE AND SHINE, BUD.
MARCO?
WAKE UP, MAN.
Uugghhh. IT'S TOO EARLY, BRO. GO AWAY.
WHERE DID MARCO GO?
YOUR MOM CAME DOWN HERE AND GOT HIM.
THANKS

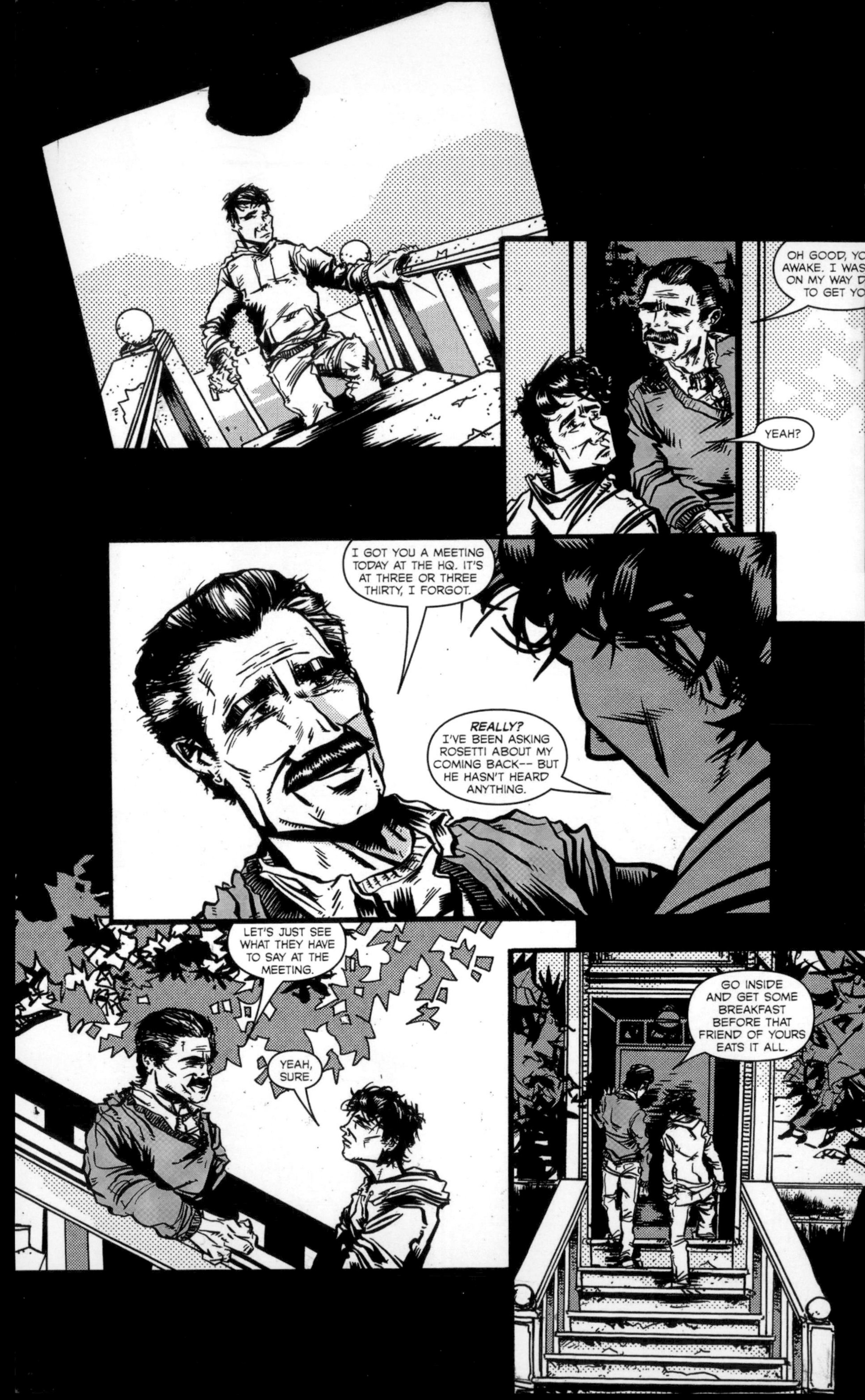
OH GOOD, AWAKE. I WAS ON MY WAY TO GET
YEAH?
I GOT YOU A MEETING TODAY AT THE HQ. IT'S AT THREE OR THREE THIRTY, I FORGOT.
REALLY? I'VE BEEN ASKING ROSETTI ABOUT MY COMING BACK-- BUT HE HASN'T HEARD ANYTHING.
LET'S JUST SEE WHAT THEY HAVE TO SAY AT THE MEETING.
YEAH, SURE.
GO INSIDE AND GET SOME BREAKFAST BEFORE THAT FRIEND OF YOURS EATS IT ALL.

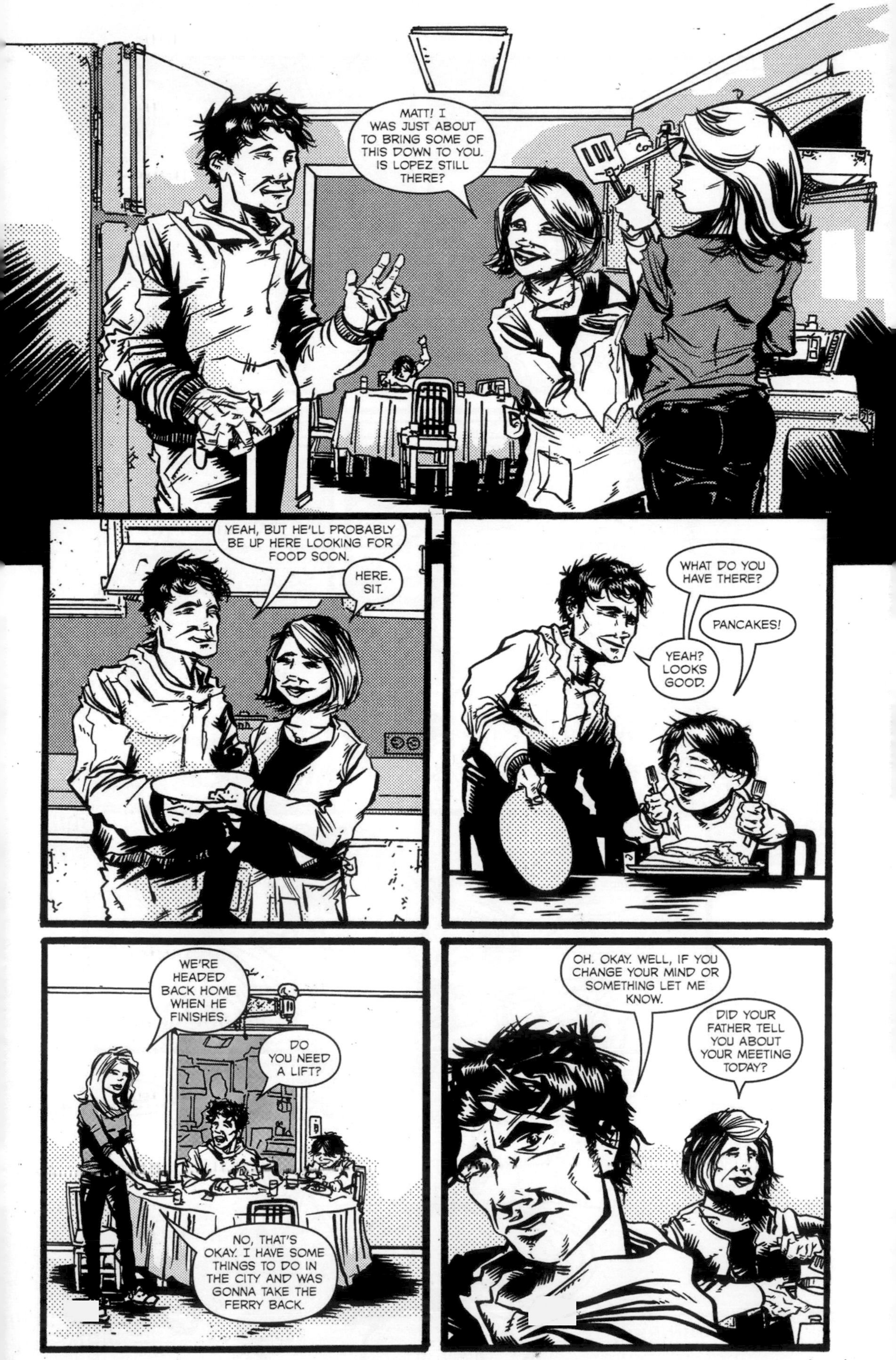
MATT! I WAS JUST ABOUT TO BRING SOME OF THIS DOWN TO YOU. IS LOPEZ STILL THERE?
YEAH, BUT HE'LL PROBABLY BE UP HERE LOOKING FOR FOOD SOON.
HERE. SIT.
WHAT DO YOU HAVE THERE?
PANCAKES!
YEAH? LOOKS GOOD.
WE'RE HEADED BACK HOME WHEN HE FINISHES.
DO YOU NEED A LIFT?
NO, THAT'S OKAY. I HAVE SOME THINGS TO DO IN THE CITY AND WAS GONNA TAKE THE FERRY BACK.
OH. OKAY. WELL, IF YOU CHANGE YOUR MIND OR SOMETHING LET ME KNOW.
DID YOUR FATHER TELL YOU ABOUT YOUR MEETING TODAY?

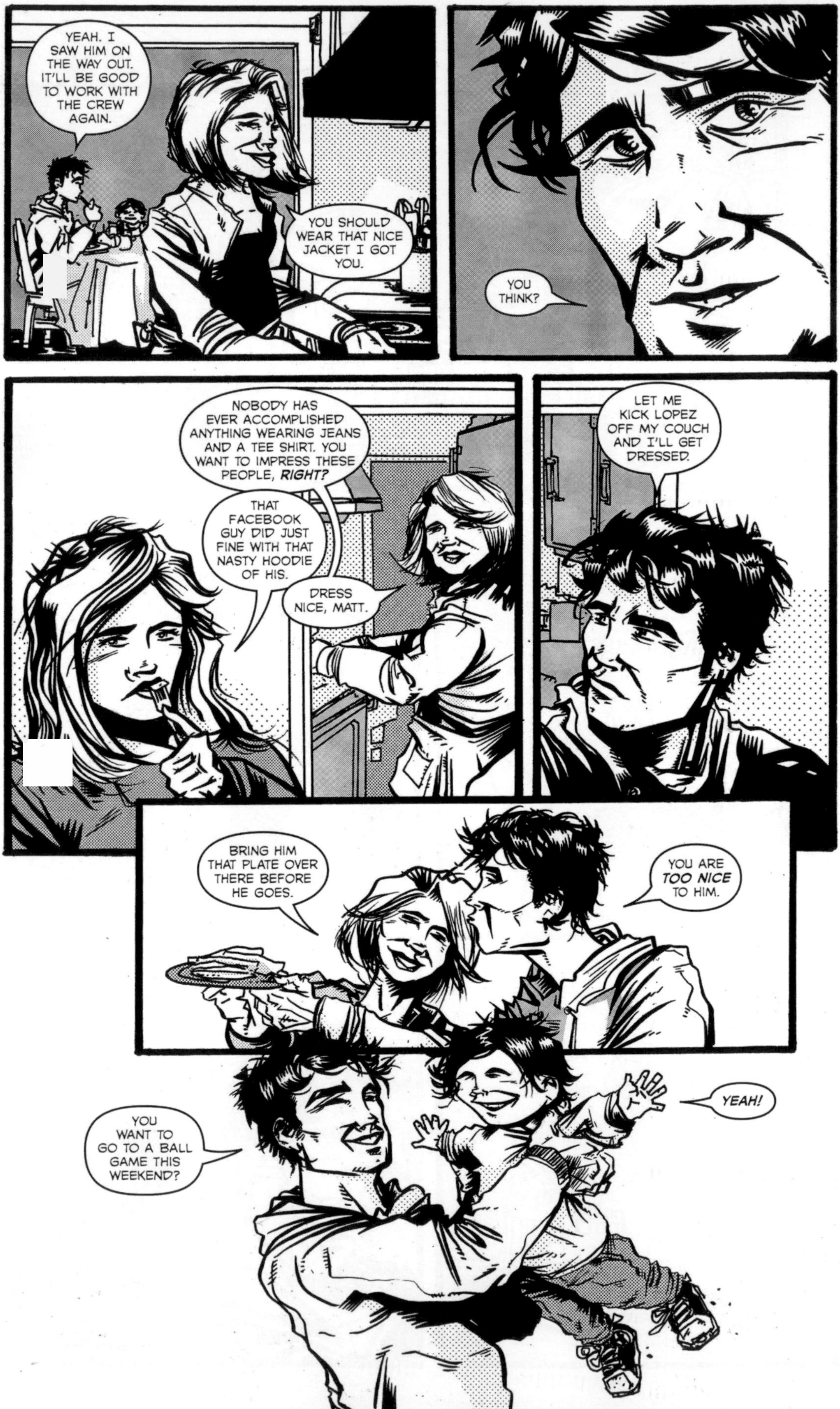
YEAH. I SAW HIM ON THE WAY OUT. IT'LL BE GOOD TO WORK WITH THE CREW AGAIN.
YOU SHOULD WEAR THAT NICE JACKET I GOT YOU.
YOU THINK?
NOBODY HAS EVER ACCOMPLISHED ANYTHING WEARING JEANS AND A TEE SHIRT. YOU WANT TO IMPRESS THESE PEOPLE, RIGHT?
THAT FACEBOOK GUY DID JUST FINE WITH THAT NASTY HOODIE OF HIS.
DRESS NICE, MATT.
LET ME KICK LOPEZ OFF MY COUCH AND I'LL GET DRESSED.
BRING HIM THAT PLATE OVER THERE BEFORE HE GOES.
YOU ARE TOO NICE TO HIM.
YOU WANT TO GO TO A BALL GAME THIS WEEKEND?
YEAH!

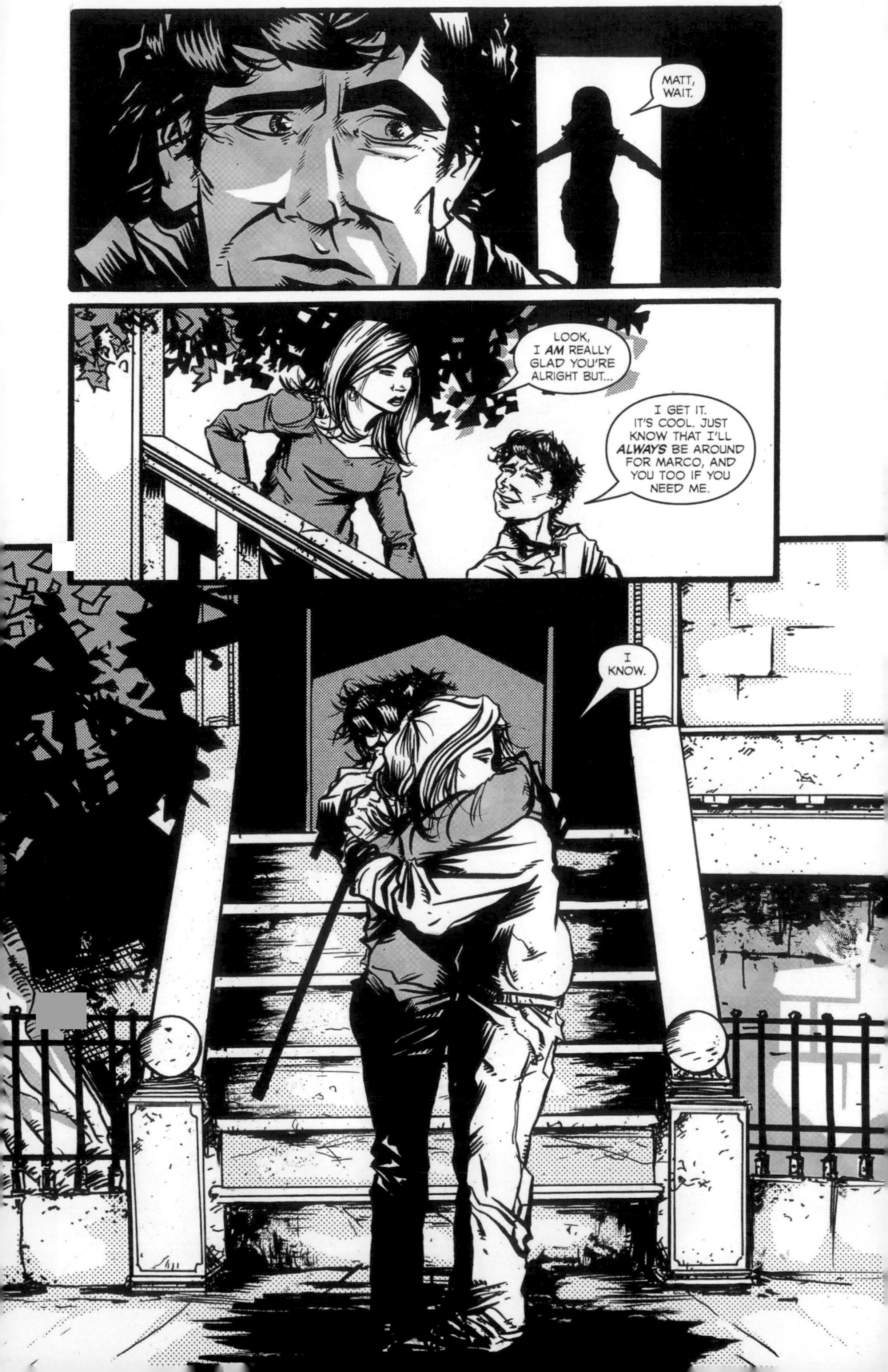
MATT, WAIT.
LOOK, I AM REALLY GLAD YOU'RE ALRIGHT BUT...
I GET IT. IT'S COOL. JUST KNOW THAT I'LL ALWAYS BE AROUND FOR MARCO, AND YOU TOO IF YOU NEED ME.
I KNOW.

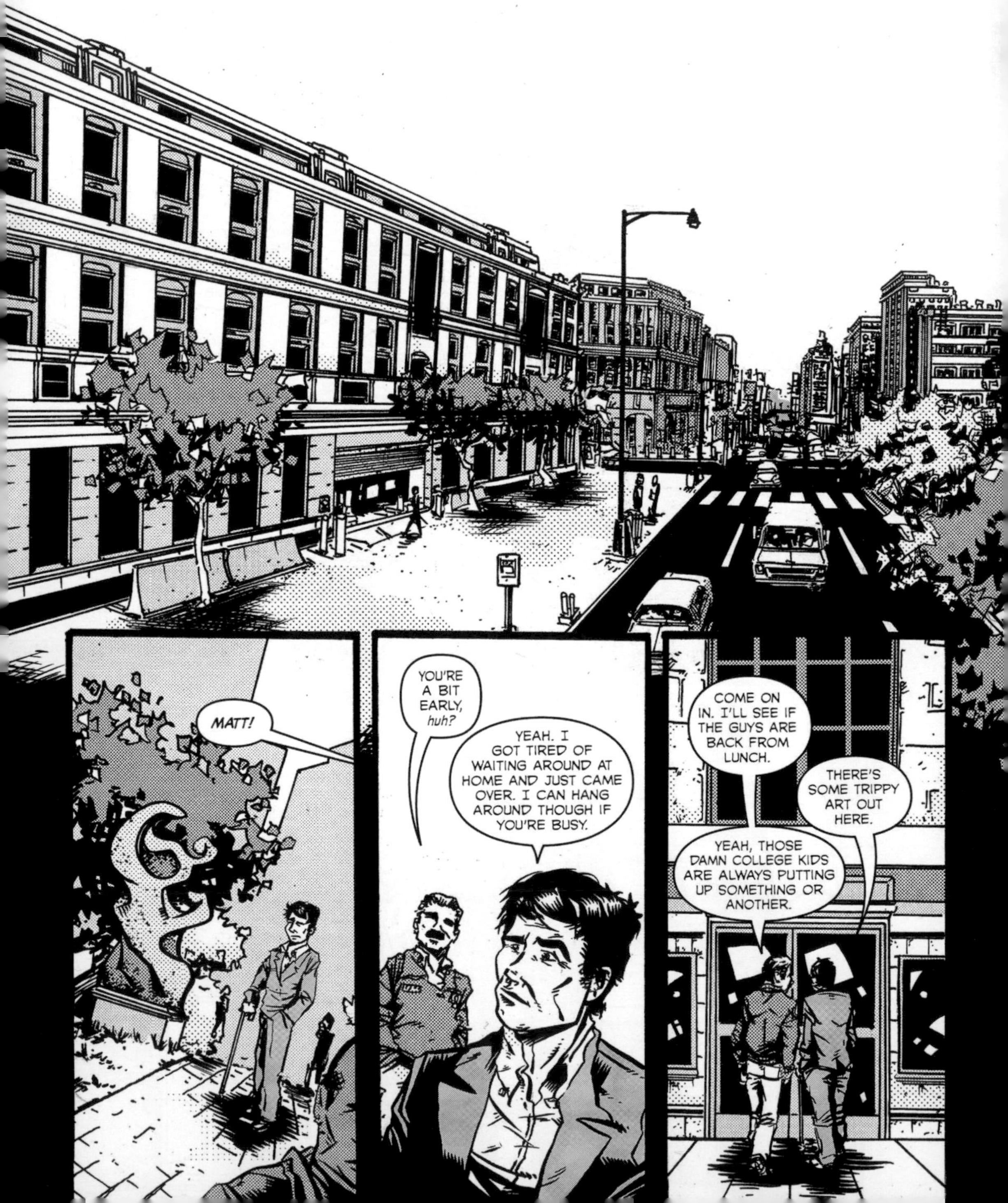

MATT!
YOU'RE A BIT EARLY, *huh?*
YEAH. I GOT TIRED OF WAITING AROUND AT HOME AND JUST CAME OVER. I CAN HANG AROUND THOUGH IF YOU'RE BUSY.
COME ON IN. I'LL SEE IF THE GUYS ARE BACK FROM LUNCH.
THERE'S SOME TRIPPY ART OUT HERE.
YEAH, THOSE DAMN COLLEGE KIDS ARE ALWAYS PUTTING UP SOMETHING OR ANOTHER.

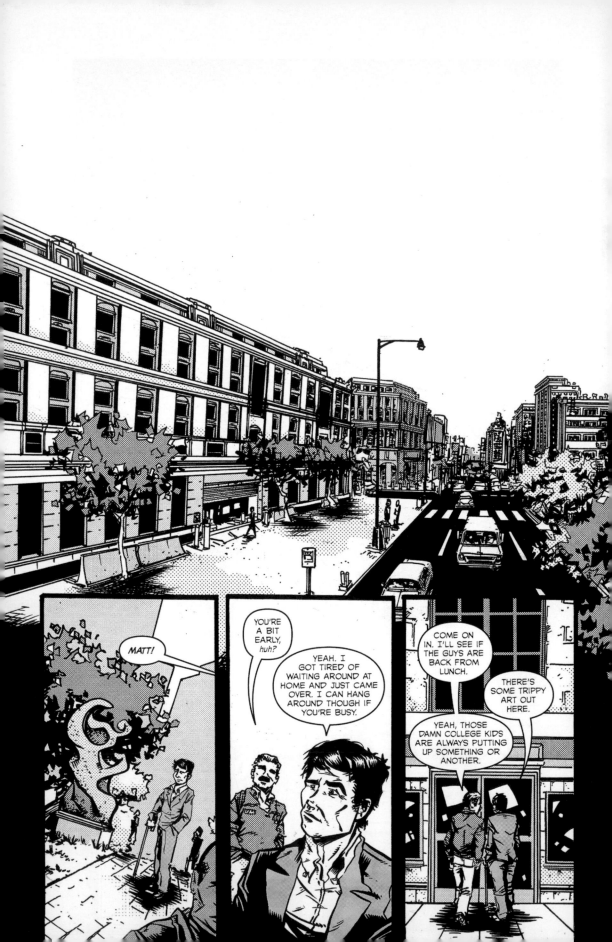

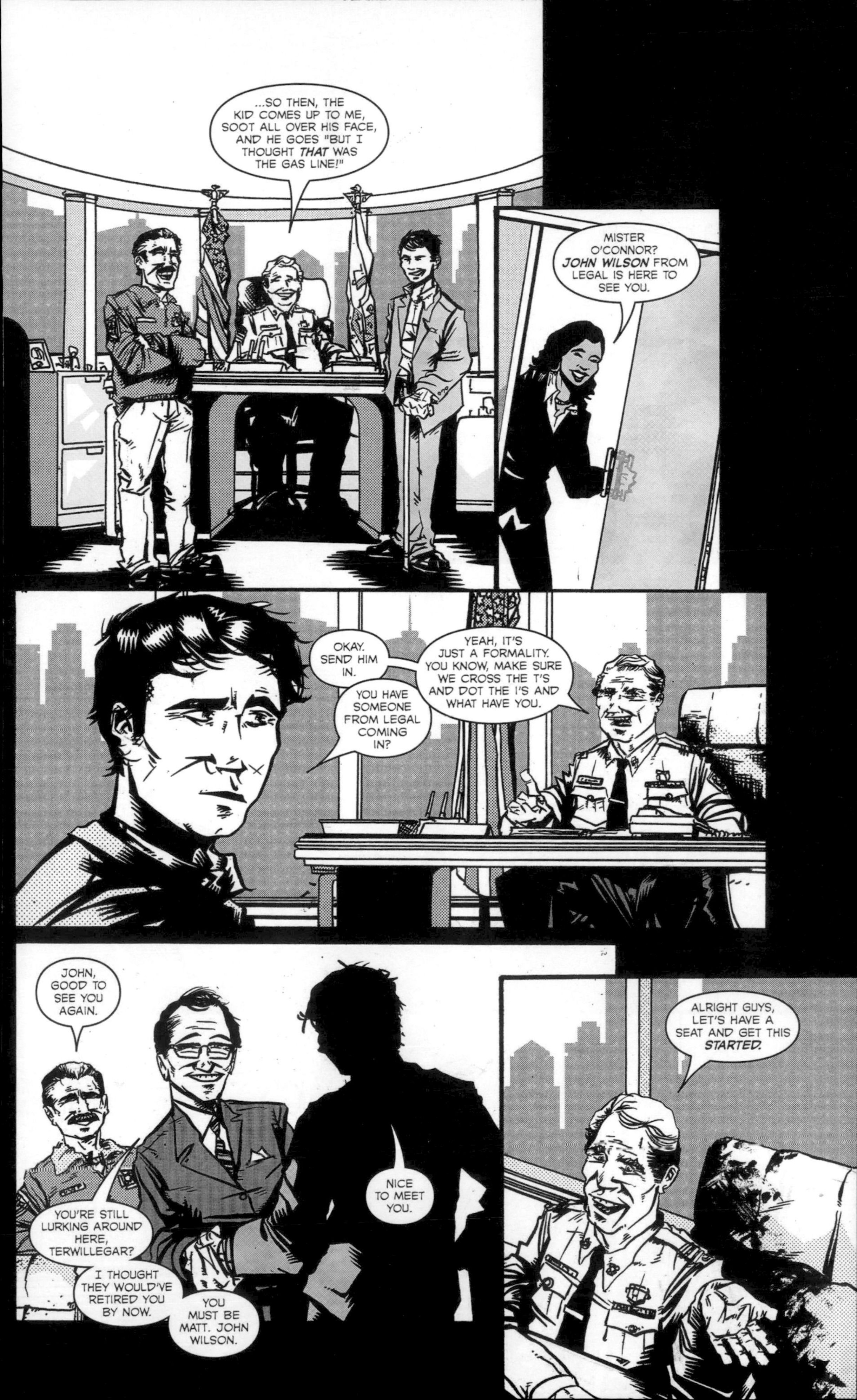
...SO THEN, THE KID COMES UP TO ME, SOOT ALL OVER HIS FACE, AND HE GOES "BUT I THOUGHT *THAT* WAS THE GAS LINE!"
MISTER O'CONNOR? ***JOHN WILSON*** FROM LEGAL IS HERE TO SEE YOU.
YOU HAVE SOMEONE FROM LEGAL COMING IN?
YEAH, IT'S JUST A FORMALITY. YOU KNOW, MAKE SURE WE CROSS THE T'S AND DOT THE I'S AND WHAT HAVE YOU.
OKAY. SEND HIM IN.
JOHN, GOOD TO SEE YOU AGAIN.
YOU'RE STILL LURKING AROUND HERE, TERWILLEGAR?
I THOUGHT THEY WOULD'VE RETIRED YOU BY NOW.
YOU MUST BE MATT. JOHN WILSON.
NICE TO MEET YOU.
ALRIGHT GUYS, LET'S HAVE A SEAT AND GET THIS ***STARTED.***

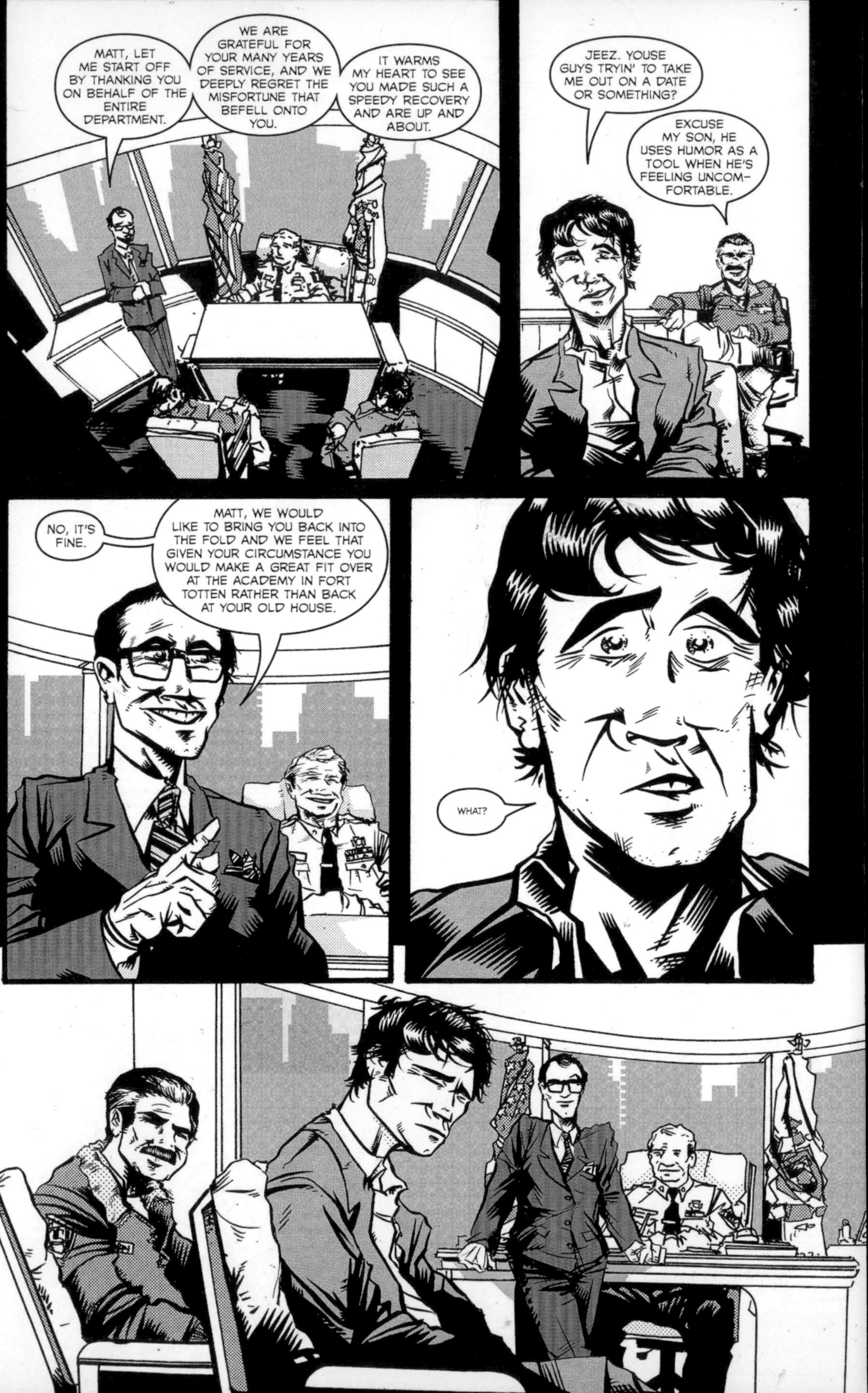
MATT, LET ME START OFF BY THANKING YOU ON BEHALF OF THE ENTIRE DEPARTMENT.
WE ARE GRATEFUL FOR YOUR MANY YEARS OF SERVICE, AND WE DEEPLY REGRET THE MISFORTUNE THAT BEFELL ONTO YOU.
IT WARMS MY HEART TO SEE YOU MADE SUCH A SPEEDY RECOVERY AND ARE UP AND ABOUT.
JEEZ. YOUSE GUYS TRYIN' TO TAKE ME OUT ON A DATE OR SOMETHING?
EXCUSE MY SON, HE USES HUMOR AS A TOOL WHEN HE'S FEELING UNCOM-FORTABLE.
NO, IT'S FINE.
MATT, WE WOULD LIKE TO BRING YOU BACK INTO THE FOLD AND WE FEEL THAT GIVEN YOUR CIRCUMSTANCE YOU WOULD MAKE A GREAT FIT OVER AT THE ACADEMY IN FORT TOTTEN RATHER THAN BACK AT YOUR OLD HOUSE.
WHAT?

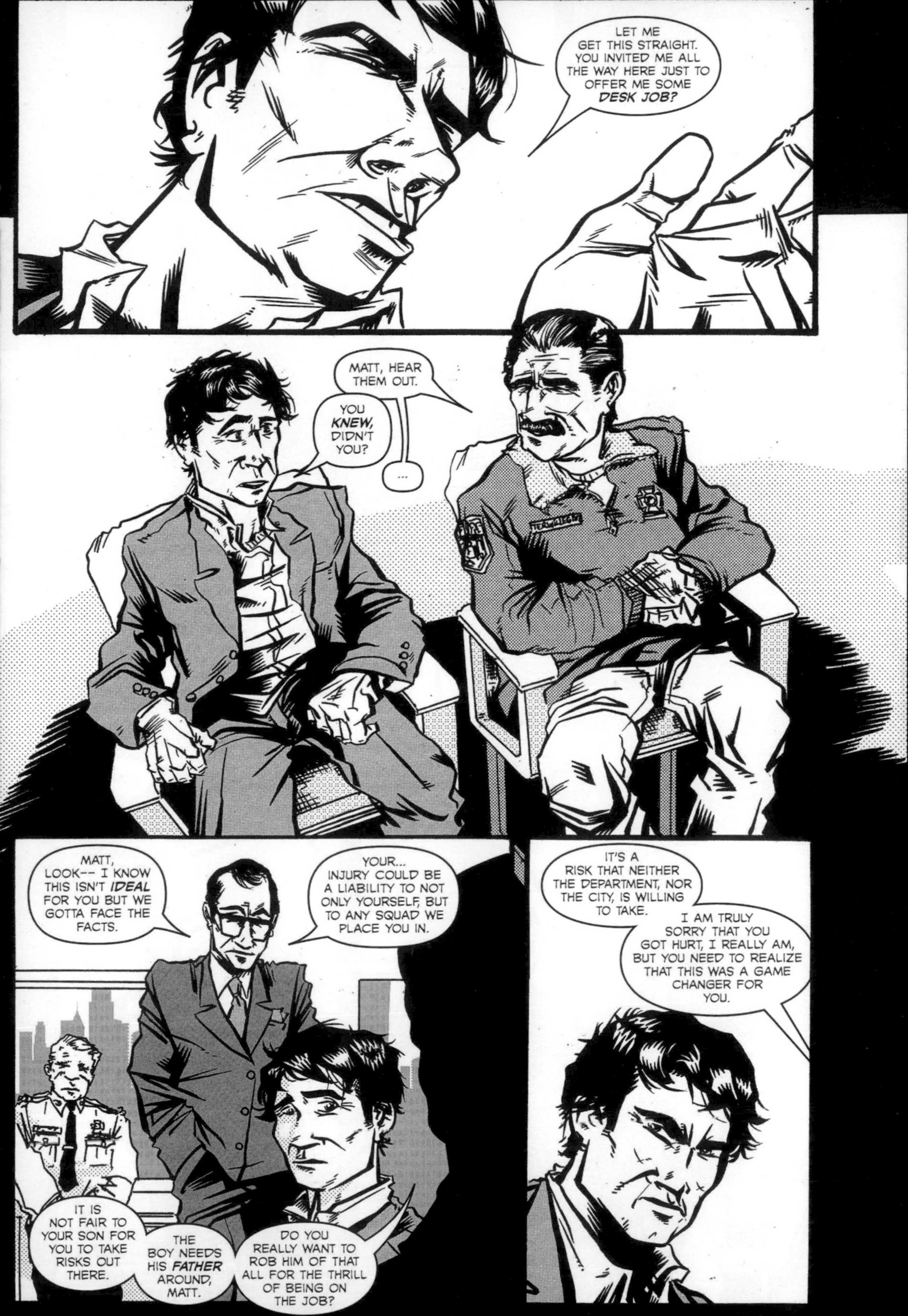
LET ME GET THIS STRAIGHT. YOU INVITED ME ALL THE WAY HERE JUST TO OFFER ME SOME *DESK JOB?*
MATT, HEAR THEM OUT.
YOU *KNEW,* DIDN'T YOU?
...
MATT, LOOK-- I KNOW THIS ISN'T *IDEAL* FOR YOU BUT WE GOTTA FACE THE FACTS.
YOUR... INJURY COULD BE A LIABILITY TO NOT ONLY YOURSELF, BUT TO ANY SQUAD WE PLACE YOU IN.
IT IS NOT FAIR TO YOUR SON FOR YOU TO TAKE RISKS OUT THERE.
THE BOY NEEDS HIS *FATHER* AROUND, MATT.
DO YOU REALLY WANT TO ROB HIM OF THAT ALL FOR THE THRILL OF BEING ON THE JOB?
IT'S A RISK THAT NEITHER THE DEPARTMENT, NOR THE CITY, IS WILLING TO TAKE.
I AM TRULY SORRY THAT YOU GOT HURT, I REALLY AM, BUT YOU NEED TO REALIZE THAT THIS WAS A GAME CHANGER FOR YOU.

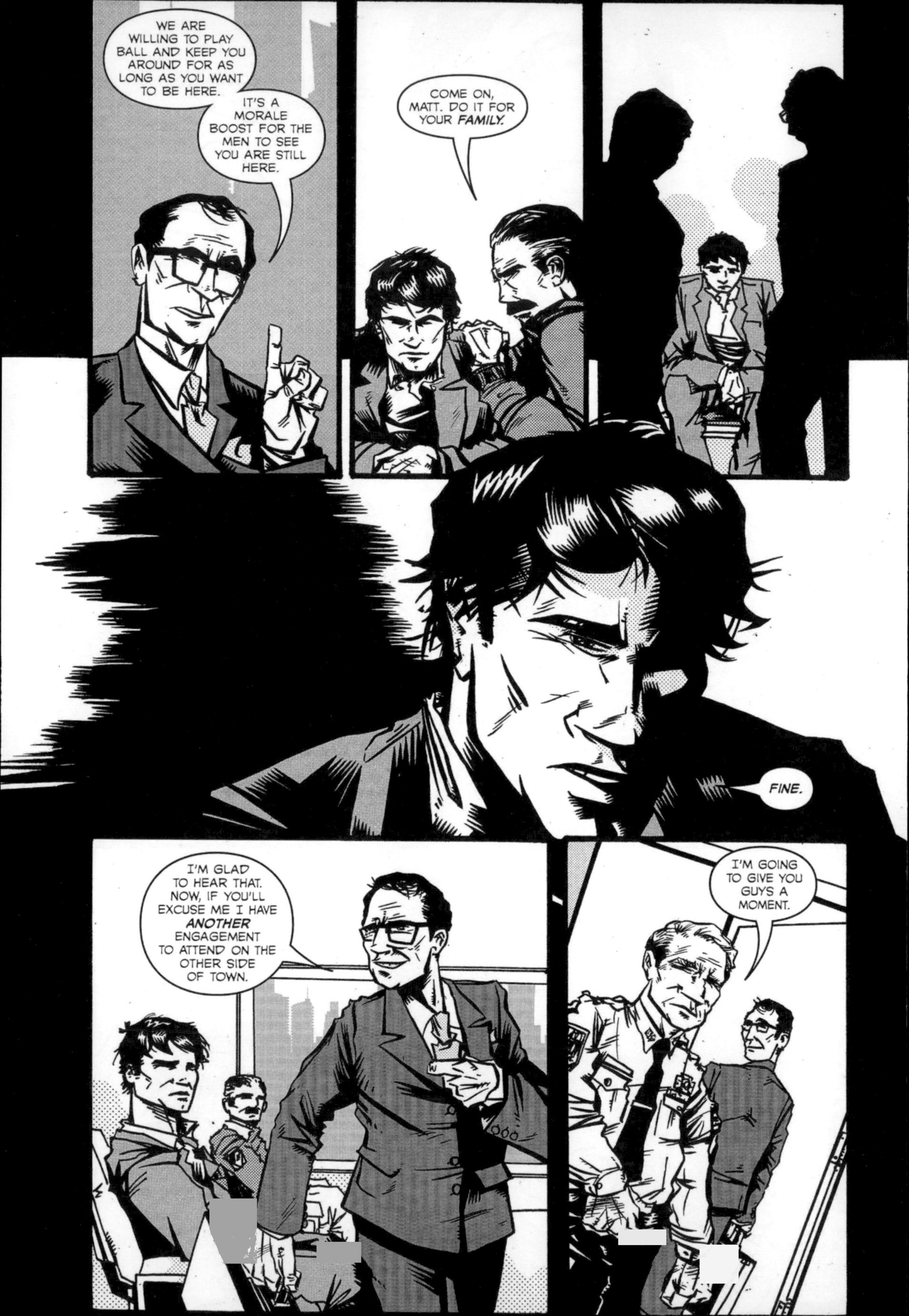
WE ARE WILLING TO PLAY BALL AND KEEP YOU AROUND FOR AS LONG AS YOU WANT TO BE HERE.
IT'S A MORALE BOOST FOR THE MEN TO SEE YOU ARE STILL HERE.
COME ON, MATT. DO IT FOR YOUR *FAMILY.*
FINE.
I'M GLAD TO HEAR THAT. NOW, IF YOU'LL EXCUSE ME I HAVE ***ANOTHER*** ENGAGEMENT TO ATTEND ON THE OTHER SIDE OF TOWN.
I'M GOING TO GIVE YOU GUYS A MOMENT.

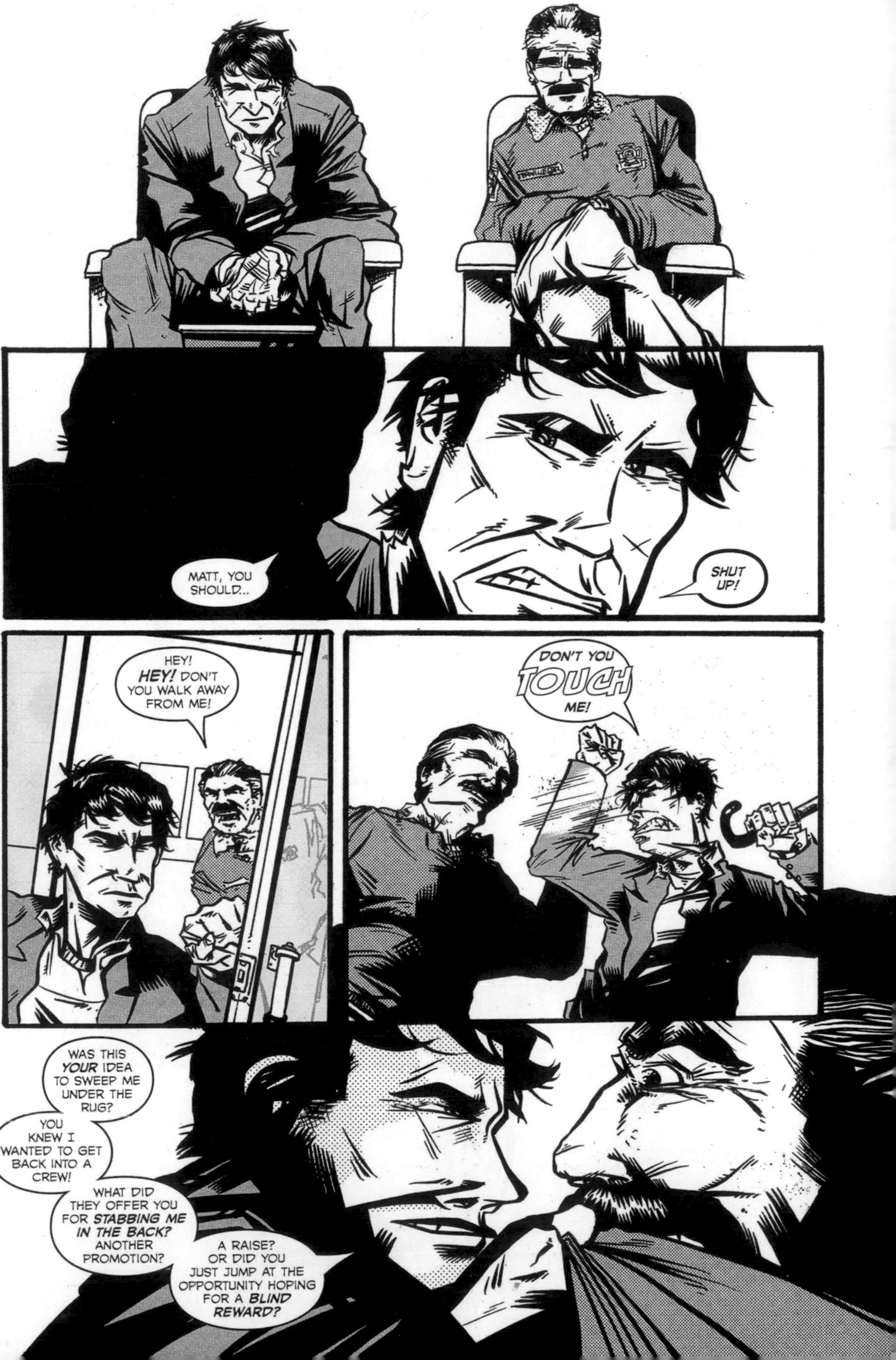
MATT, YOU SHOULD...
SHUT UP!
HEY! HEY! DON'T YOU WALK AWAY FROM ME!
DON'T YOU TOUCH ME!
WAS THIS YOUR IDEA TO SWEEP ME UNDER THE RUG?
YOU KNEW I WANTED TO GET BACK INTO A CREW!
WHAT DID THEY OFFER YOU FOR STABBING ME IN THE BACK? ANOTHER PROMOTION?
A RAISE? OR DID YOU JUST JUMP AT THE OPPORTUNITY HOPING FOR A BLIND REWARD?

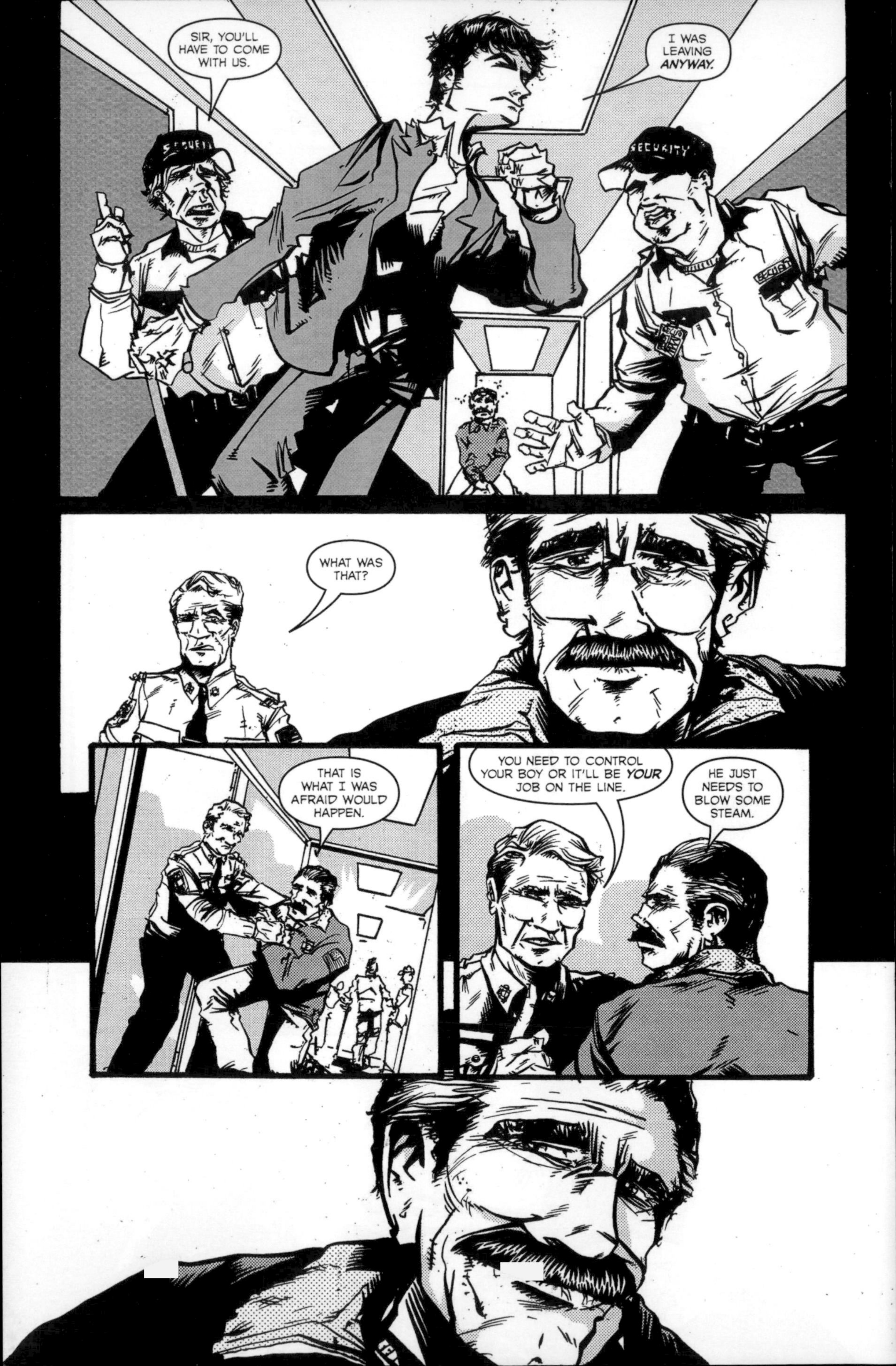
SIR, YOU'LL HAVE TO COME WITH US.
I WAS LEAVING ANYWAY.
SECURITY
SECURITY
WHAT WAS THAT?
THAT IS WHAT I WAS AFRAID WOULD HAPPEN.
YOU NEED TO CONTROL YOUR BOY OR IT'LL BE YOUR JOB ON THE LINE.
HE JUST NEEDS TO BLOW SOME STEAM.

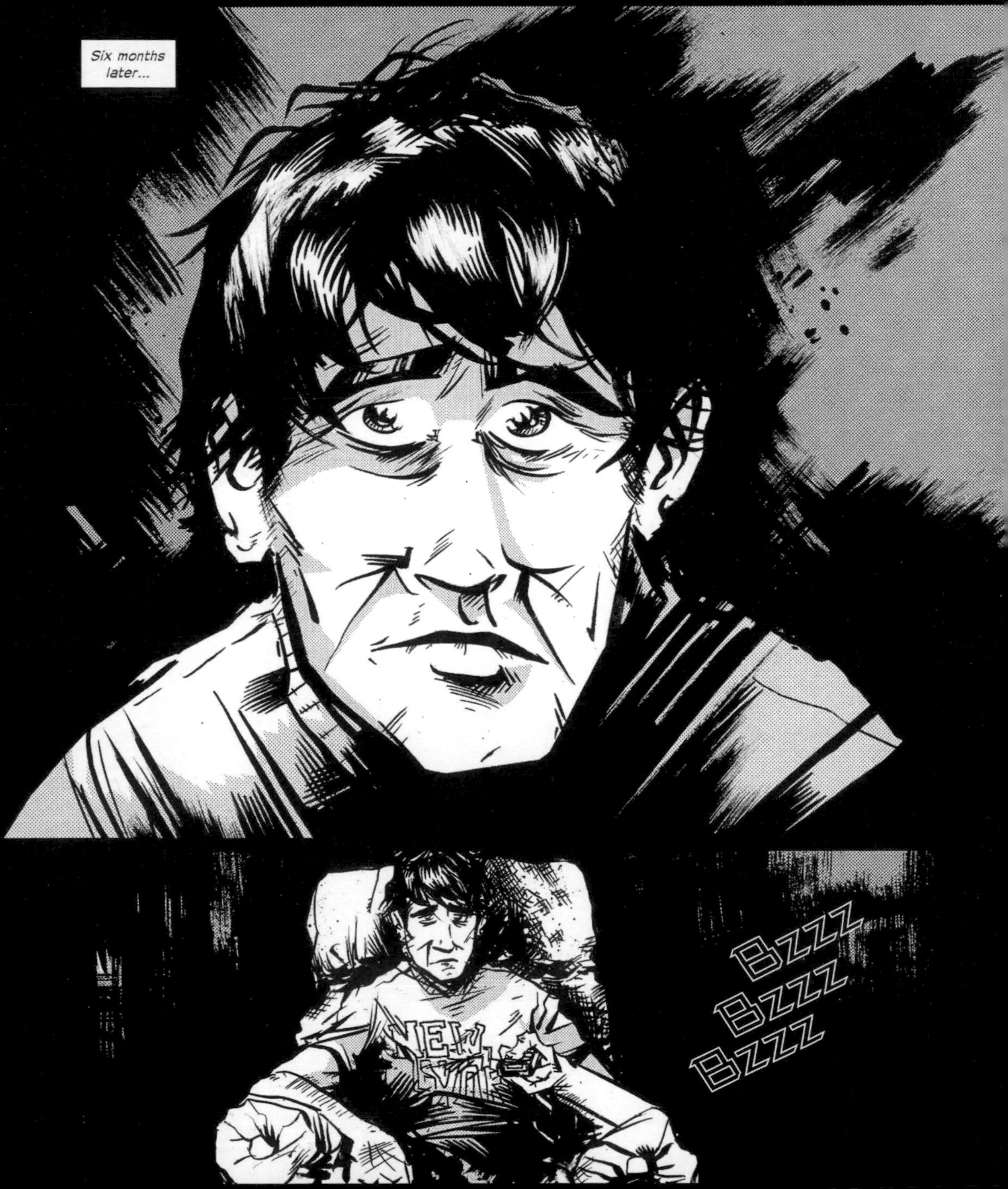
Six months later...
Bzzz
Bzzz
Bzzz

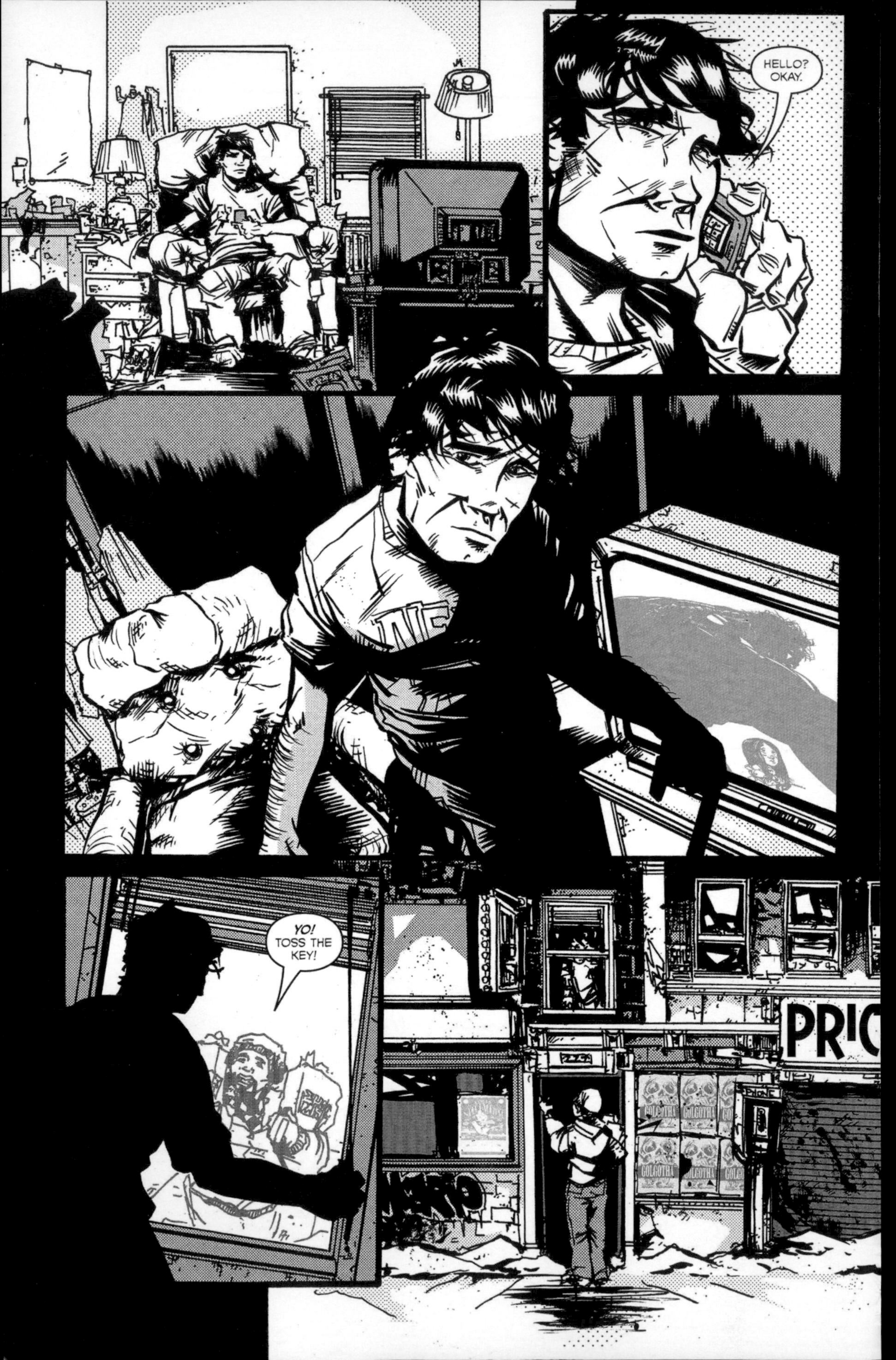
HELLO? OKAY.
YO! TOSS THE KEY!
PRIC
GOLGOTHA
PHONE

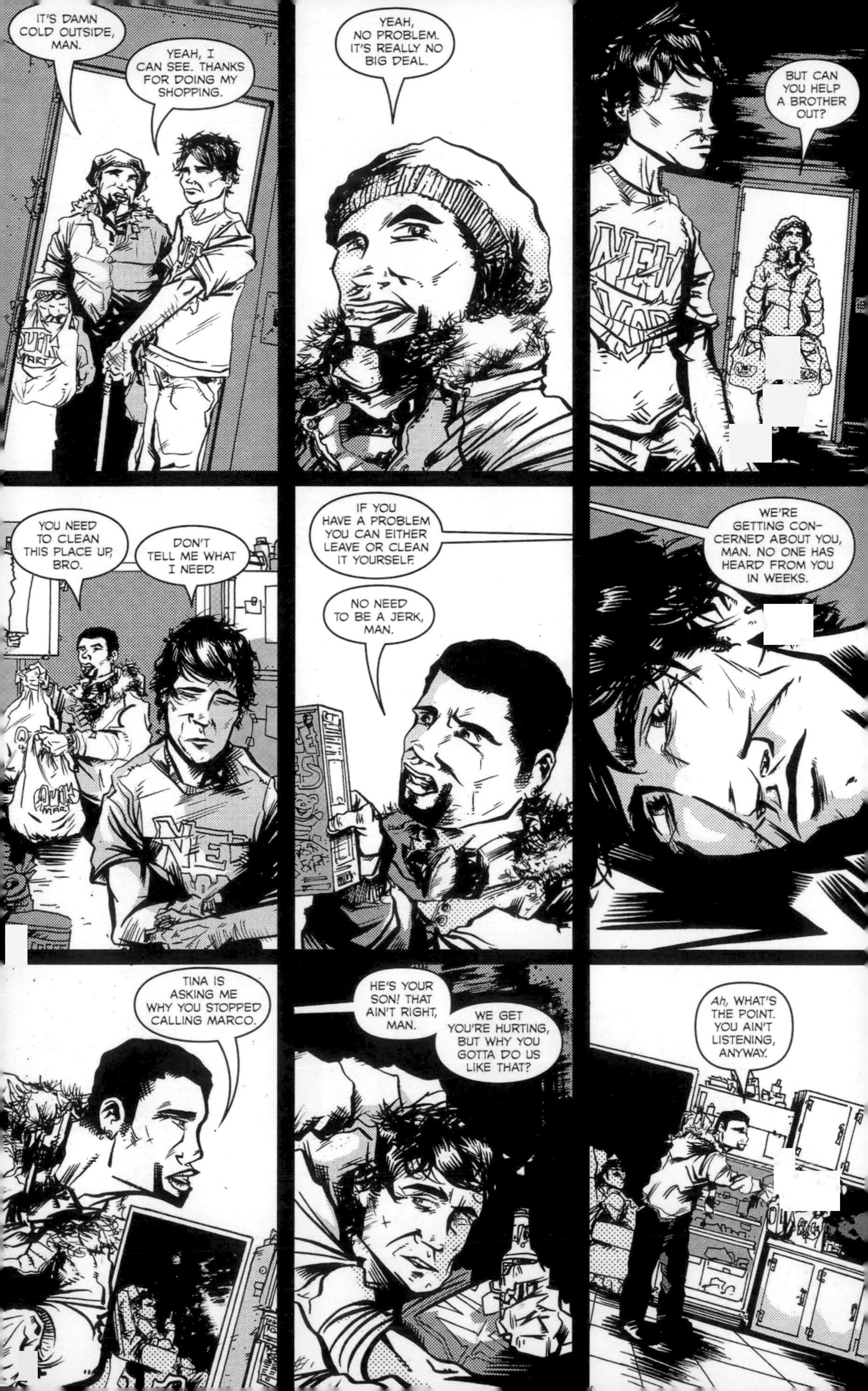
IT'S DAMN COLD OUTSIDE, MAN.
YEAH, I CAN SEE. THANKS FOR DOING MY SHOPPING.
YEAH, NO PROBLEM. IT'S REALLY NO BIG DEAL.
BUT CAN YOU HELP A BROTHER OUT?
YOU NEED TO CLEAN THIS PLACE UP, BRO.
DON'T TELL ME WHAT I NEED.
IF YOU HAVE A PROBLEM YOU CAN EITHER LEAVE OR CLEAN IT YOURSELF.
NO NEED TO BE A JERK, MAN.
WE'RE GETTING CON- CERNED ABOUT YOU, MAN. NO ONE HAS HEARD FROM YOU IN WEEKS.
TINA IS ASKING ME WHY YOU STOPPED CALLING MARCO.
HE'S YOUR SON! THAT AIN'T RIGHT, MAN.
WE GET YOU'RE HURTING, BUT WHY YOU GOTTA DO US LIKE THAT?
Ah, WHAT'S THE POINT. YOU AIN'T LISTENING, ANYWAY.

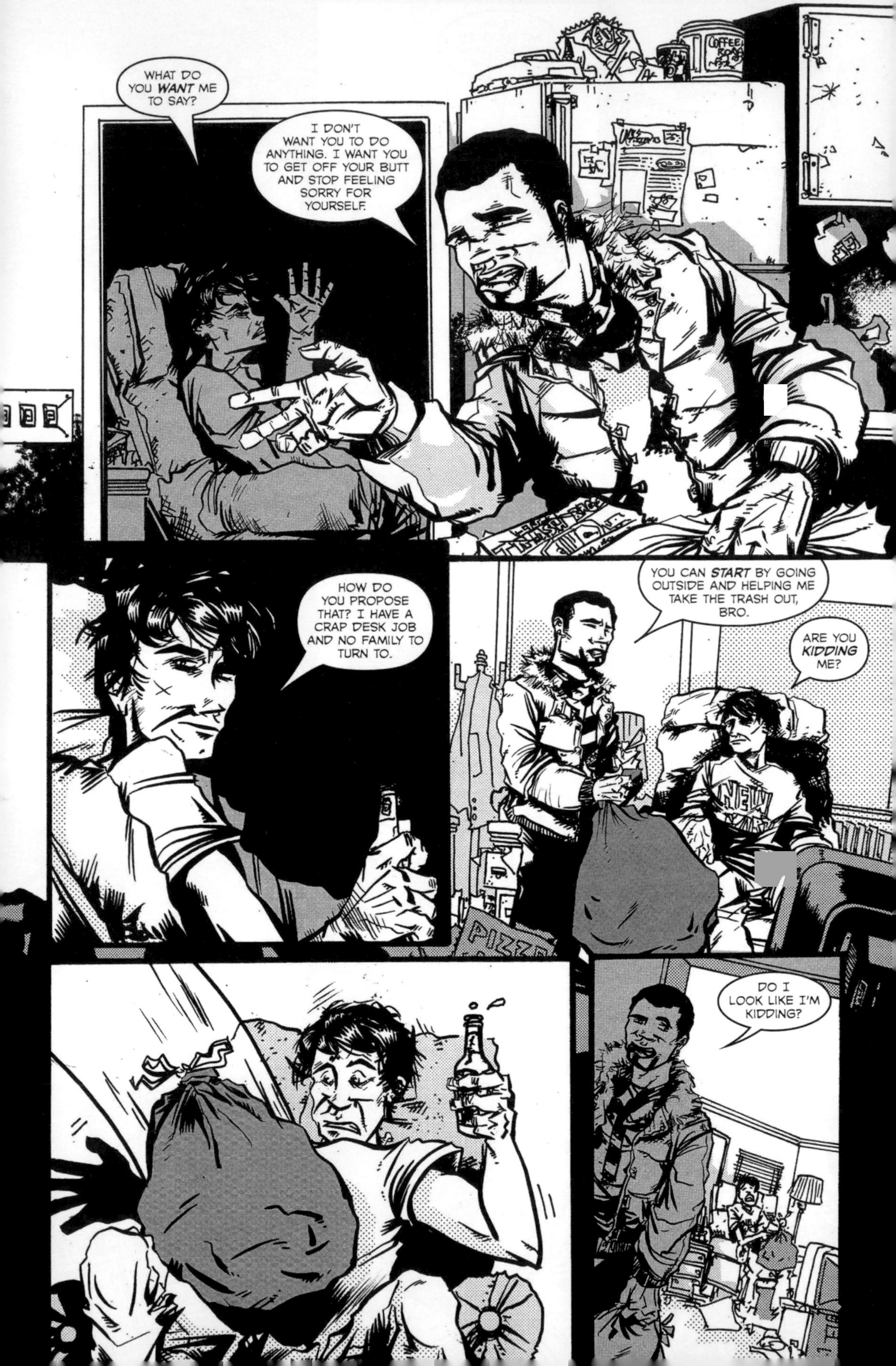
WHAT DO YOU WANT ME TO SAY?
I DON'T WANT YOU TO DO ANYTHING. I WANT YOU TO GET OFF YOUR BUTT AND STOP FEELING SORRY FOR YOURSELF.
HOW DO YOU PROPOSE THAT? I HAVE A CRAP DESK JOB AND NO FAMILY TO TURN TO.
YOU CAN START BY GOING OUTSIDE AND HELPING ME TAKE THE TRASH OUT, BRO.
ARE YOU KIDDING ME?
DO I LOOK LIKE I'M KIDDING?

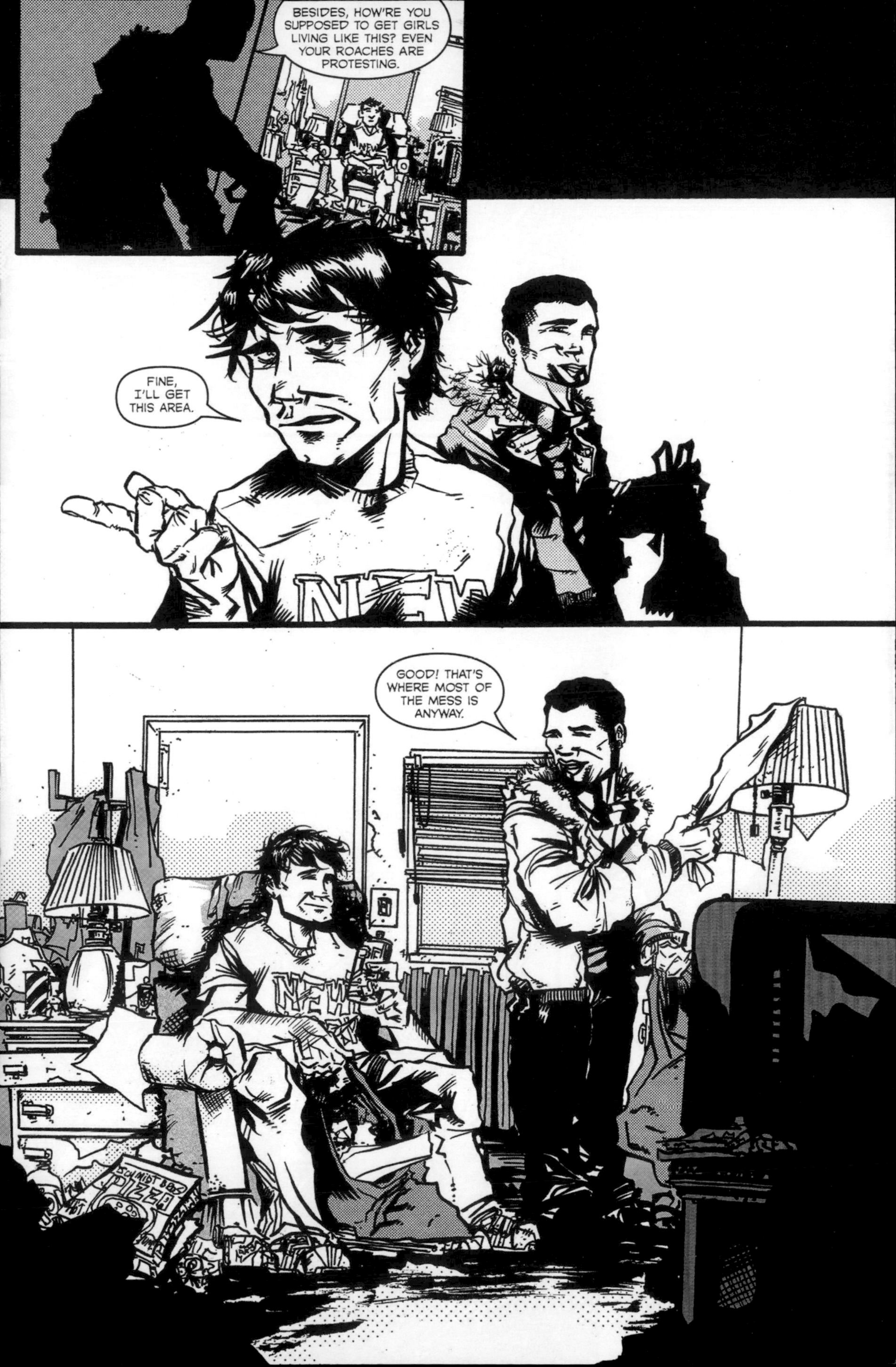
BESIDES, HOW'RE YOU SUPPOSED TO GET GIRLS LIVING LIKE THIS? EVEN YOUR ROACHES ARE PROTESTING.
FINE, I'LL GET THIS AREA.
GOOD! THAT'S WHERE MOST OF THE MESS IS ANYWAY.

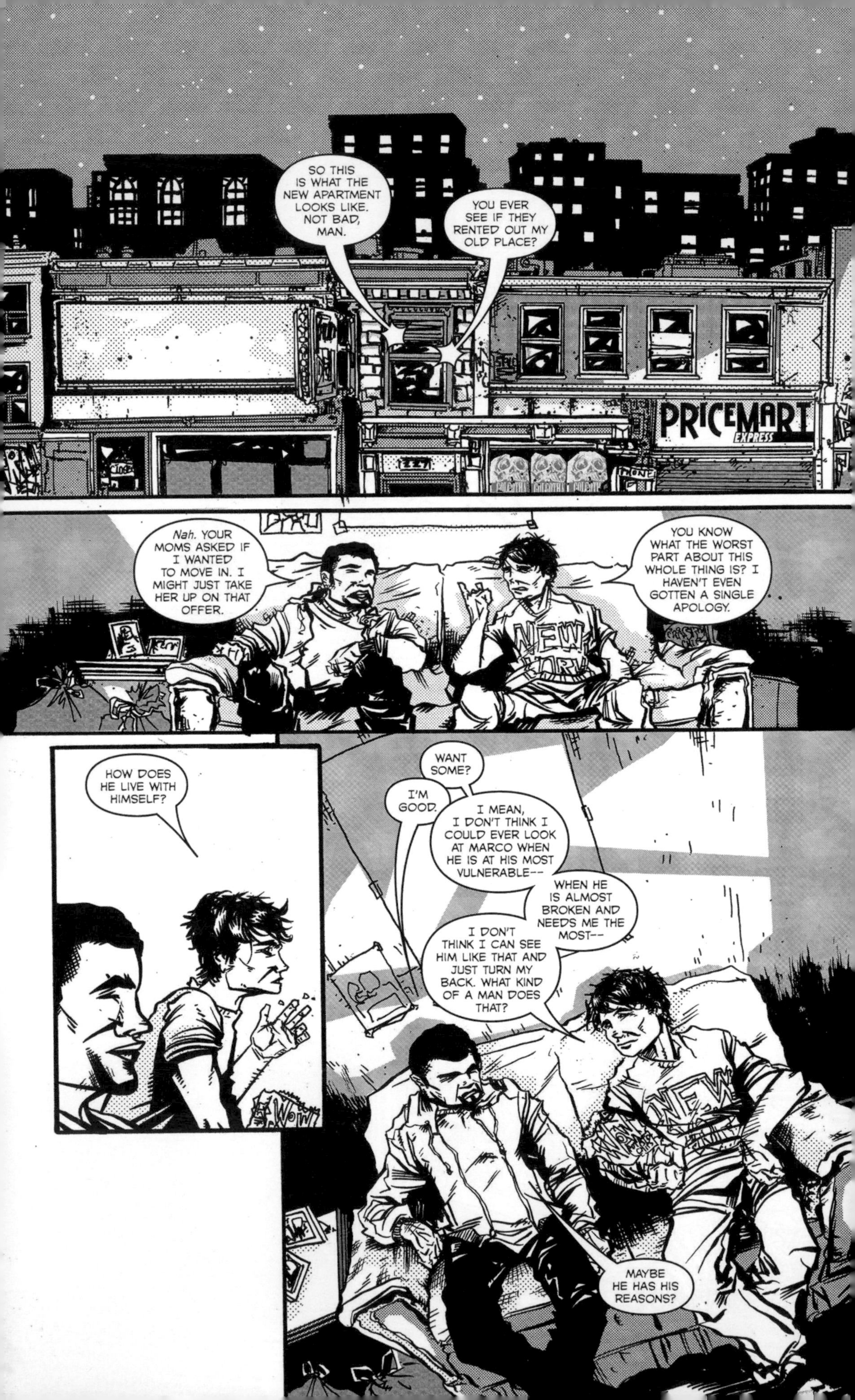
SO THIS IS WHAT THE NEW APARTMENT LOOKS LIKE. NOT BAD, MAN.
YOU EVER SEE IF THEY RENTED OUT MY OLD PLACE?
PRICEMART EXPRESS
Nah. YOUR MOMS ASKED IF I WANTED TO MOVE IN. I MIGHT JUST TAKE HER UP ON THAT OFFER.
YOU KNOW WHAT THE WORST PART ABOUT THIS WHOLE THING IS? I HAVEN'T EVEN GOTTEN A SINGLE APOLOGY.
HOW DOES HE LIVE WITH HIMSELF?
WANT SOME?
I'M GOOD.
I MEAN, I DON'T THINK I COULD EVER LOOK AT MARCO WHEN HE IS AT HIS MOST VULNERABLE--
WHEN HE IS ALMOST BROKEN AND NEEDS ME THE MOST--
I DON'T THINK I CAN SEE HIM LIKE THAT AND JUST TURN MY BACK. WHAT KIND OF A MAN DOES THAT?
MAYBE HE HAS HIS REASONS?

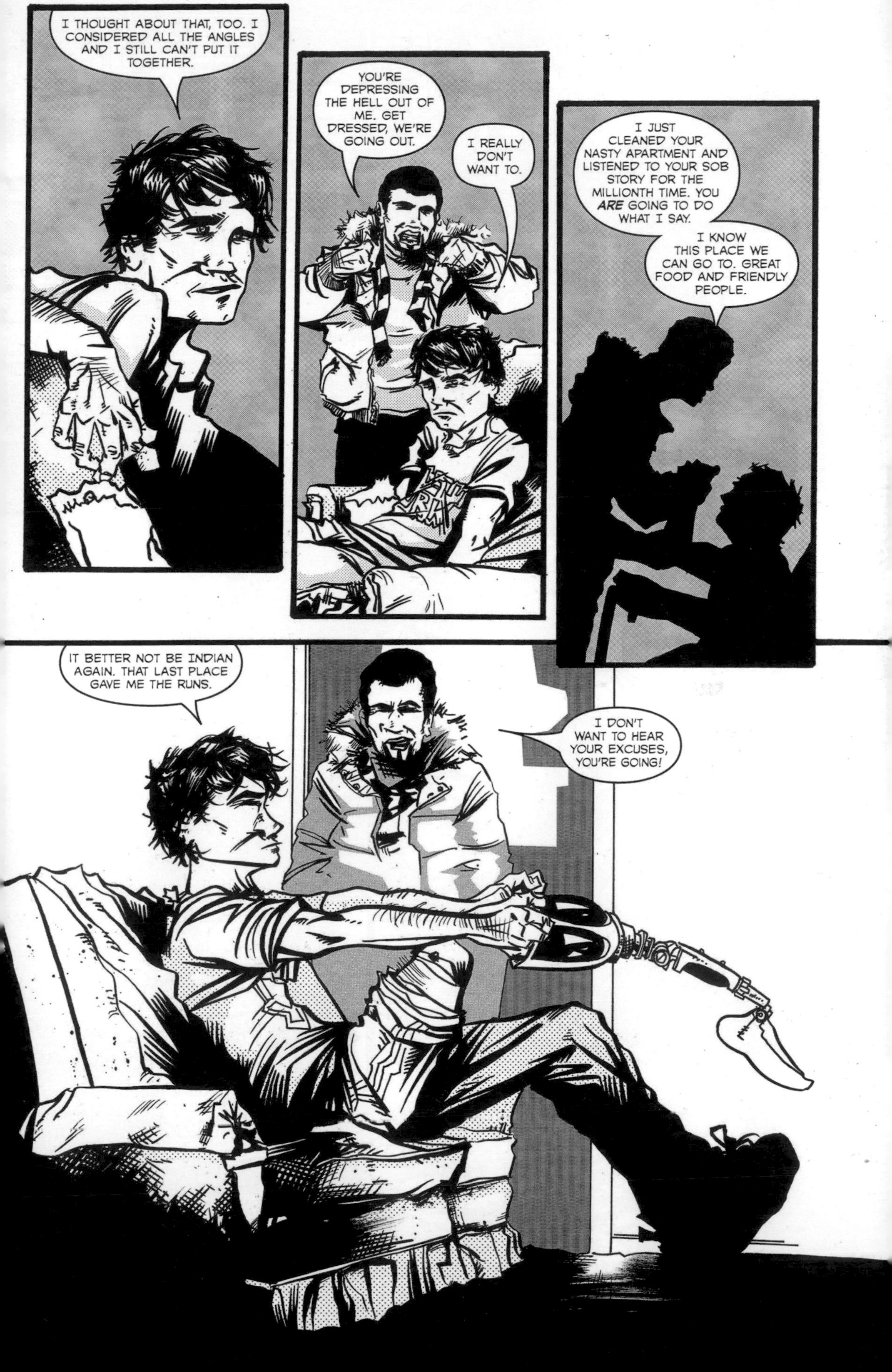
I THOUGHT ABOUT THAT, TOO. I CONSIDERED ALL THE ANGLES AND I STILL CAN'T PUT IT TOGETHER.
YOU'RE DEPRESSING THE HELL OUT OF ME. GET DRESSED, WE'RE GOING OUT.
I REALLY DON'T WANT TO.
I JUST CLEANED YOUR NASTY APARTMENT AND LISTENED TO YOUR SOB STORY FOR THE MILLIONTH TIME. YOU ***ARE*** GOING TO DO WHAT I SAY.
I KNOW THIS PLACE WE CAN GO TO. GREAT FOOD AND FRIENDLY PEOPLE.
IT BETTER NOT BE INDIAN AGAIN. THAT LAST PLACE GAVE ME THE RUNS.
I DON'T WANT TO HEAR YOUR EXCUSES, YOU'RE GOING!

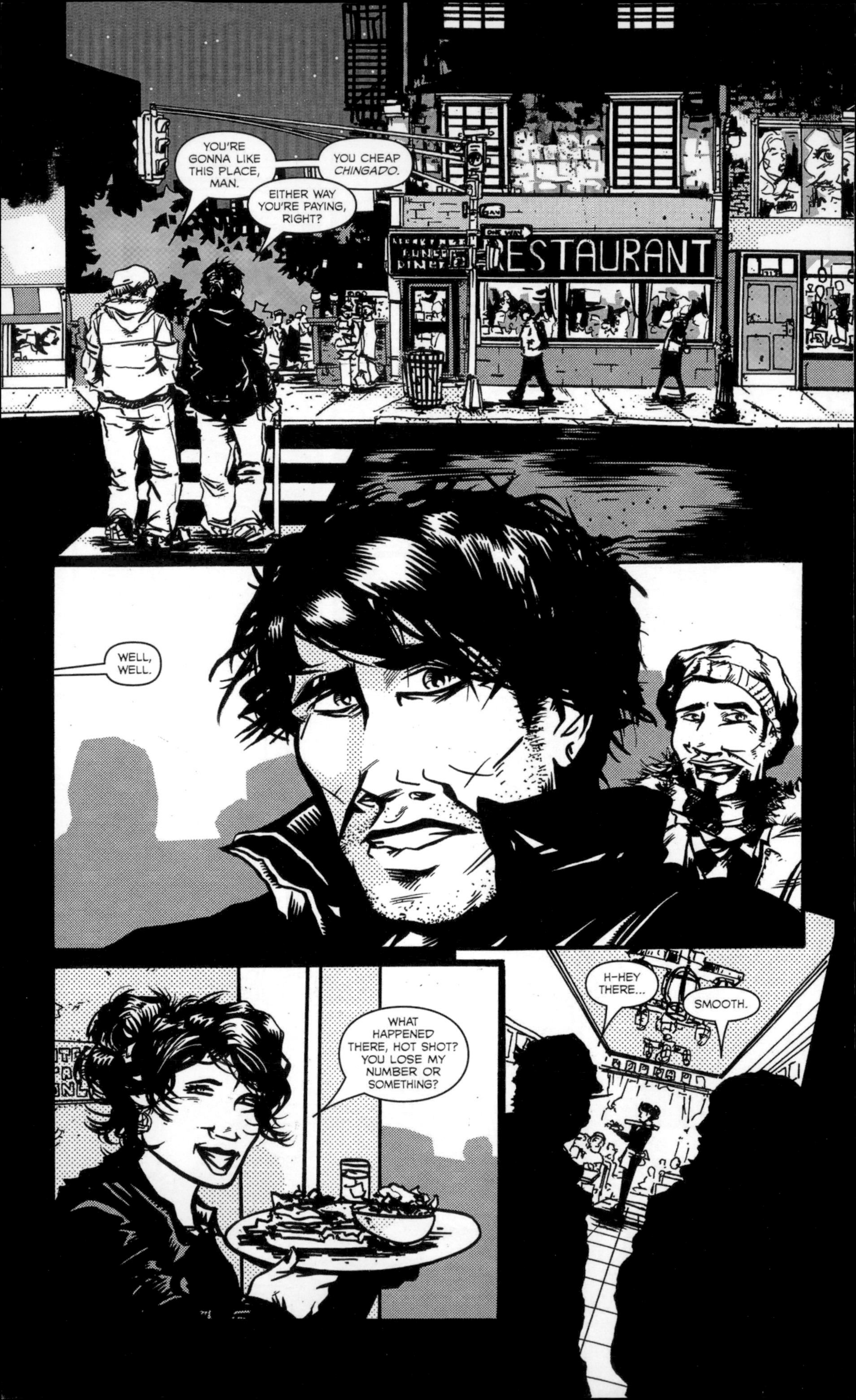
YOU'RE GONNA LIKE THIS PLACE, MAN.
YOU CHEAP *CHINGADO.*
EITHER WAY YOU'RE PAYING, RIGHT?
ONE WAY
RESTAURANT
WELL, WELL.
WHAT HAPPENED THERE, HOT SHOT? YOU LOSE MY NUMBER OR SOMETHING?
H-HEY THERE...
SMOOTH.

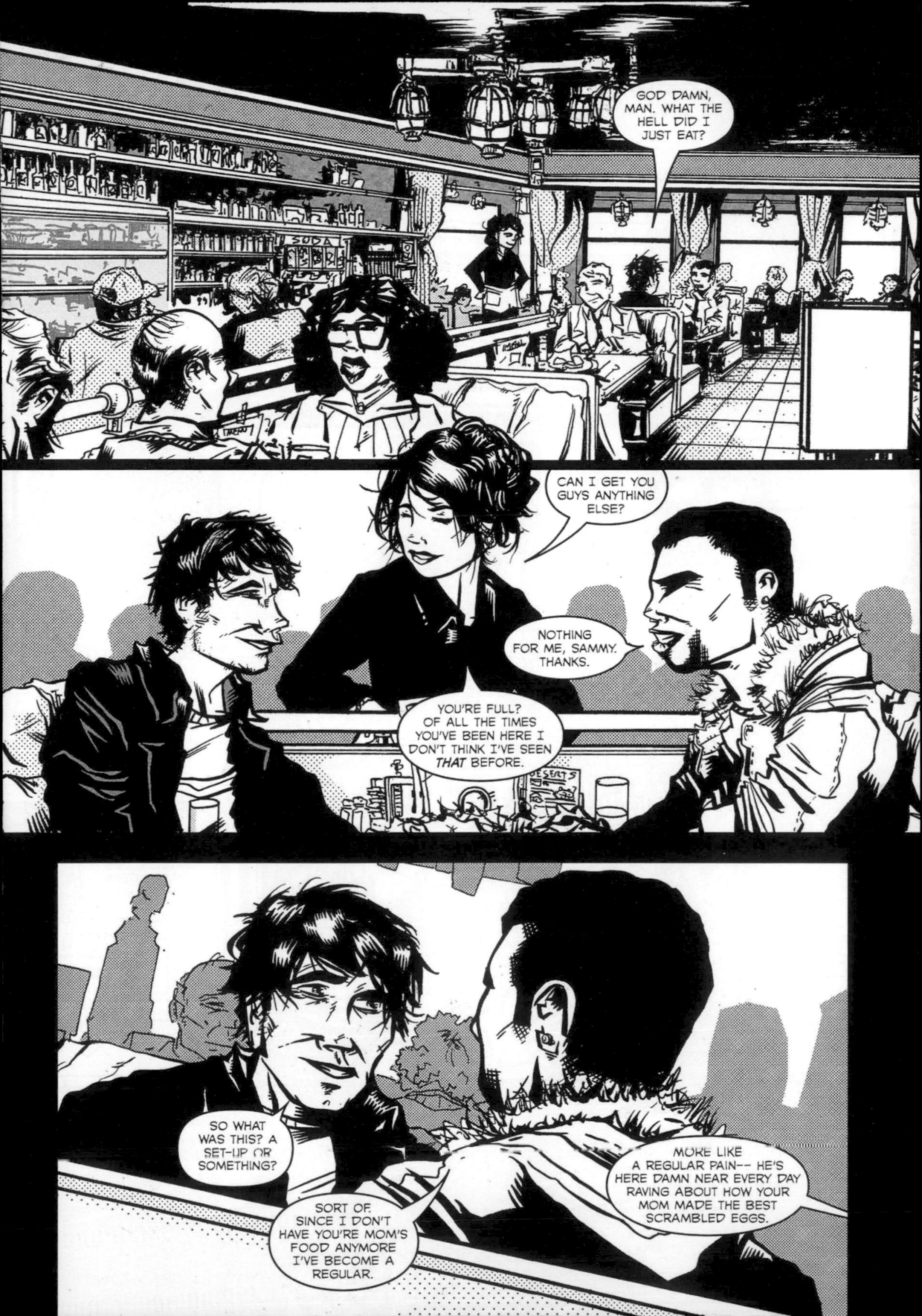
GOD DAMN, MAN. WHAT THE HELL DID I JUST EAT?
SODA
CAN I GET YOU GUYS ANYTHING ELSE?
NOTHING FOR ME, SAMMY. THANKS.
YOU'RE FULL? OF ALL THE TIMES YOU'VE BEEN HERE I DON'T THINK I'VE SEEN *THAT* BEFORE.
SO WHAT WAS THIS? A SET-UP OR SOMETHING?
SORT OF. SINCE I DON'T HAVE YOU'RE MOM'S FOOD ANYMORE I'VE BECOME A REGULAR.
MORE LIKE A REGULAR PAIN-- HE'S HERE DAMN NEAR EVERY DAY RAVING ABOUT HOW YOUR MOM MADE THE BEST SCRAMBLED EGGS.

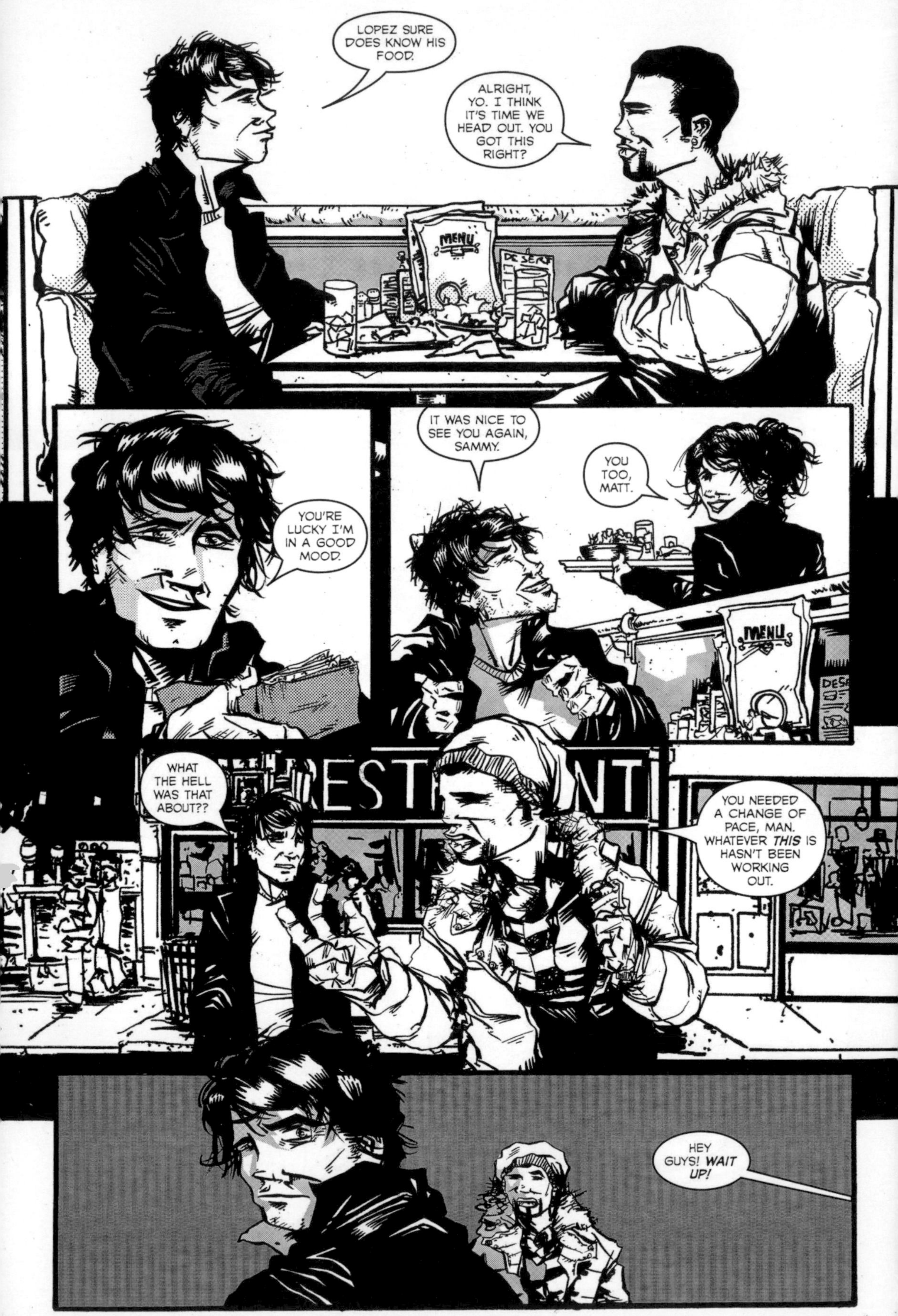
LOPEZ SURE DOES KNOW HIS FOOD.
ALRIGHT, YO. I THINK IT'S TIME WE HEAD OUT. YOU GOT THIS RIGHT?
YOU'RE LUCKY I'M IN A GOOD MOOD.
IT WAS NICE TO SEE YOU AGAIN, SAMMY.
YOU TOO, MATT.
MENU
WHAT THE HELL WAS THAT ABOUT??
YOU NEEDED A CHANGE OF PACE, MAN. WHATEVER *THIS* IS HASN'T BEEN WORKING OUT.
HEY GUYS! ***WAIT UP!***

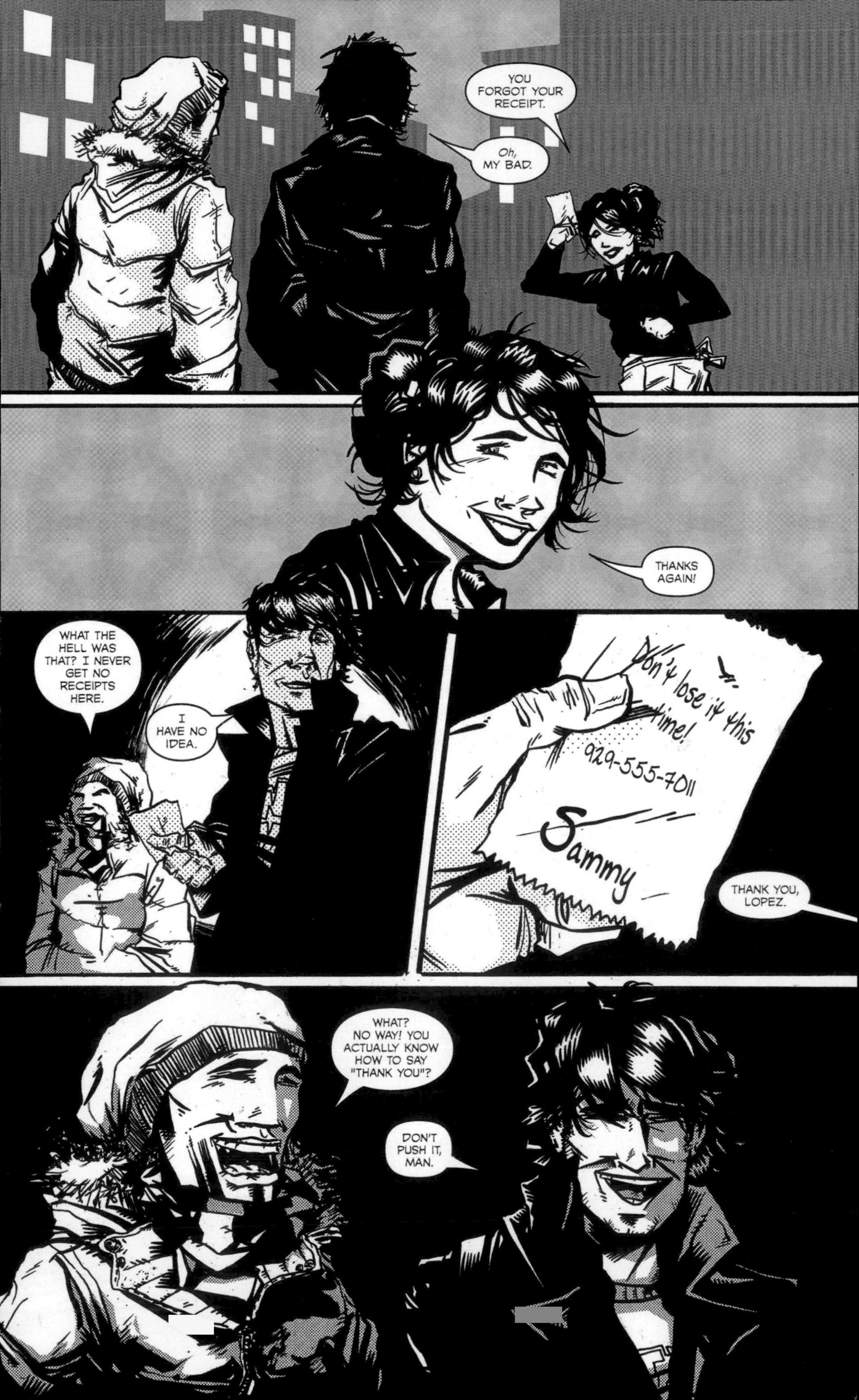
YOU FORGOT YOUR RECEIPT.
Oh, MY BAD.
THANKS AGAIN!
WHAT THE HELL WAS THAT? I NEVER GET NO RECEIPTS HERE.
I HAVE NO IDEA.
Don't lose it this time!
929-555-7011
Sammy
THANK YOU, LOPEZ.
WHAT? NO WAY! YOU ACTUALLY KNOW HOW TO SAY "THANK YOU"?
DON'T PUSH IT, MAN.

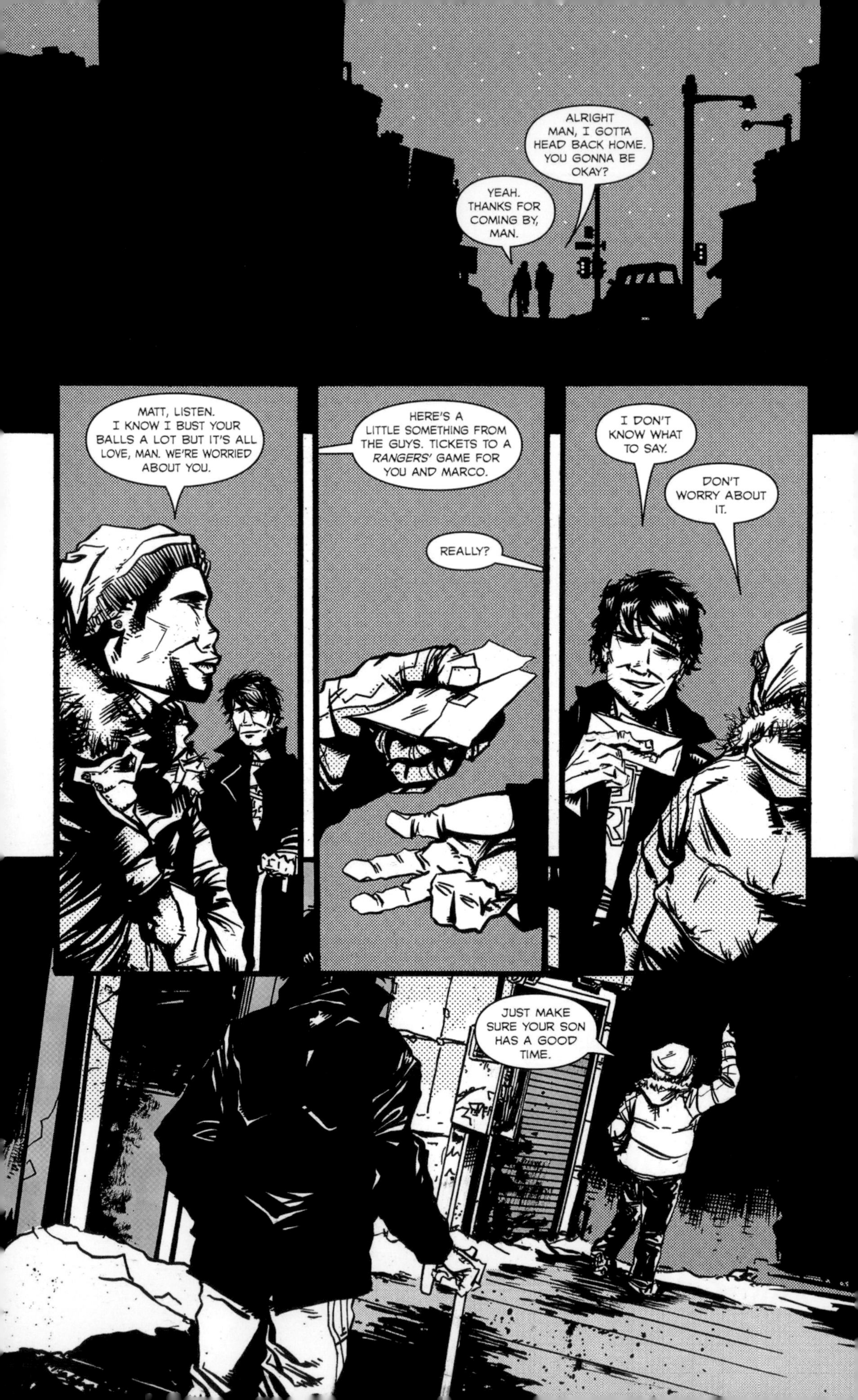

ALRIGHT MAN, I GOTTA HEAD BACK HOME. YOU GONNA BE OKAY?
YEAH. THANKS FOR COMING BY, MAN.
MATT, LISTEN. I KNOW I BUST YOUR BALLS A LOT BUT IT'S ALL LOVE, MAN. WE'RE WORRIED ABOUT YOU.
HERE'S A LITTLE SOMETHING FROM THE GUYS. TICKETS TO A *RANGERS'* GAME FOR YOU AND MARCO.
REALLY?
I DON'T KNOW WHAT TO SAY.
DON'T WORRY ABOUT IT.
JUST MAKE SURE YOUR SON HAS A GOOD TIME.

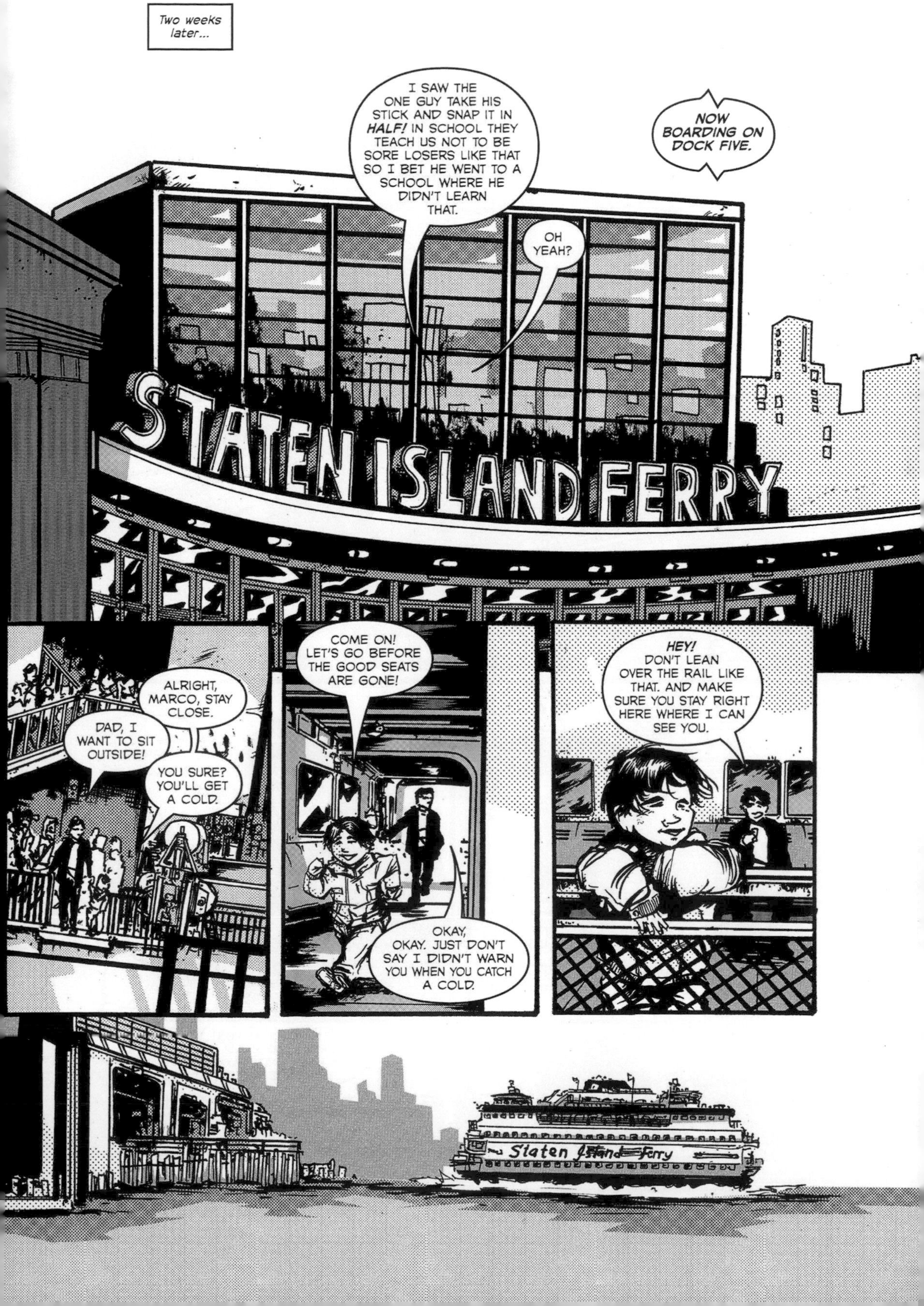
Two weeks later...
I SAW THE ONE GUY TAKE HIS STICK AND SNAP IT IN HALF! IN SCHOOL THEY TEACH US NOT TO BE SORE LOSERS LIKE THAT SO I BET HE WENT TO A SCHOOL WHERE HE DIDN'T LEARN THAT.
OH YEAH?
NOW BOARDING ON DOCK FIVE.
STATEN ISLAND FERRY
ALRIGHT, MARCO, STAY CLOSE.
DAD, I WANT TO SIT OUTSIDE!
YOU SURE? YOU'LL GET A COLD.
COME ON! LET'S GO BEFORE THE GOOD SEATS ARE GONE!
OKAY, OKAY. JUST DON'T SAY I DIDN'T WARN YOU WHEN YOU CATCH A COLD.
HEY! DON'T LEAN OVER THE RAIL LIKE THAT. AND MAKE SURE YOU STAY RIGHT HERE WHERE I CAN SEE YOU.
Staten Island Ferry

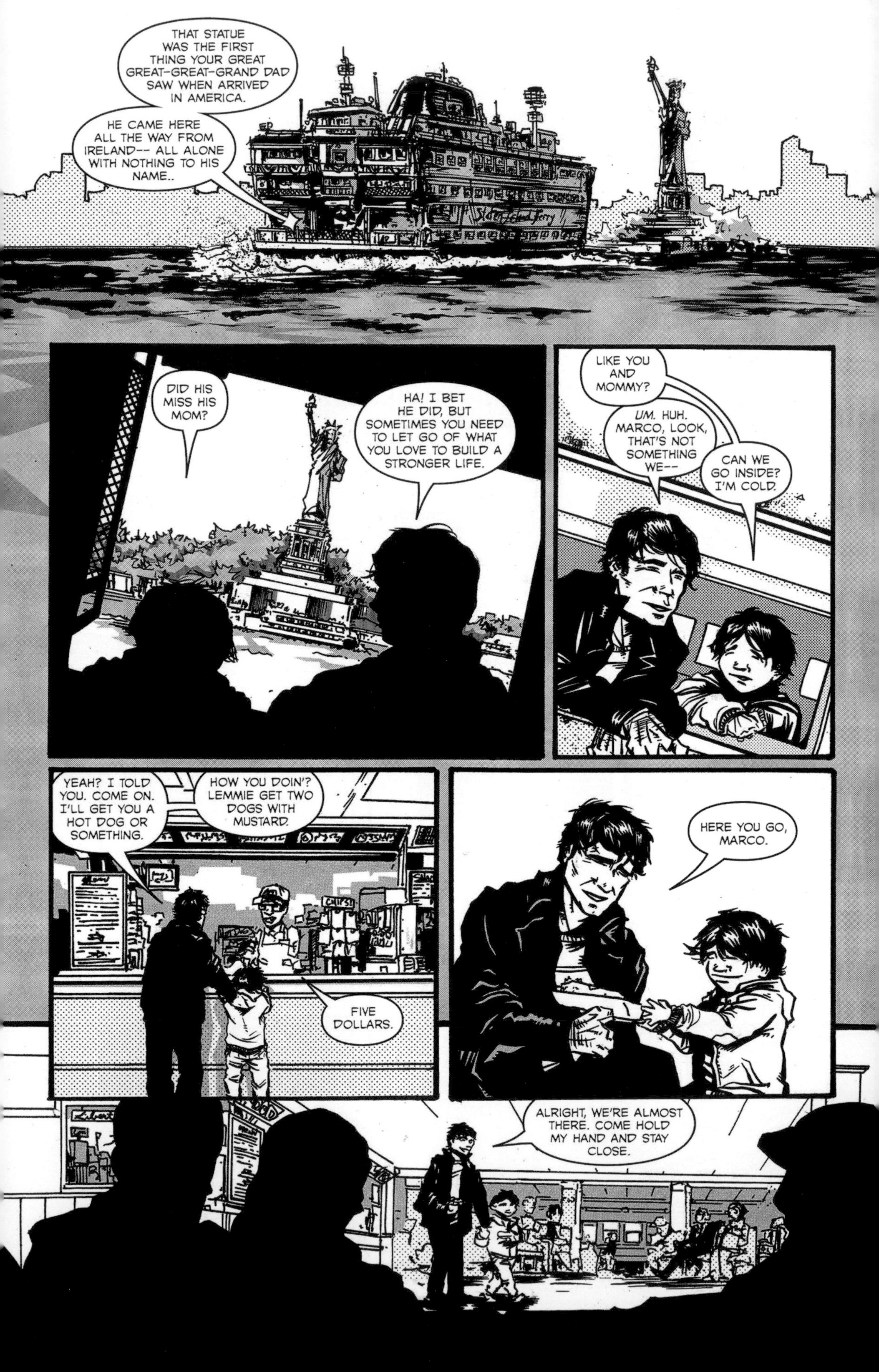
THAT STATUE WAS THE FIRST THING YOUR GREAT GREAT-GREAT-GRAND DAD SAW WHEN ARRIVED IN AMERICA.
HE CAME HERE ALL THE WAY FROM IRELAND-- ALL ALONE WITH NOTHING TO HIS NAME..
DID HIS MISS HIS MOM?
HA! I BET HE DID, BUT SOMETIMES YOU NEED TO LET GO OF WHAT YOU LOVE TO BUILD A STRONGER LIFE.
LIKE YOU AND MOMMY?
UM. HUH. MARCO, LOOK, THAT'S NOT SOMETHING WE--
CAN WE GO INSIDE? I'M COLD.
YEAH? I TOLD YOU. COME ON. I'LL GET YOU A HOT DOG OR SOMETHING.
HOW YOU DOIN'? LEMMIE GET TWO DOGS WITH MUSTARD.
FIVE DOLLARS.
HERE YOU GO, MARCO.
ALRIGHT, WE'RE ALMOST THERE. COME HOLD MY HAND AND STAY CLOSE.

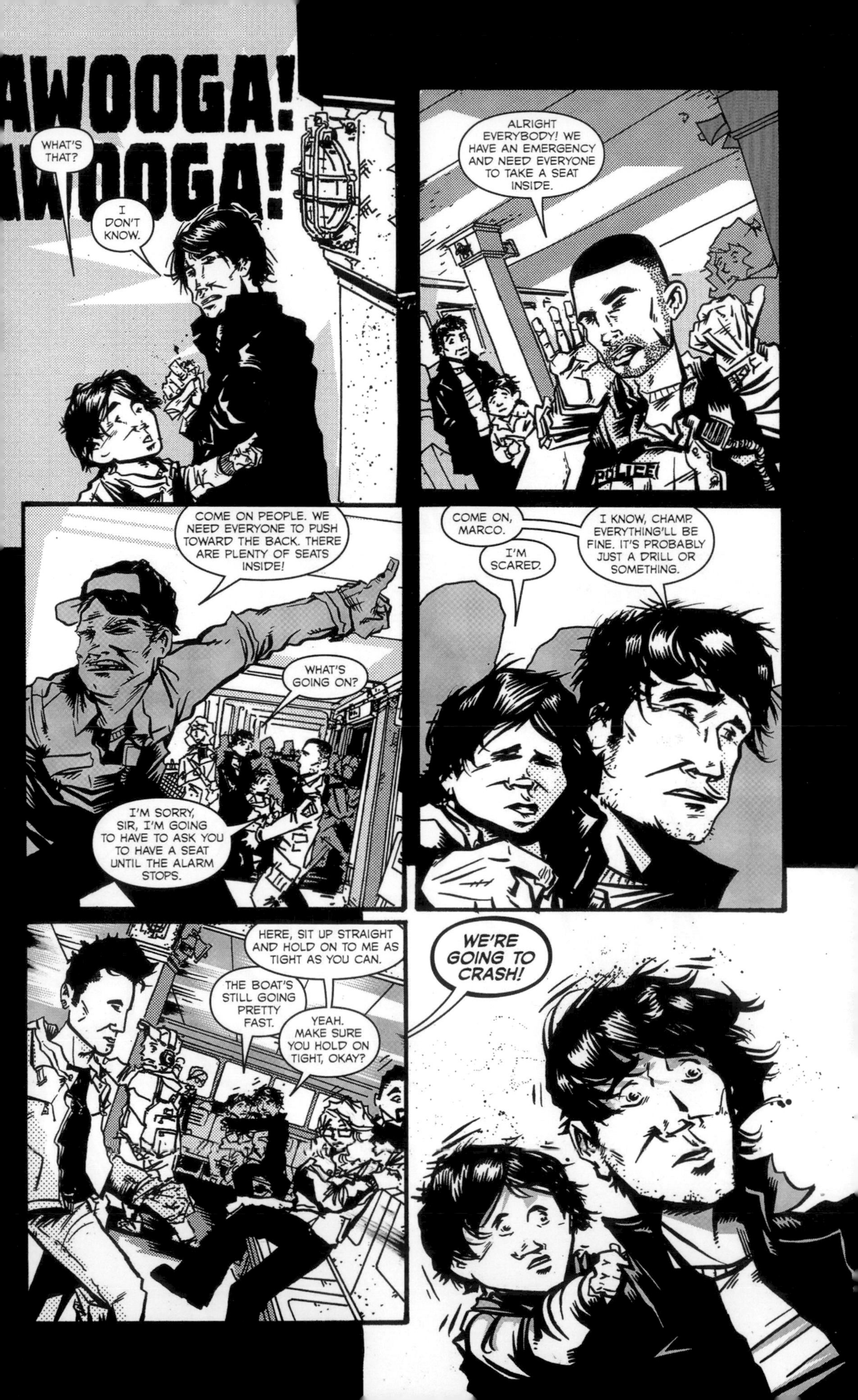
AWOOGA! AWOOGA!
WHAT'S THAT?
I DON'T KNOW.
ALRIGHT EVERYBODY! WE HAVE AN EMERGENCY AND NEED EVERYONE TO TAKE A SEAT INSIDE.
POLICE
COME ON PEOPLE. WE NEED EVERYONE TO PUSH TOWARD THE BACK. THERE ARE PLENTY OF SEATS INSIDE!
WHAT'S GOING ON?
I'M SORRY, SIR, I'M GOING TO HAVE TO ASK YOU TO HAVE A SEAT UNTIL THE ALARM STOPS.
COME ON, MARCO.
I'M SCARED.
I KNOW, CHAMP. EVERYTHING'LL BE FINE. IT'S PROBABLY JUST A DRILL OR SOMETHING.
HERE, SIT UP STRAIGHT AND HOLD ON TO ME AS TIGHT AS YOU CAN.
THE BOAT'S STILL GOING PRETTY FAST.
YEAH. MAKE SURE YOU HOLD ON TIGHT, OKAY?
WE'RE GOING TO CRASH!

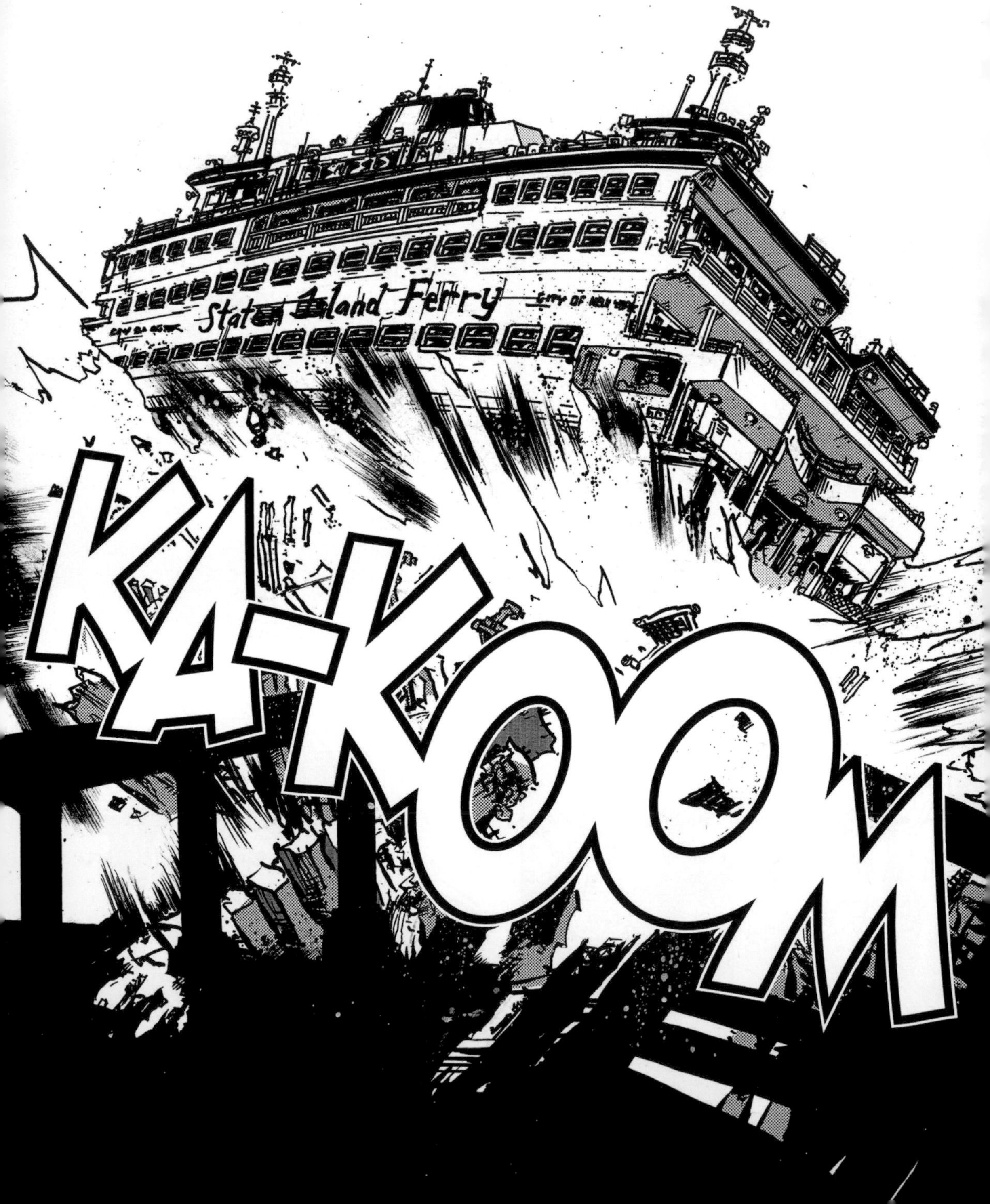
Staten Island Ferry
KA-KOOM

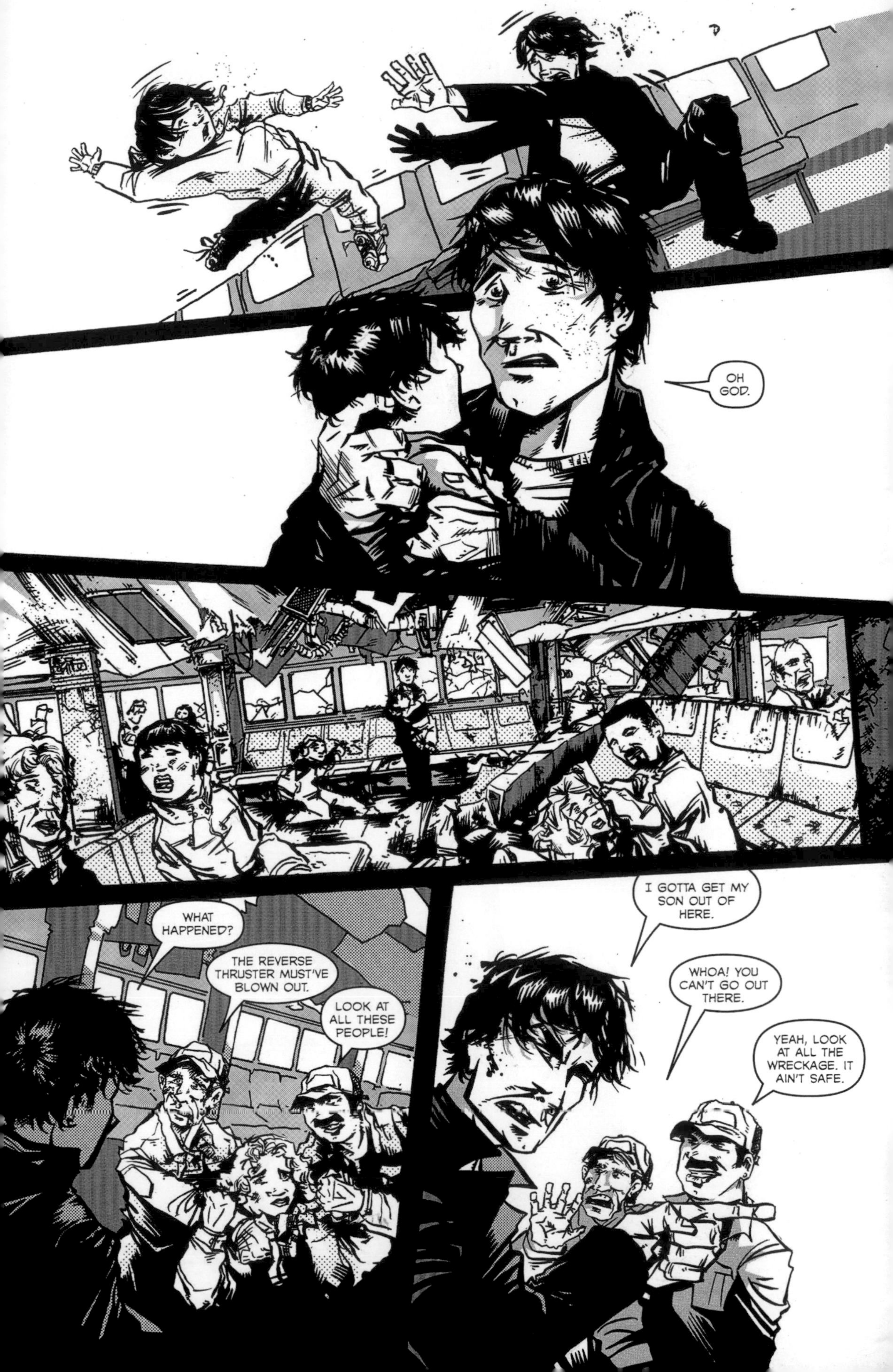
OH GOD.
WHAT HAPPENED?
THE REVERSE THRUSTER MUST'VE BLOWN OUT.
LOOK AT ALL THESE PEOPLE!
I GOTTA GET MY SON OUT OF HERE.
WHOA! YOU CAN'T GO OUT THERE.
YEAH, LOOK AT ALL THE WRECKAGE. IT AIN'T SAFE.

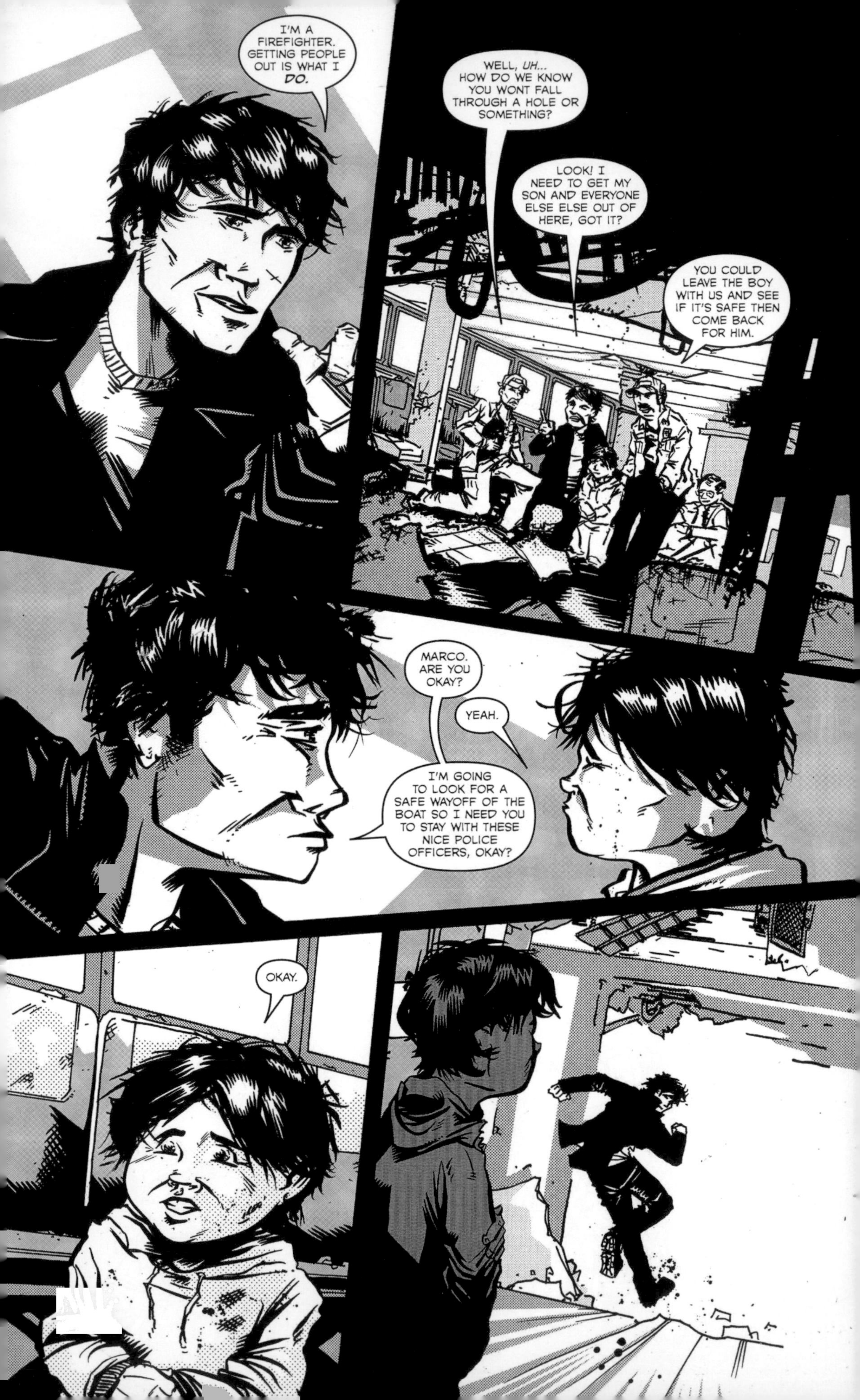
I'M A FIREFIGHTER. GETTING PEOPLE OUT IS WHAT I *DO.*
WELL, *UH...* HOW DO WE KNOW YOU WONT FALL THROUGH A HOLE OR SOMETHING?
LOOK! I NEED TO GET MY SON AND EVERYONE ELSE ELSE OUT OF HERE, GOT IT?
YOU COULD LEAVE THE BOY WITH US AND SEE IF IT'S SAFE THEN COME BACK FOR HIM.
MARCO. ARE YOU OKAY?
YEAH.
I'M GOING TO LOOK FOR A SAFE WAYOFF OF THE BOAT SO I NEED YOU TO STAY WITH THESE NICE POLICE OFFICERS, OKAY?
OKAY.

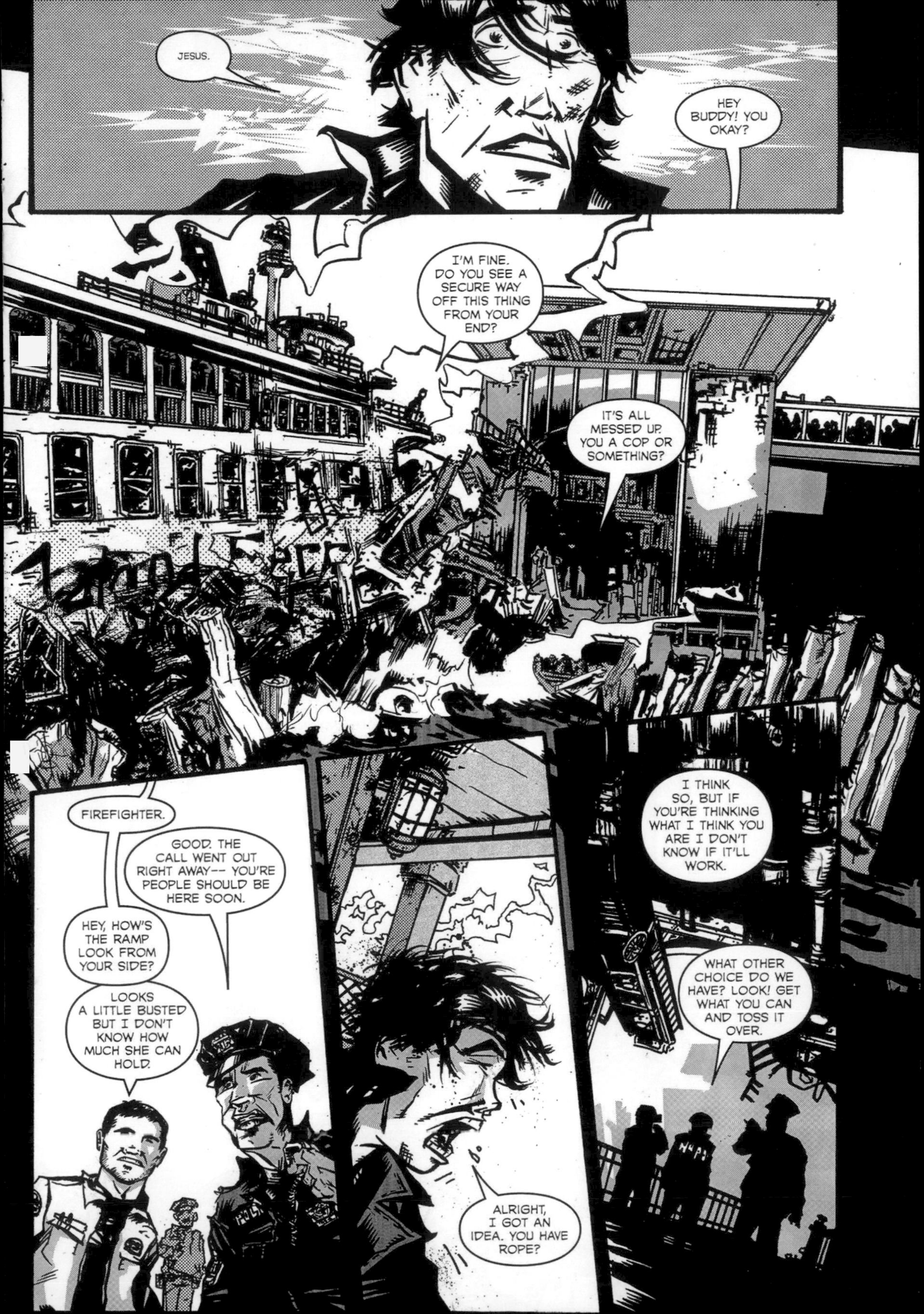

JESUS.
HEY BUDDY! YOU OKAY?
I'M FINE. DO YOU SEE A SECURE WAY OFF THIS THING FROM YOUR END?
IT'S ALL MESSED UP. YOU A COP OR SOMETHING?
FIREFIGHTER.
GOOD. THE CALL WENT OUT RIGHT AWAY-- YOU'RE PEOPLE SHOULD BE HERE SOON.
HEY, HOW'S THE RAMP LOOK FROM YOUR SIDE?
LOOKS A LITTLE BUSTED BUT I DON'T KNOW HOW MUCH SHE CAN HOLD.
I THINK SO, BUT IF YOU'RE THINKING WHAT I THINK YOU ARE I DON'T KNOW IF IT'LL WORK.
WHAT OTHER CHOICE DO WE HAVE? LOOK! GET WHAT YOU CAN AND TOSS IT OVER.
ALRIGHT, I GOT AN IDEA. YOU HAVE ROPE?

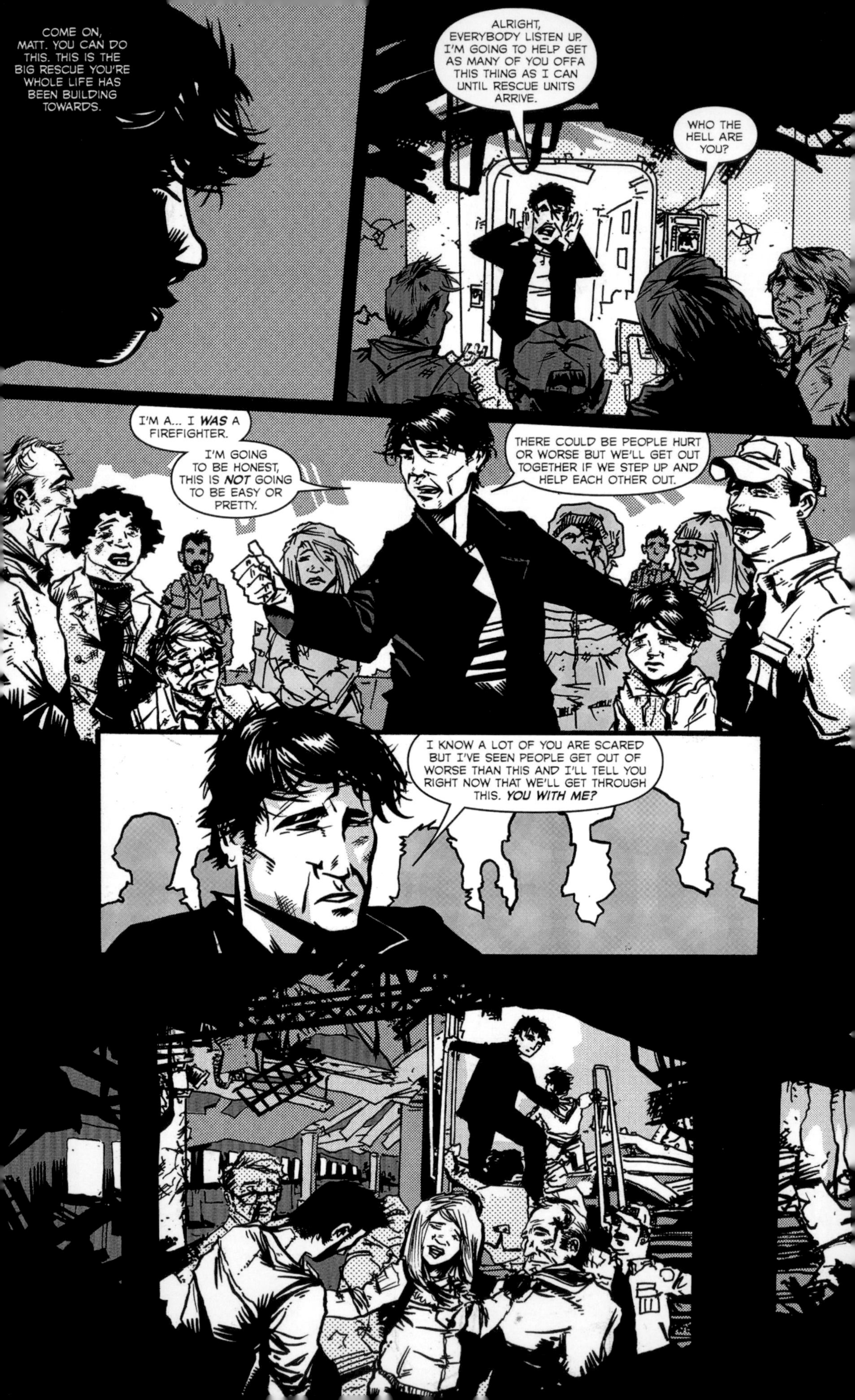
COME ON, MATT. YOU CAN DO THIS. THIS IS THE BIG RESCUE YOU'RE WHOLE LIFE HAS BEEN BUILDING TOWARDS.
ALRIGHT, EVERYBODY LISTEN UP. I'M GOING TO HELP GET AS MANY OF YOU OFFA THIS THING AS I CAN UNTIL RESCUE UNITS ARRIVE.
WHO THE HELL ARE YOU?
I'M A... I **WAS** A FIREFIGHTER.
I'M GOING TO BE HONEST, THIS IS **NOT** GOING TO BE EASY OR PRETTY.
THERE COULD BE PEOPLE HURT OR WORSE BUT WE'LL GET OUT TOGETHER IF WE STEP UP AND HELP EACH OTHER OUT.
I KNOW A LOT OF YOU ARE SCARED BUT I'VE SEEN PEOPLE GET OUT OF WORSE THAN THIS AND I'LL TELL YOU RIGHT NOW THAT WE'LL GET THROUGH THIS. ***YOU WITH ME?***

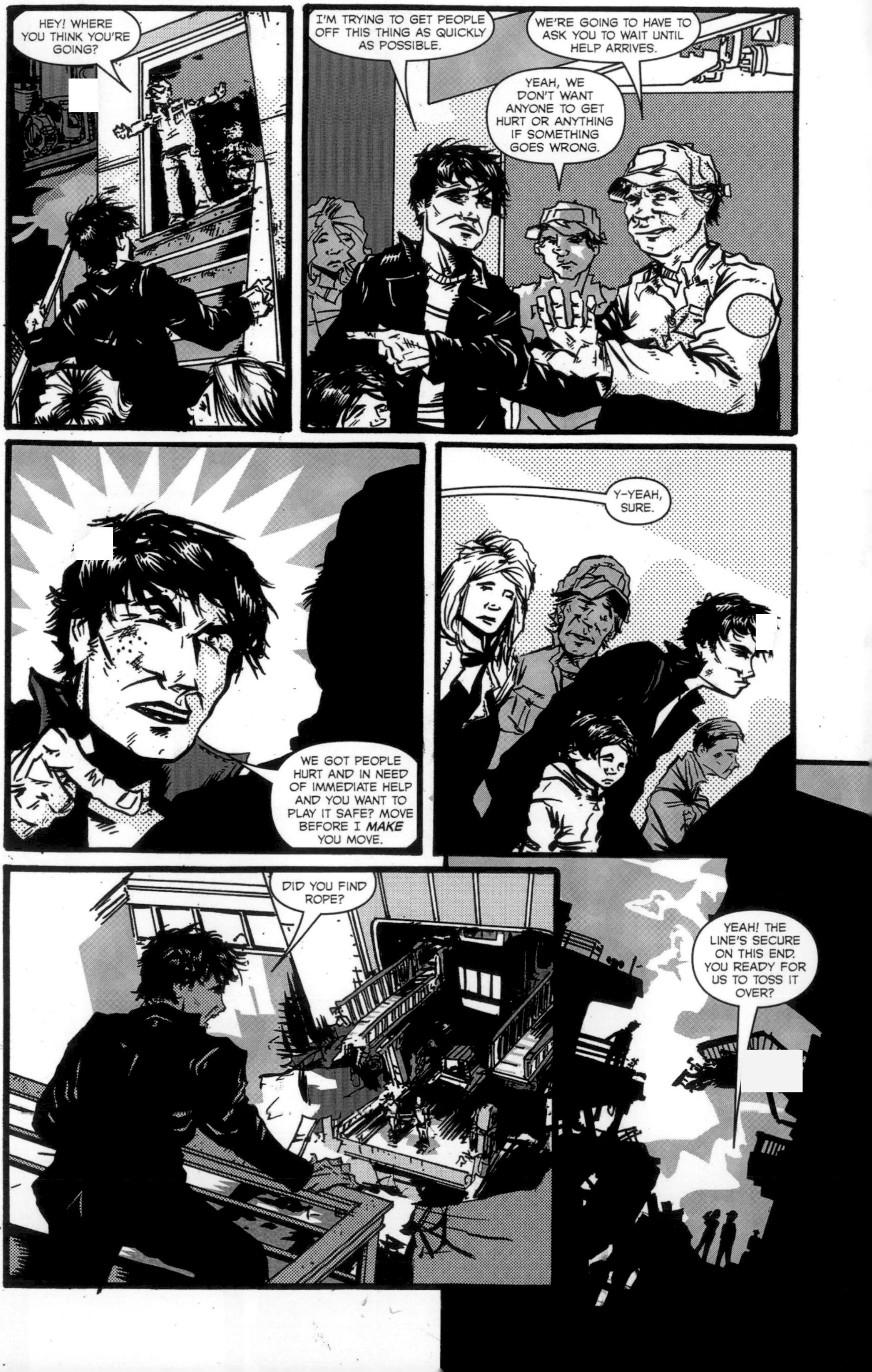
HEY! WHERE YOU THINK YOU'RE GOING?
I'M TRYING TO GET PEOPLE OFF THIS THING AS QUICKLY AS POSSIBLE.
WE'RE GOING TO HAVE TO ASK YOU TO WAIT UNTIL HELP ARRIVES.
YEAH, WE DON'T WANT ANYONE TO GET HURT OR ANYTHING IF SOMETHING GOES WRONG.
WE GOT PEOPLE HURT AND IN NEED OF IMMEDIATE HELP AND YOU WANT TO PLAY IT SAFE? MOVE BEFORE I *MAKE* YOU MOVE.
Y-YEAH, SURE.
DID YOU FIND ROPE?
YEAH! THE LINE'S SECURE ON THIS END. YOU READY FOR US TO TOSS IT OVER?

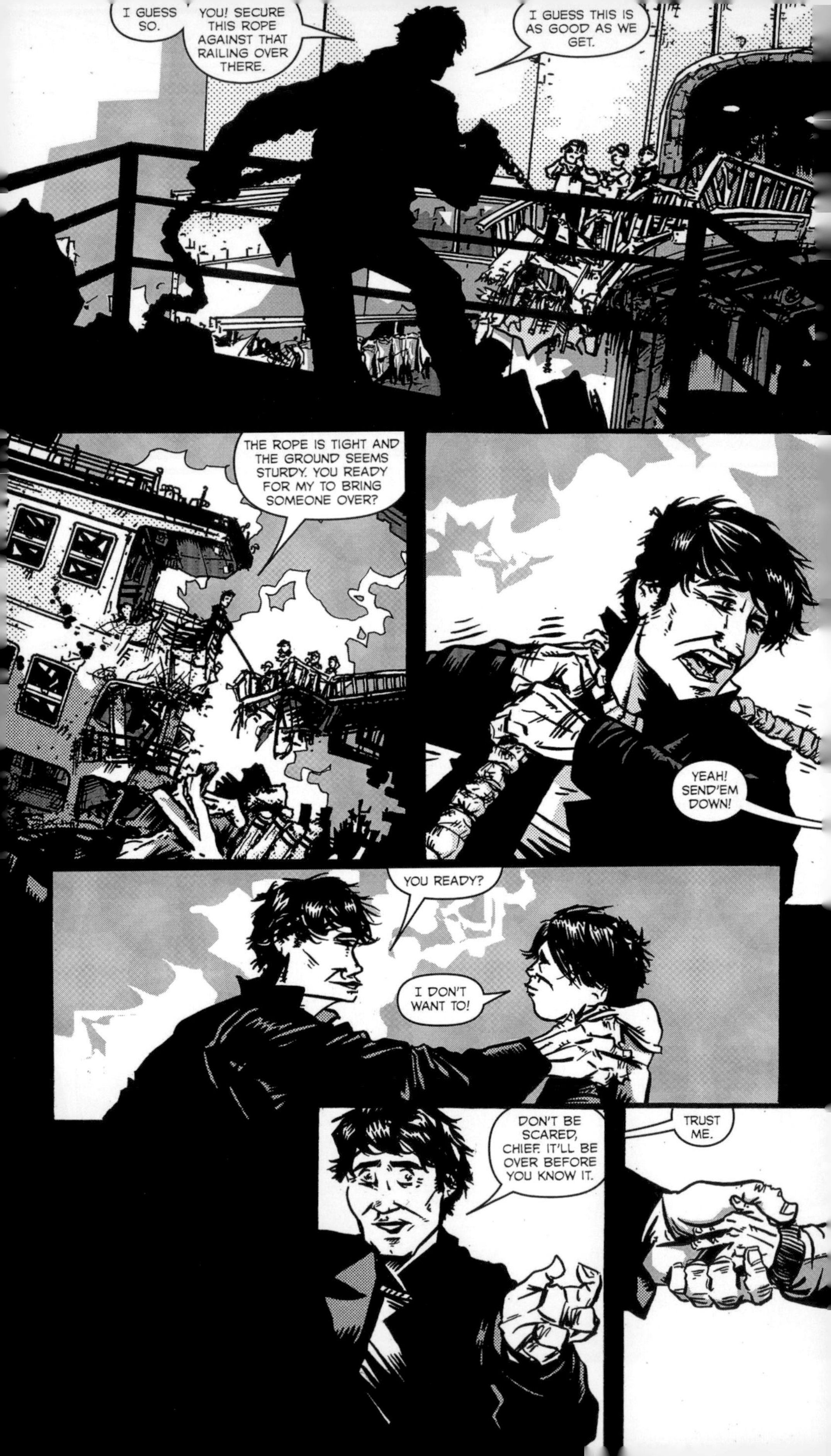
I GUESS SO.
YOU! SECURE THIS ROPE AGAINST THAT RAILING OVER THERE.
I GUESS THIS IS AS GOOD AS WE GET.
THE ROPE IS TIGHT AND THE GROUND SEEMS STURDY. YOU READY FOR MY TO BRING SOMEONE OVER?
YEAH! SEND'EM DOWN!
YOU READY?
I DON'T WANT TO!
DON'T BE SCARED, CHIEF. IT'LL BE OVER BEFORE YOU KNOW IT.
TRUST ME.

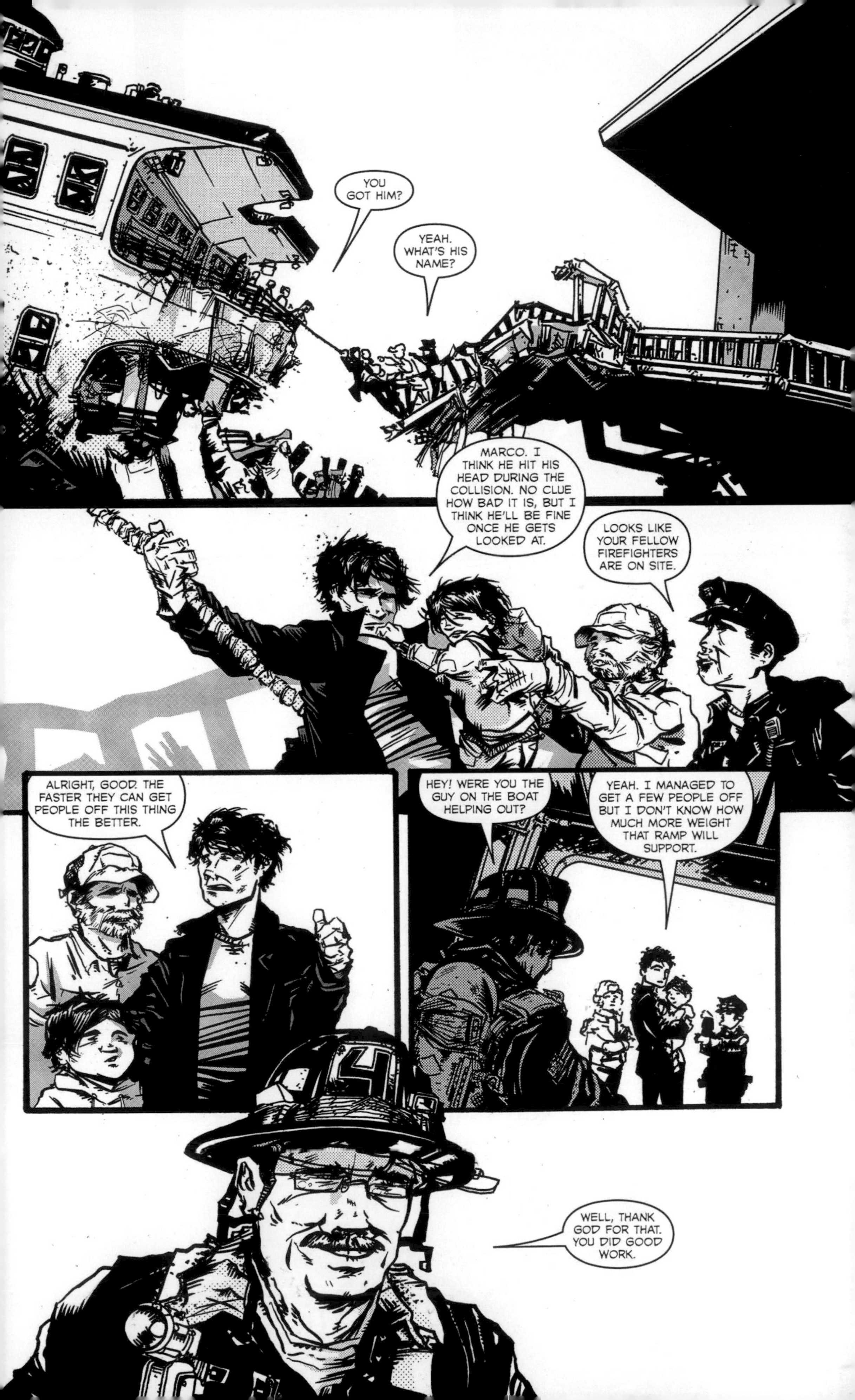
YOU GOT HIM?
YEAH. WHAT'S HIS NAME?
MARCO. I THINK HE HIT HIS HEAD DURING THE COLLISION. NO CLUE HOW BAD IT IS, BUT I THINK HE'LL BE FINE ONCE HE GETS LOOKED AT.
LOOKS LIKE YOUR FELLOW FIREFIGHTERS ARE ON SITE.
ALRIGHT, GOOD. THE FASTER THEY CAN GET PEOPLE OFF THIS THING THE BETTER.
HEY! WERE YOU THE GUY ON THE BOAT HELPING OUT?
YEAH. I MANAGED TO GET A FEW PEOPLE OFF BUT I DON'T KNOW HOW MUCH MORE WEIGHT THAT RAMP WILL SUPPORT.
WELL, THANK GOD FOR THAT. YOU DID GOOD WORK.

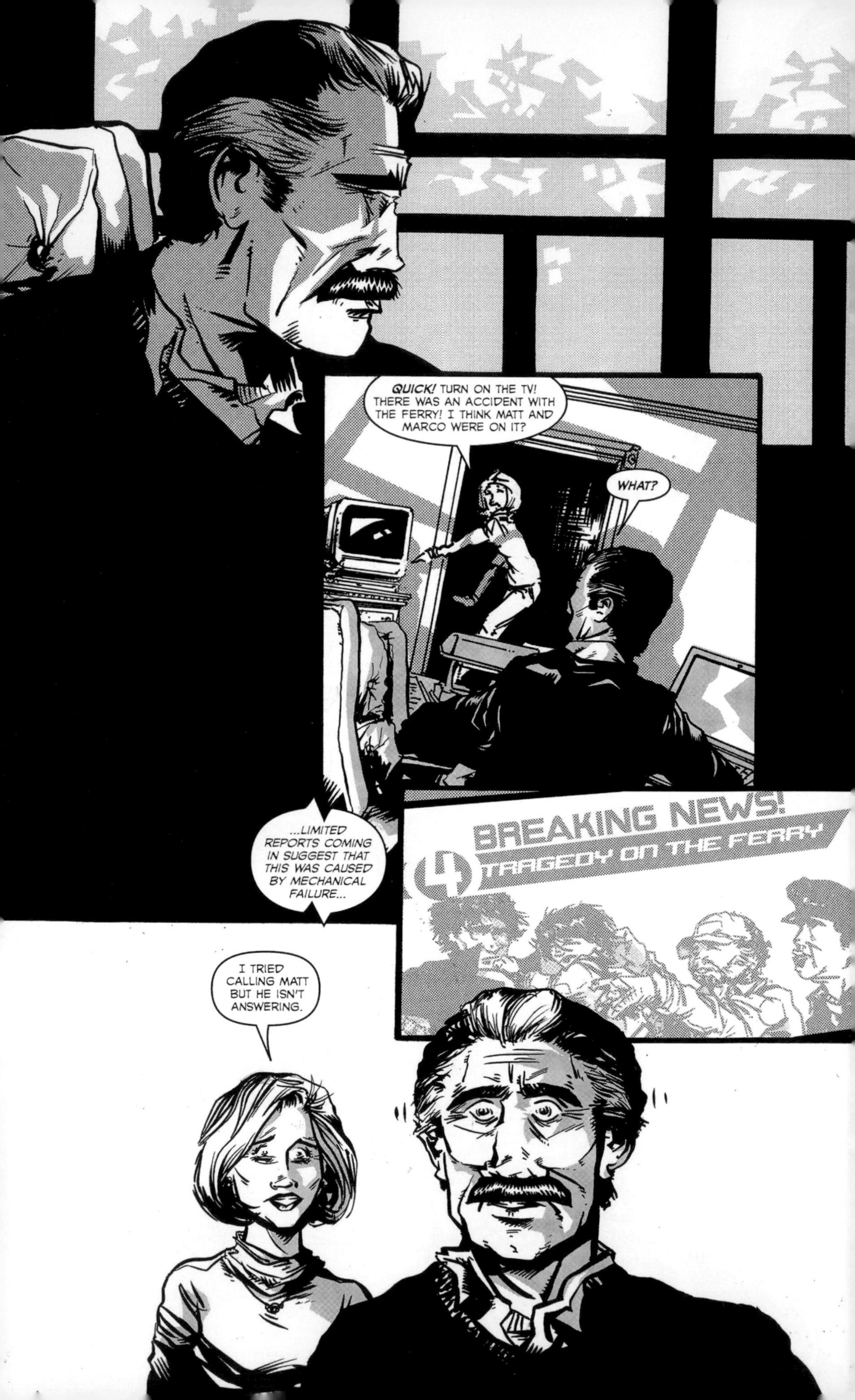
QUICK! TURN ON THE TV! THERE WAS AN ACCIDENT WITH THE FERRY! I THINK MATT AND MARCO WERE ON IT?
WHAT?
BREAKING NEWS!
4
TRAGEDY ON THE FERRY
...LIMITED REPORTS COMING IN SUGGEST THAT THIS WAS CAUSED BY MECHANICAL FAILURE...
I TRIED CALLING MATT BUT HE ISN'T ANSWERING.

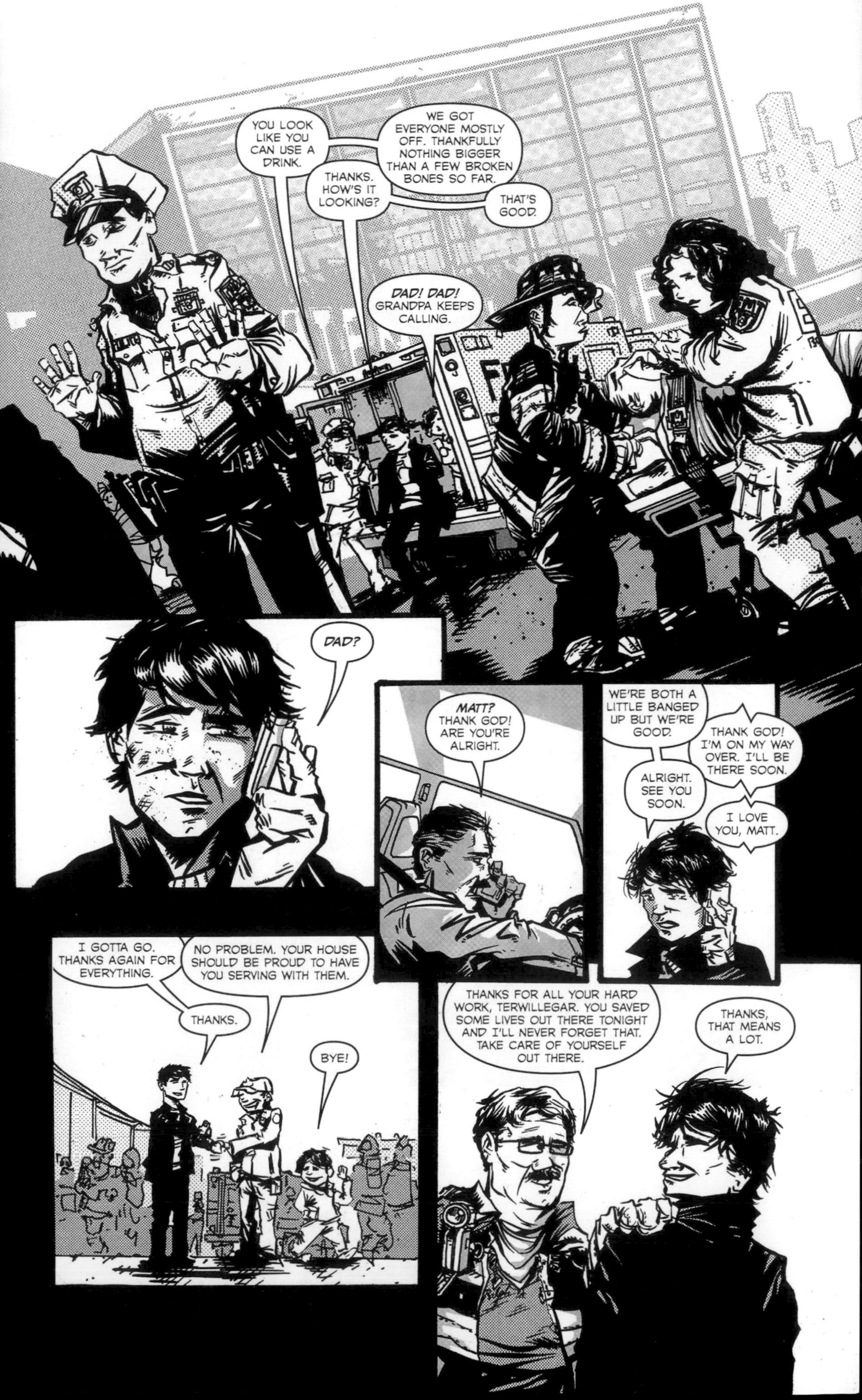

YOU LOOK LIKE YOU CAN USE A DRINK.
THANKS. HOW'S IT LOOKING?
WE GOT EVERYONE MOSTLY OFF. THANKFULLY NOTHING BIGGER THAN A FEW BROKEN BONES SO FAR.
THAT'S GOOD.
DAD! DAD! GRANDPA KEEPS CALLING.
DAD?
MATT? THANK GOD! ARE YOU'RE ALRIGHT.
WE'RE BOTH A LITTLE BANGED UP BUT WE'RE GOOD.
THANK GOD! I'M ON MY WAY OVER. I'LL BE THERE SOON.
ALRIGHT. SEE YOU SOON.
I LOVE YOU, MATT.
I GOTTA GO. THANKS AGAIN FOR EVERYTHING.
NO PROBLEM. YOUR HOUSE SHOULD BE PROUD TO HAVE YOU SERVING WITH THEM.
THANKS.
BYE!
THANKS FOR ALL YOUR HARD WORK, TERWILLEGAR. YOU SAVED SOME LIVES OUT THERE TONIGHT AND I'LL NEVER FORGET THAT. TAKE CARE OF YOURSELF OUT THERE.
THANKS, THAT MEANS A LOT.

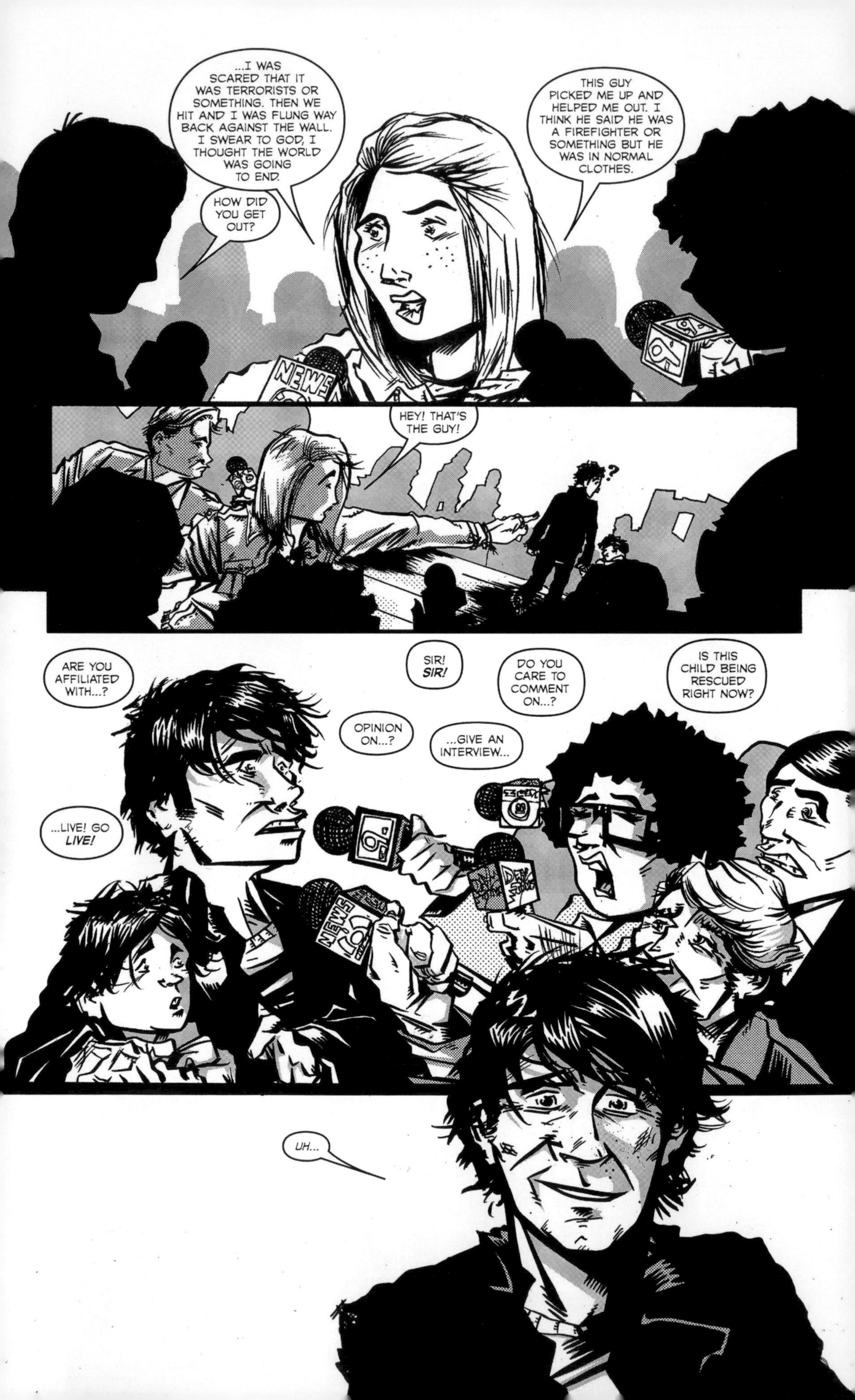
...I WAS SCARED THAT IT WAS TERRORISTS OR SOMETHING. THEN WE HIT AND I WAS FLUNG WAY BACK AGAINST THE WALL. I SWEAR TO GOD, I THOUGHT THE WORLD WAS GOING TO END.
HOW DID YOU GET OUT?
THIS GUY PICKED ME UP AND HELPED ME OUT. I THINK HE SAID HE WAS A FIREFIGHTER OR SOMETHING BUT HE WAS IN NORMAL CLOTHES.
NEWS
HEY! THAT'S THE GUY!
ARE YOU AFFILIATED WITH...?
SIR! SIR!
DO YOU CARE TO COMMENT ON...?
IS THIS CHILD BEING RESCUED RIGHT NOW?
OPINION ON...?
...GIVE AN INTERVIEW...
...LIVE! GO LIVE!
NEWS
UH...

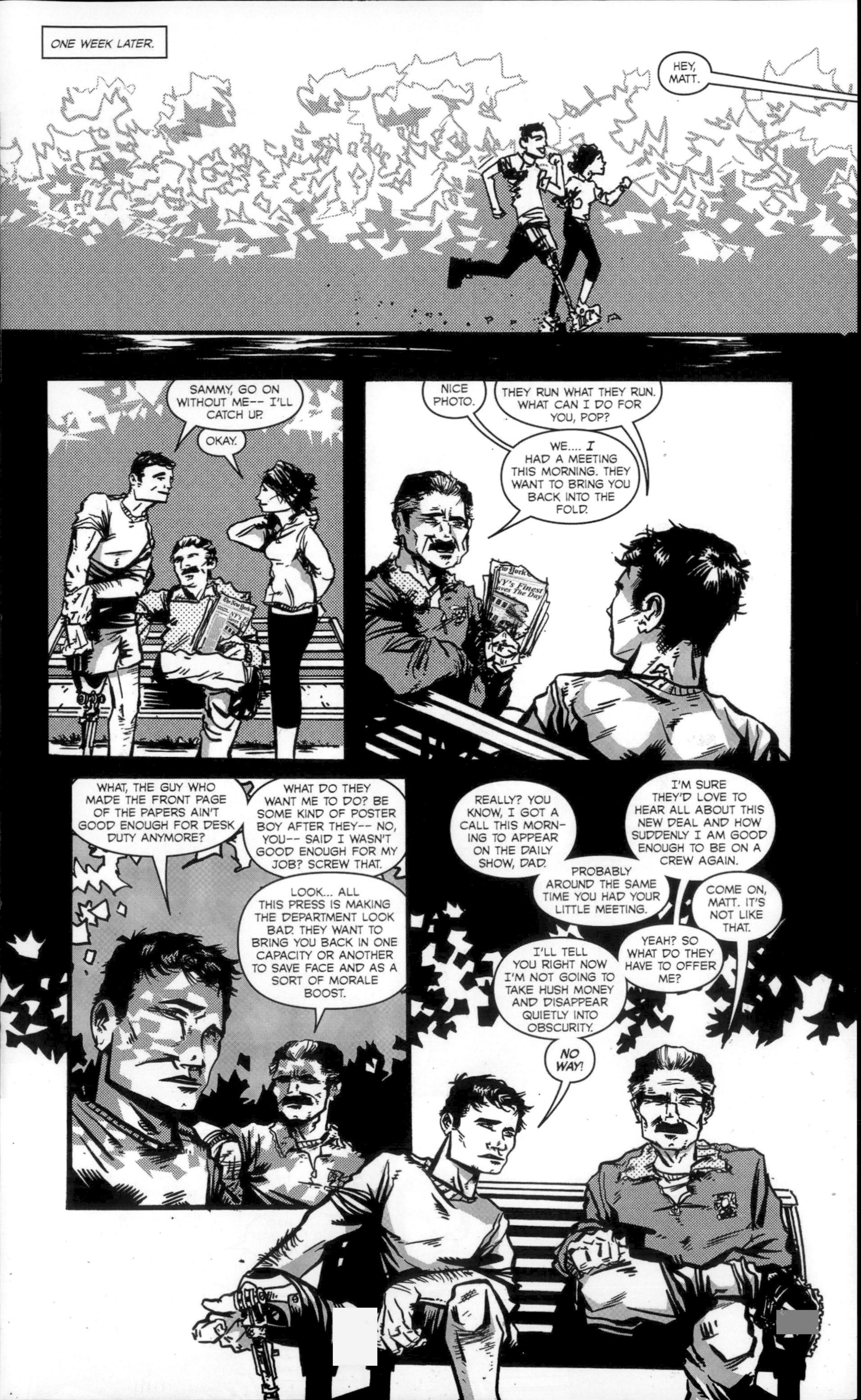
ONE WEEK LATER.
HEY, MATT.
SAMMY, GO ON WITHOUT ME-- I'LL CATCH UP.
OKAY.
NICE PHOTO.
THEY RUN WHAT THEY RUN. WHAT CAN I DO FOR YOU, POP?
WE.... *I* HAD A MEETING THIS MORNING. THEY WANT TO BRING YOU BACK INTO THE FOLD.
WHAT, THE GUY WHO MADE THE FRONT PAGE OF THE PAPERS AIN'T GOOD ENOUGH FOR DESK DUTY ANYMORE?
WHAT DO THEY WANT ME TO DO? BE SOME KIND OF POSTER BOY AFTER THEY-- NO, YOU-- SAID I WASN'T GOOD ENOUGH FOR MY JOB? SCREW THAT.
LOOK... ALL THIS PRESS IS MAKING THE DEPARTMENT LOOK BAD. THEY WANT TO BRING YOU BACK IN ONE CAPACITY OR ANOTHER TO SAVE FACE AND AS A SORT OF MORALE BOOST.
REALLY? YOU KNOW, I GOT A CALL THIS MORNING TO APPEAR ON THE DAILY SHOW, DAD.
I'M SURE THEY'D LOVE TO HEAR ALL ABOUT THIS NEW DEAL AND HOW SUDDENLY I AM GOOD ENOUGH TO BE ON A CREW AGAIN.
PROBABLY AROUND THE SAME TIME YOU HAD YOUR LITTLE MEETING.
COME ON, MATT. IT'S NOT LIKE THAT.
YEAH? SO WHAT DO THEY HAVE TO OFFER ME?
I'LL TELL YOU RIGHT NOW I'M NOT GOING TO TAKE HUSH MONEY AND DISAPPEAR QUIETLY INTO OBSCURITY.
NO WAY!

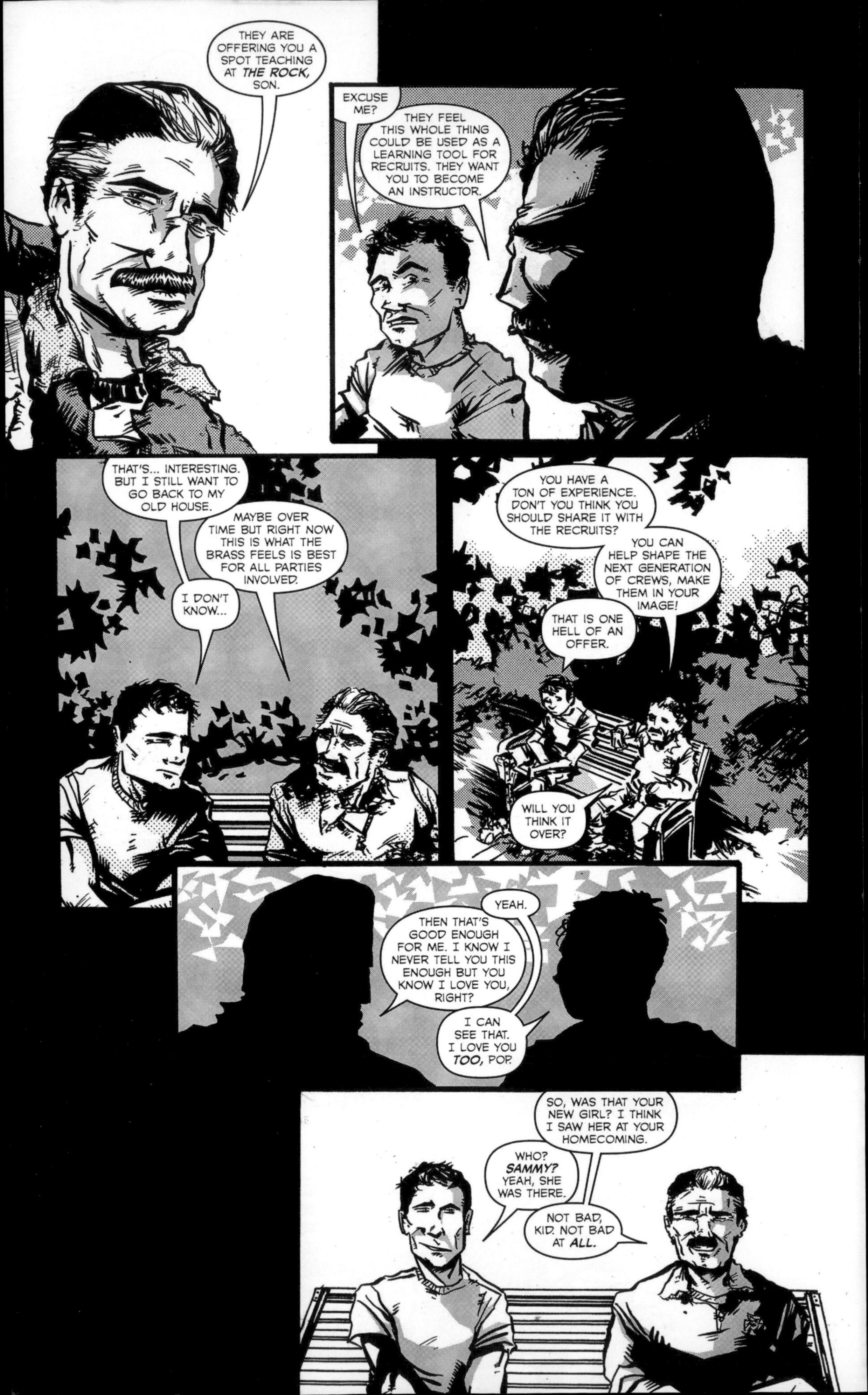
THEY ARE OFFERING YOU A SPOT TEACHING AT THE ROCK, SON.
EXCUSE ME?
THEY FEEL THIS WHOLE THING COULD BE USED AS A LEARNING TOOL FOR RECRUITS. THEY WANT YOU TO BECOME AN INSTRUCTOR.
THAT'S... INTERESTING. BUT I STILL WANT TO GO BACK TO MY OLD HOUSE.
MAYBE OVER TIME BUT RIGHT NOW THIS IS WHAT THE BRASS FEELS IS BEST FOR ALL PARTIES INVOLVED.
I DON'T KNOW...
YOU HAVE A TON OF EXPERIENCE. DON'T YOU THINK YOU SHOULD SHARE IT WITH THE RECRUITS?
YOU CAN HELP SHAPE THE NEXT GENERATION OF CREWS, MAKE THEM IN YOUR IMAGE!
THAT IS ONE HELL OF AN OFFER.
WILL YOU THINK IT OVER?
YEAH.
THEN THAT'S GOOD ENOUGH FOR ME. I KNOW I NEVER TELL YOU THIS ENOUGH BUT YOU KNOW I LOVE YOU, RIGHT?
I CAN SEE THAT. I LOVE YOU TOO, POP.
SO, WAS THAT YOUR NEW GIRL? I THINK I SAW HER AT YOUR HOMECOMING.
WHO? SAMMY? YEAH, SHE WAS THERE.
NOT BAD, KID. NOT BAD AT ALL.

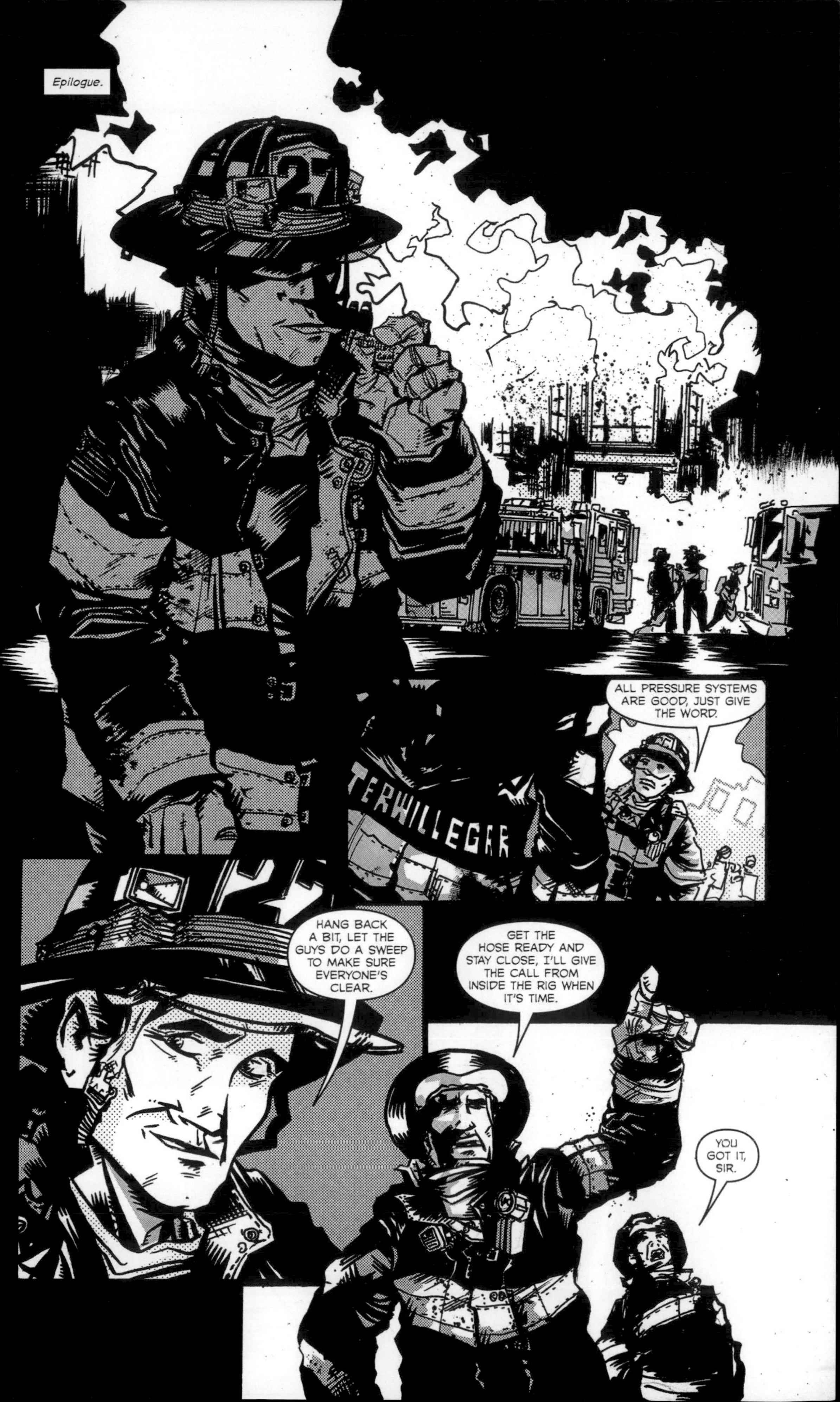
Epilogue.
27
ALL PRESSURE SYSTEMS ARE GOOD, JUST GIVE THE WORD.
TERWILLEGRR
HANG BACK A BIT, LET THE GUYS DO A SWEEP TO MAKE SURE EVERYONE'S CLEAR.
GET THE HOSE READY AND STAY CLOSE, I'LL GIVE THE CALL FROM INSIDE THE RIG WHEN IT'S TIME.
YOU GOT IT, SIR.

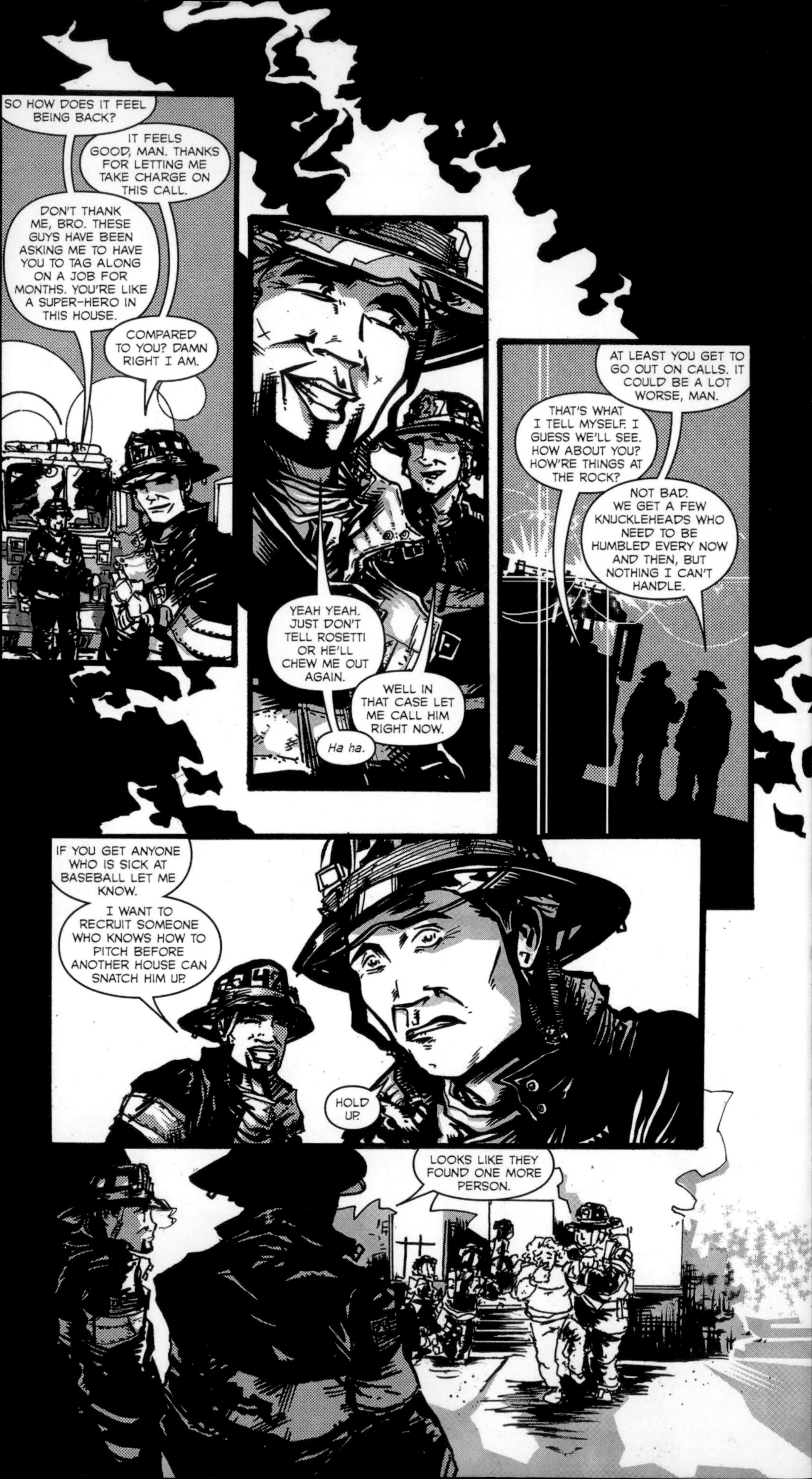
SO HOW DOES IT FEEL BEING BACK?
IT FEELS GOOD, MAN. THANKS FOR LETTING ME TAKE CHARGE ON THIS CALL.
DON'T THANK ME, BRO. THESE GUYS HAVE BEEN ASKING ME TO HAVE YOU TO TAG ALONG ON A JOB FOR MONTHS. YOU'RE LIKE A SUPER-HERO IN THIS HOUSE.
COMPARED TO YOU? DAMN RIGHT I AM.
YEAH YEAH. JUST DON'T TELL ROSETTI OR HE'LL CHEW ME OUT AGAIN.
WELL IN THAT CASE LET ME CALL HIM RIGHT NOW.
Ha ha.
AT LEAST YOU GET TO GO OUT ON CALLS. IT COULD BE A LOT WORSE, MAN.
THAT'S WHAT I TELL MYSELF. I GUESS WE'LL SEE. HOW ABOUT YOU? HOW'RE THINGS AT THE ROCK?
NOT BAD. WE GET A FEW KNUCKLEHEADS WHO NEED TO BE HUMBLED EVERY NOW AND THEN, BUT NOTHING I CAN'T HANDLE.
IF YOU GET ANYONE WHO IS SICK AT BASEBALL LET ME KNOW.
I WANT TO RECRUIT SOMEONE WHO KNOWS HOW TO PITCH BEFORE ANOTHER HOUSE CAN SNATCH HIM UP.
HOLD UP.
LOOKS LIKE THEY FOUND ONE MORE PERSON.

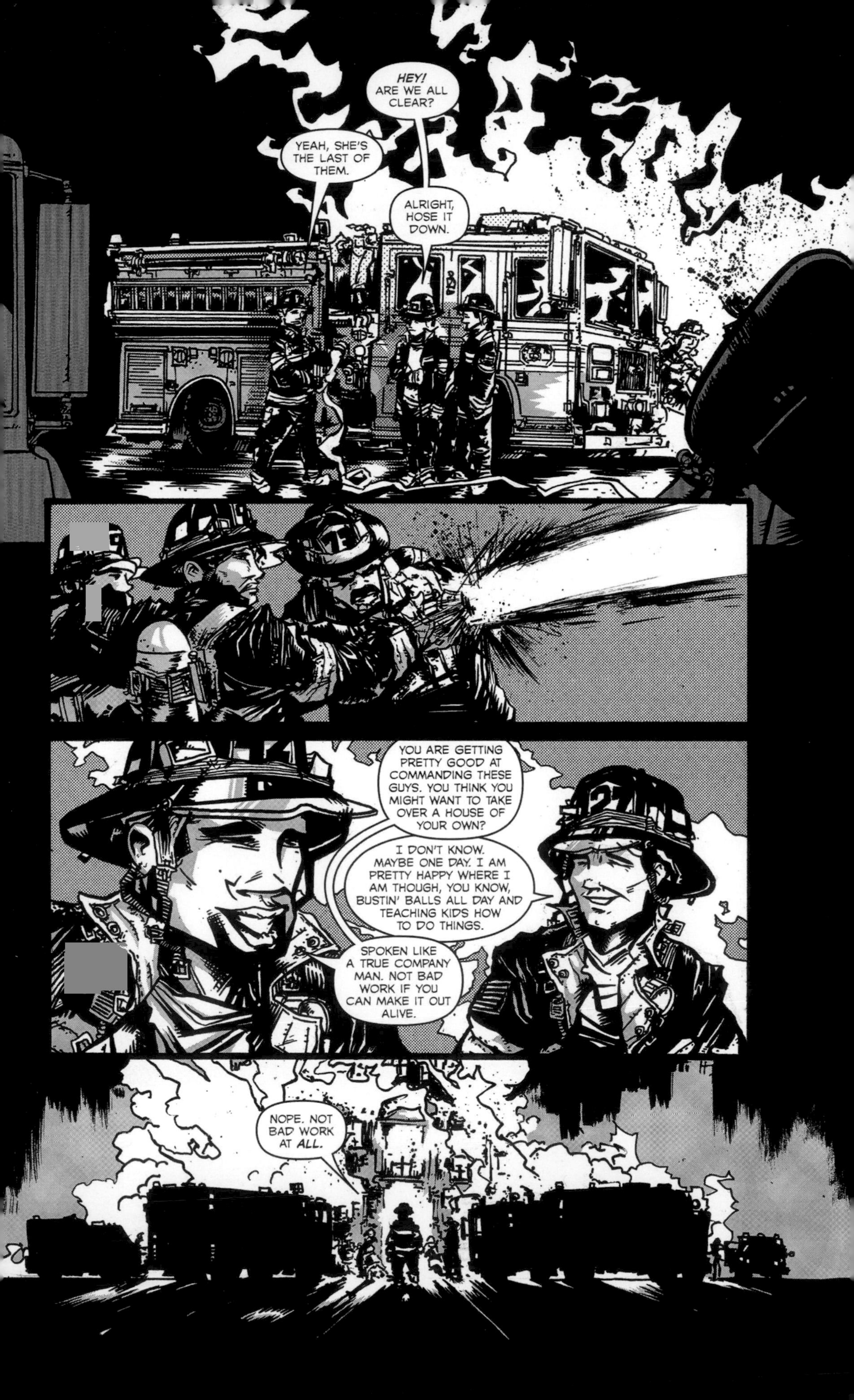

HEY! ARE WE ALL CLEAR?
YEAH, SHE'S THE LAST OF THEM.
ALRIGHT, HOSE IT DOWN.
YOU ARE GETTING PRETTY GOOD AT COMMANDING THESE GUYS. YOU THINK YOU MIGHT WANT TO TAKE OVER A HOUSE OF YOUR OWN?
I DON'T KNOW. MAYBE ONE DAY. I AM PRETTY HAPPY WHERE I AM THOUGH, YOU KNOW, BUSTIN' BALLS ALL DAY AND TEACHING KIDS HOW TO DO THINGS.
SPOKEN LIKE A TRUE COMPANY MAN. NOT BAD WORK IF YOU CAN MAKE IT OUT ALIVE.
NOPE. NOT BAD WORK AT ALL.

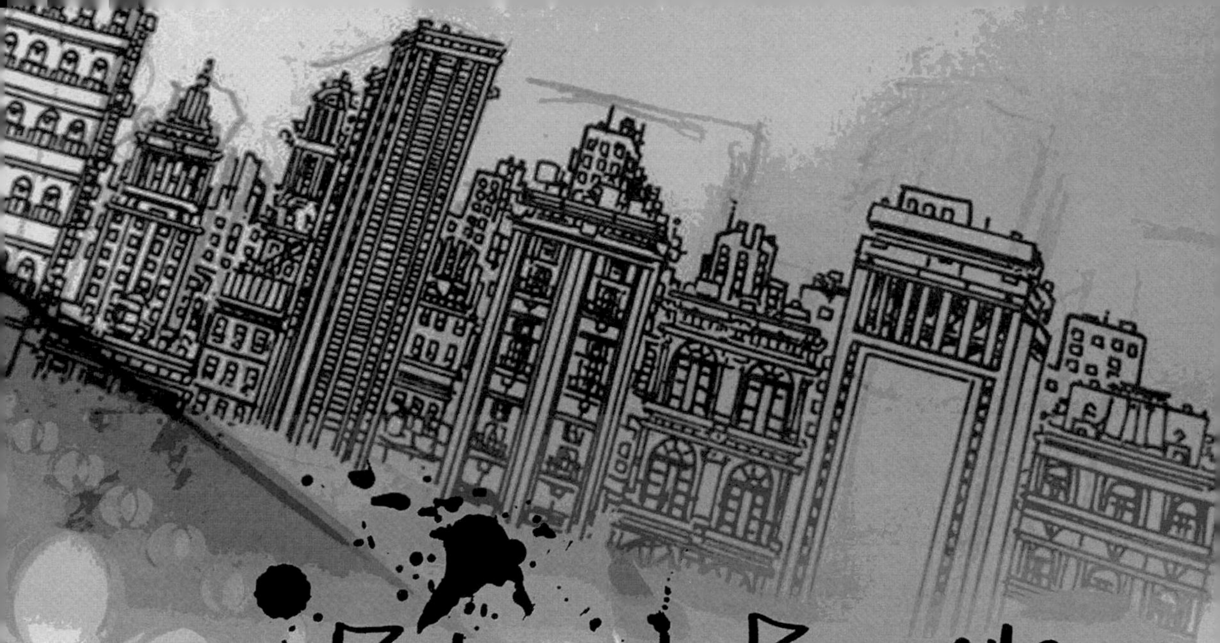

BEYOND THE BUROUGHS

INSIDE *ASHES: A FIREFIGHTER'S TALE*

New York is important to me; it's a city that serves as a character in itself in modern fiction. When I originally began conceptualizing the look of ASHES, I found myself grafting the brownstones and crumbling, aged sidewalks of Brooklyn with fervent nostalgia. I was drawing the city I came to love; a city held together by the people that inhabit it. Matt's world is far-removed from the reflective concrete streets glamorized so often in movies; it's a roughneck, blue-collar grind usually overlooked in the shuffle. It has been an unwavering honor to depict the Brooklyn I love and the men and women that keep it alive.

Thanks for reading!

xoxo

Karl Slominski, 2015

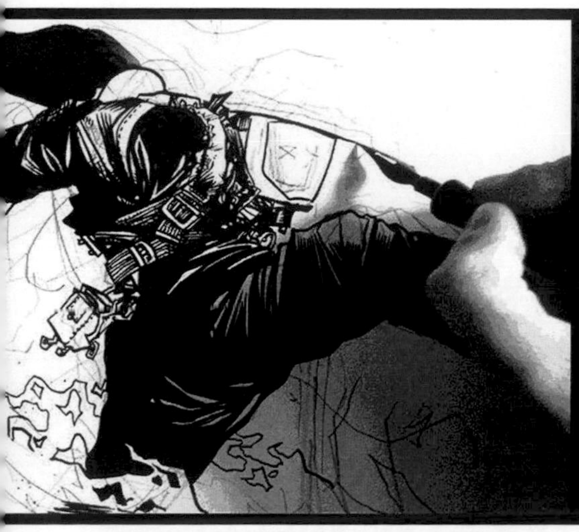

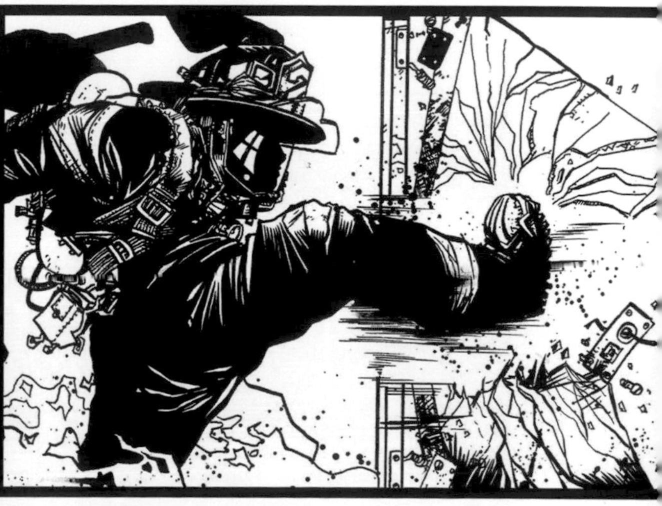

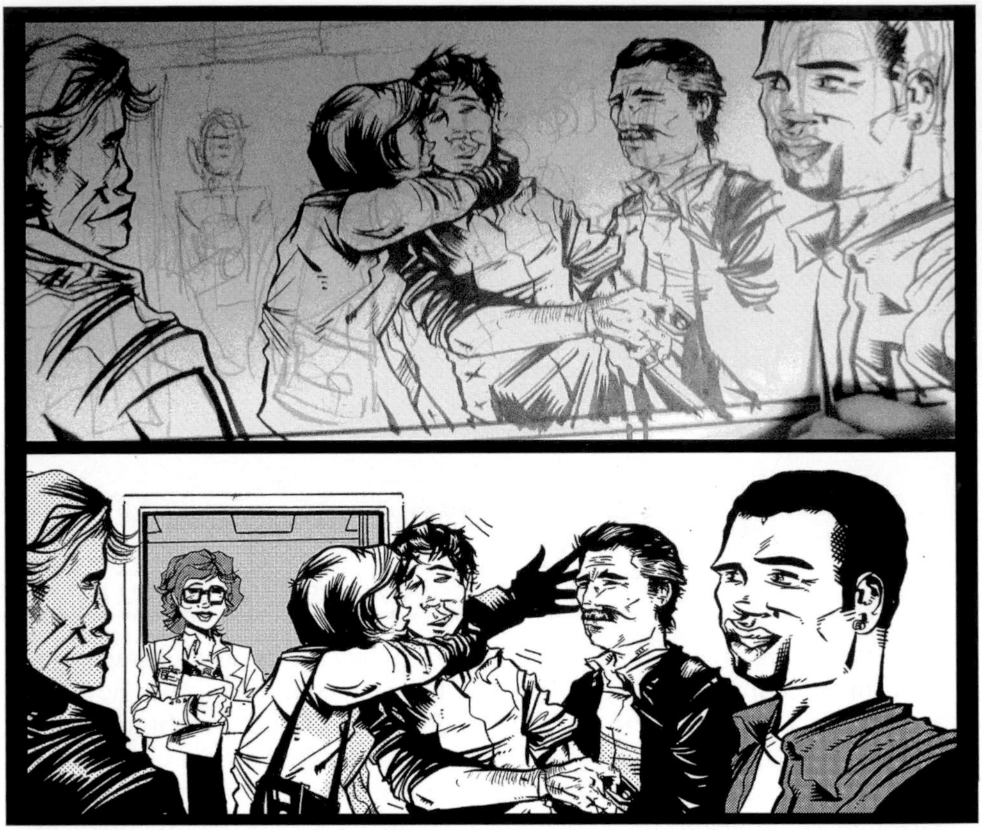

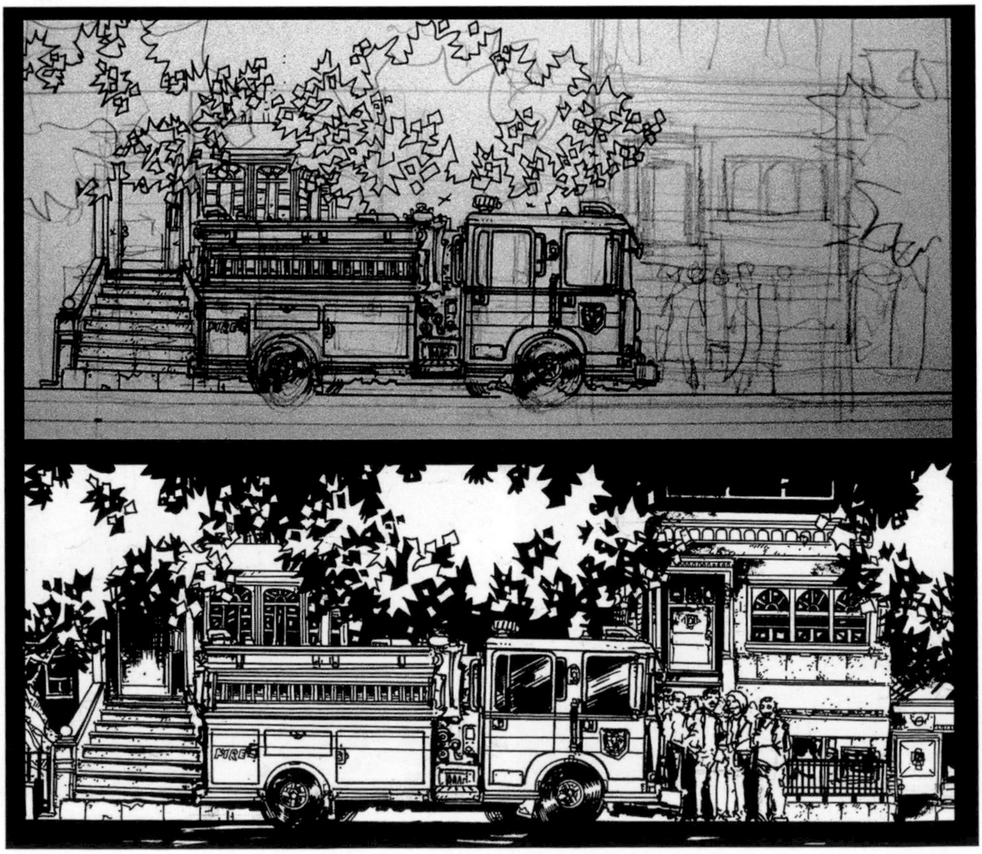

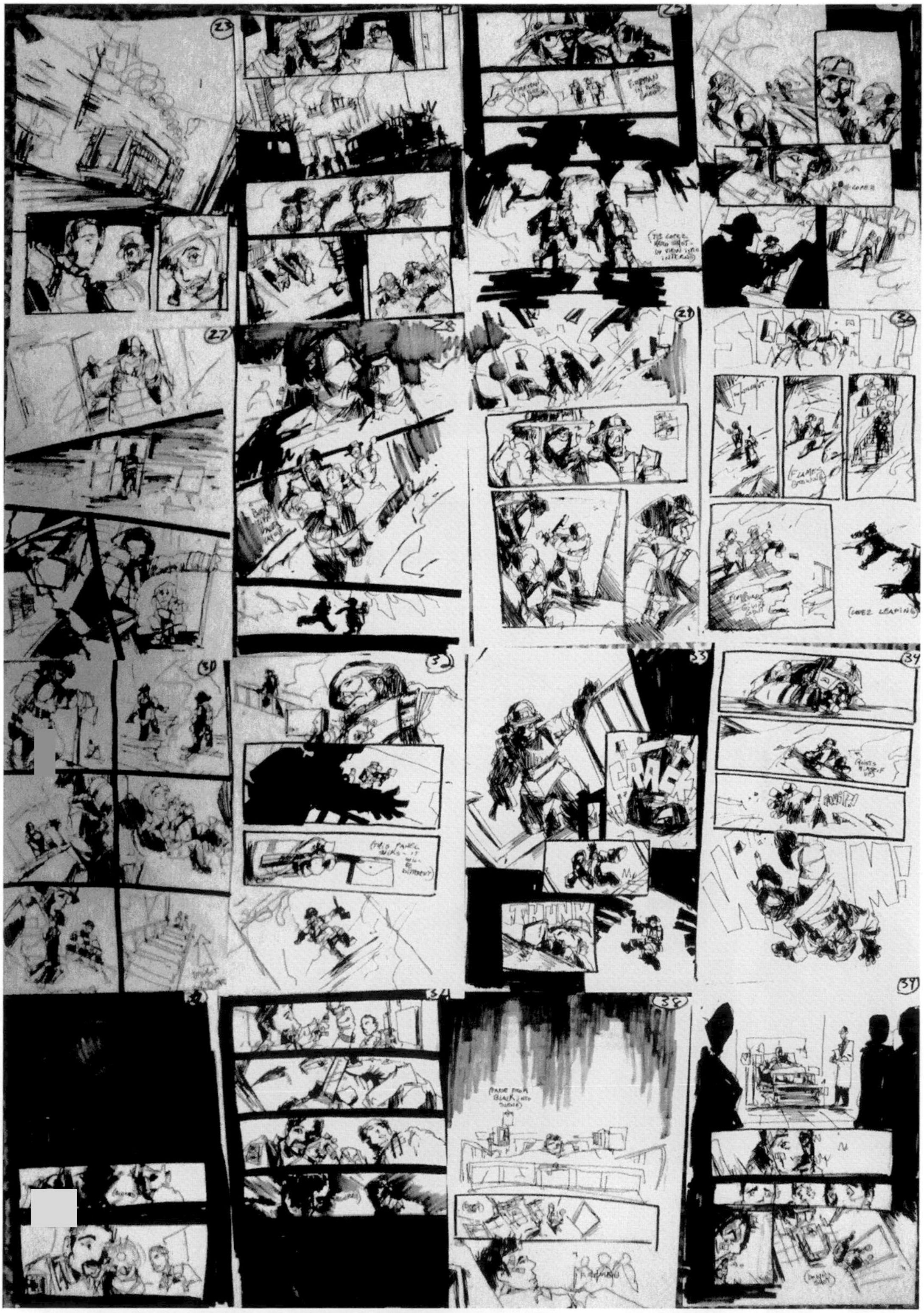

ORIGINAL THUMBNAILS

Initial layouts for the sequence that would go on to be the first pages completed for ASHES as the book came to fruition.

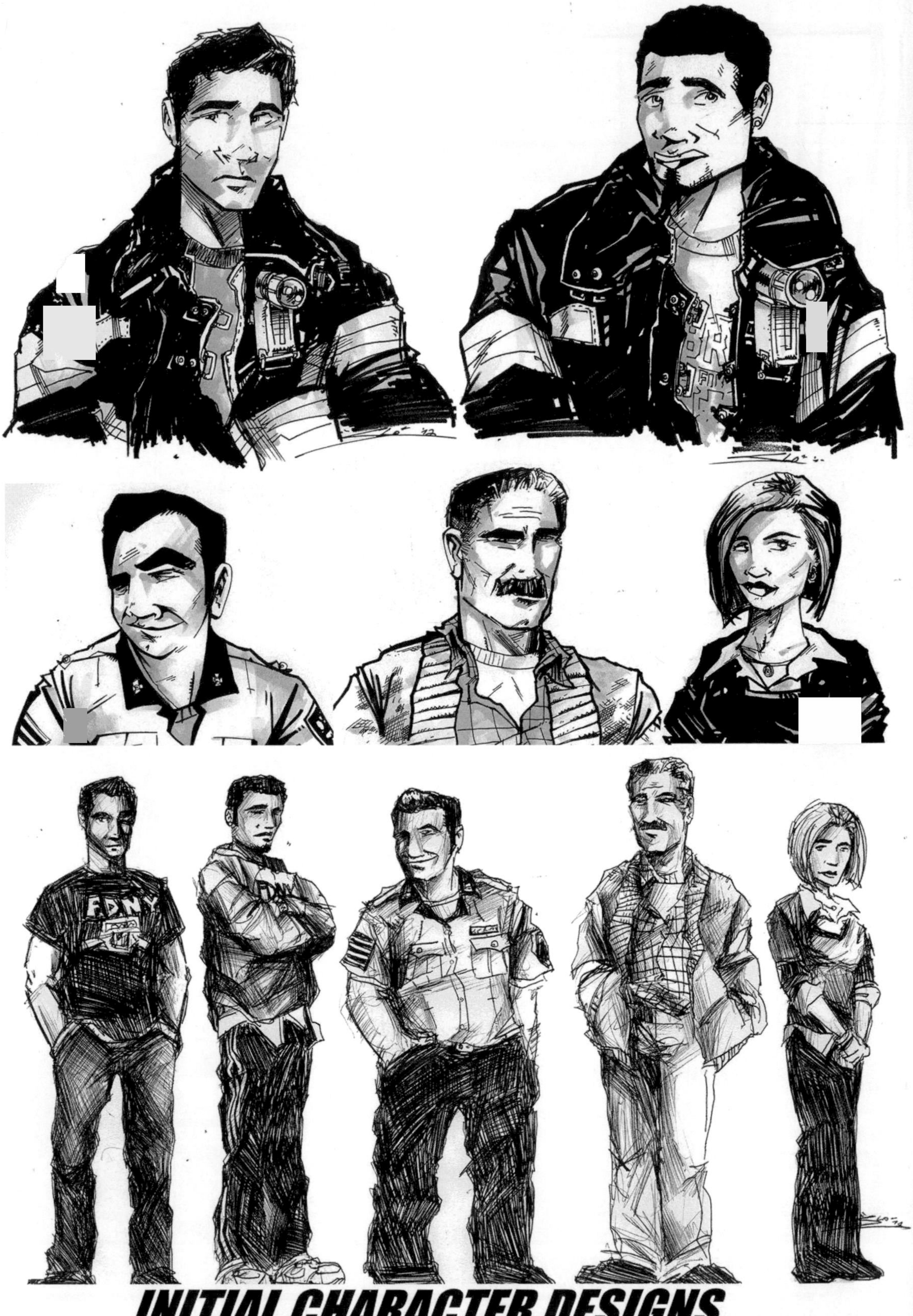
FDNY

INITIAL CHARACTER DESIGNS

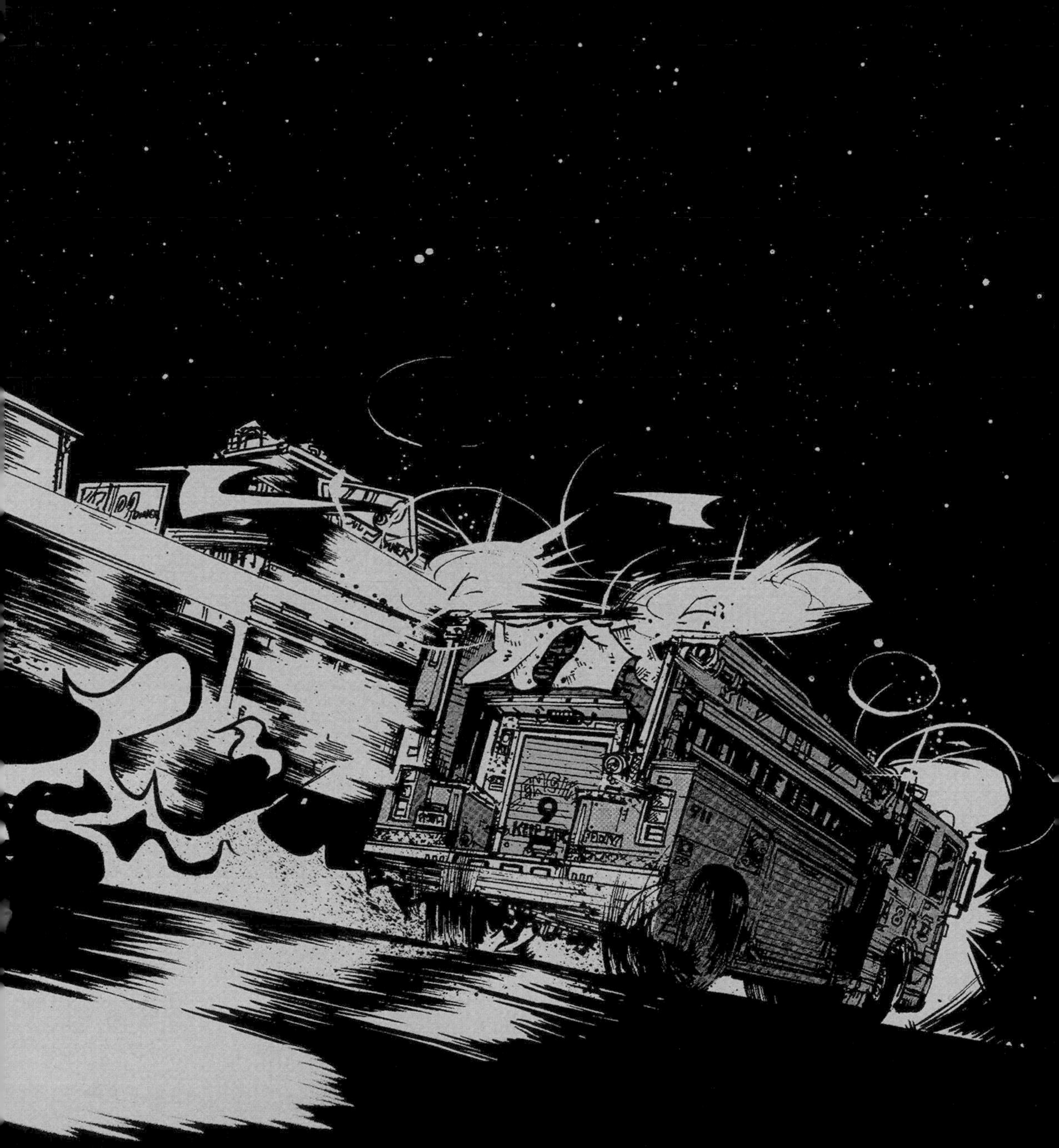

Z2 COMICS
New York City
Publishers: Josh Frankel and Sridhar Reddy
Book Design: Karl Slominski and Tyler Boss

ISBN 978-1940878034

First Printing: October 2015
Printed in The USA